D1303084

PRINT REFERENCE SOURCES:

A SELECT BIBLIOGRAPHY 18th-20th CENTURIES

Compiled by: Lauris Mason
Assisted by: Joan Ludman

KRAUS-THOMSON ORGANIZATION LIMITED
Millwood, N.Y.
1975

NE
850
.Z9
M37
1975

Library of Congress Cataloging in Publication Data

Mason, Lauris.
    Print reference sources.

    1. Prints—Bibliography.   2. Printmakers—Bibli-
ography.   I. Ludman, Joan.   II. Title.
Z5947.A3M37   016.769'92'2   74-79901
ISBN 0-527-00372-7

Printed in U.S.A.

ii

For Danny
with whom life is a
continuing education

For Eric, Lee and Gary
who have my love
and my love of knowledge

INTRODUCTION

Everyone who works with graphics knows how hard it is to find information about printmakers and prints. Major museums and libraries offer some aid, frequently a great deal. Their *catalogues raisonnés* on individual artists, where they exist; their collections of essays and article material; and ephemeral exhibition catalogs can be searched. But nowhere has there been a single reliable source listing a large body of available material about the artists and the prints of the last few centuries. The need for such a source has of course long been recognized. Everyone knew it had to be done, and everyone wished somebody else would do it! The job is at once so huge and the labor required so painstaking that the metaphors are classic: The task is Herculean, the Augean stables are referred to, and Sisyphus is invoked. Grants are applied for, plans are charted, and foundations are approached. In time all this activity will result in the masterwork that the print world awaits.

But once in a while someone comes along who gets the smaller (though still vast) and more pressing job done. A need is felt—no, not just a need—a sharp necessity bites and scratches, and there is no choice but to bound ahead and do the work as quickly and thoroughly as possible. Lauris Mason, first a collector and now an established dealer in prints, needed just such a book for her work with the prints of the 18th, 19th, and 20th centuries. So does everyone else who works with prints—museum curators, collectors, dealers. Like them, she visited the libraries and museums to authenticate and verify prints when the resources of her own excellent library were insufficient. And when the need for the sourcebook you are now reading became intense, she intrepidly went ahead and put it together.

The result of her labor is this unique volume. In it you will find an excellent supply of answers to questions you ask constantly. Not that the answer to every question has been found, but a few days' use will confirm your sense of the book's importance. And whenever you discover a nugget of information not included here, you will be doing everyone in the print world a service if you pass the material on to Mrs. Mason to incorporate in future editions. In this way other scholars will be able to build on her sturdy foundations. That, indeed, may be this catalog of catalog's greatest long-term value, for it should and will serve to stimulate further research and publication of the specific information continually needed in the world of the print.

David Shapiro
Professor of Fine Art
Hofstra University

A NOTE TO THE USER:

This bibliography is designed for the use of collectors, curators, librarians, dealers, auction cataloguers, and print lovers. The purpose of this book is to simplify research by providing a selected bibliography of the literature on printmakers of the 18th through 20th centuries. Close to 1,300 printmakers have been listed with an average of 3 references under each name. The printmakers are listed alphabetically with the references for each one arranged chronologically. The dates in the left-hand column are the dates of publication for each entry and they serve to guide the reader to the most appropriate reference. Included as entries are the following sources of primary and secondary information on printmakers: catalogues raisonnés, œuvre-catalogues, museum and dealer publications, and check-lists and essays from books and periodicals. References to unpublished material about certain printmakers have also been included; where the information has been available, the title and the projected date of publication of the work have been listed. When information about an artist is scarce, reference is made to listings in group exhibitions, general books and articles. The hope is that the user of this book shares the feeling that locating even the smallest fact is frequently pertinent and rewarding.

All of the listings in this bibliography are as complete as we have been able to make them. In entries where information such as the publisher or the name of the author is omitted, it is because the information is unavailable to us at the present time. This is particularly applicable to many of the early pamphlets and catalogues listed. In cases where a gallery, workshop, or association has been the author and publisher of a certain work, please note that the full name of the organization is listed first and it is not repeated in the place where the publisher is usually listed.

Prints are a democratic art form, since people can appreciate and collect similar impressions of an original work of art. The scholarship involved in locating print reference sources and the subsequent documentation of the print enhances the appreciation and almost always helps determine the relative value of the particular impression.

The works cited in this selected bibliography range from publications still in print and readily available to those that are extremely rare and difficult to locate. As the interest in print scholarship continues to grow, sources now out-of-print will be reprinted, new works will be written and become valuable additions to reference collections in print study rooms, public and private libraries.

Lauris Mason,
Director,
Mason Fine Prints

The following journals have undergone title changes. In the bibliography these journals are cited under the title used at the time of publication of the specific article.

Arts. Hopewell, N.J.; N.Y. 1, N 1, 1926+
    N 1926-Jl 1954 as **Art Digest**
    Ag 1954-S 1955 as **Arts Digest**

Collector's Magazine. London. 1-4, Ja 1903-My 1906
    Arts. Ja-F 1903 as **Printseller**
    Mr-Ag 1903 as **Printseller and Print Collector**
    S 1903-Jl 1904 as **Printseller and Collector**

Magazine of Art. (American Federation of Arts) Washington; N.Y. vl-46 no.5, N 1909-My 1953
    1909-D 1915 as **Art and Progress**
    Ja 1916-Ag 1936 as **American Magazine of Art**
    S-D 1936 as **Art, Including Creative Art**

Richly deserved thanks to:

Harold Ludman, M.D., our "Devil's Advocate."

Herbert Gstalder, our editor, who said that the best reference books
are written by the people who need them.

Elizabeth E. Roth, the oracle at the Print Room,
New York Public Library.

Cecile and David Shapiro, the voices of experience.

Carol Sirefman and Ruth Janssen, for their skill with details.

Curators, Librarians and Dealers who answered our questionnaires, sent
us exhibition catalogues, and requested the first copy of this book!

Lauris Mason
Joan Ludman

ABBÉ, S. VAN (1883–   )

1939   Bender, J. H. "The Drypoints of S. Van Abbé." *Print Collector's Quarterly* 26 (1939): 293–309.

ABERLI, J.-L. (1723–1786)

1927   Lonchamp, Frédéric Charles. *J.-L. Aberli, son temps, sa vie et son oeuvre, avec un catalogue complet.* Paris: Librairie des bibliophiles, 1927.

ACHENER, MAURICE (1881–   )

1923   "Catalogue Raisonné of the Etchings of Maurice Achener." *Print Connoisseur* 3(1923): 327.

1923   Sedeyn, Louis. "The Etchings of Maurice Achener." *Print Connoisseur* 3 (1923): 322.

ADAM, HENRI-GEORGES (1904–1967)

1957   Gheerbrant, Bernard. *Adam: oeuvre gravé 1939–1957.* Paris: La Hune, 1957.

1963   Musée d'art et d'histoire, Cabinet des estampes. *Henri-Georges Adam: gravures-décors: exposition.* Geneva, 1963.

ADAMS, CLINTON (1918–   )

1970   Library of Congress. *American Prints in the Library of Congress: A Catalog of the Collection.* Compiled by Karen F. Beall. p.2. Baltimore: The Library of Congress, The Johns Hopkins Press, 1970.

1973   University of New Mexico Art Museum. *Clinton Adams: A Retrospective Exhibition of Lithographs.* Albuquerque, N. Mex., 1973.

ALBEE, GRACE (1890–   )

1949   Reese, Albert. *American Prize Prints of the 20th Century.* p. 2. New York: American Artists Group, 1949.

1970   Library of Congress. *American Prints in the Library of Congress: A Catalog of the Collection.* Compiled by Karen F. Beall. p. 3. Baltimore: The Library of Congress, The Johns Hopkins Press, 1970.

ALBERS, JOSEF (1888–   )

1965   Wingler, H. M. *Graphic Work from the Bauhaus.* Greenwich, Conn.: New York Graphic Society, 1965.

1968   Grohmann, W. and de Sujo, C. *Josef Albers*. Starnberg: J. Keller, 1968.

1968   Staber, Margit, ed. *Josef Albers: graphic tectonic; ein zyklus von acht lithographien aus dem jahr 1942*. German, English, French and Italian editions. Cologne: Galerie der Spiegel, 1968.

1970   Library of Congress. *American Prints in the Library of Congress: A Catalog of the Collection*. Compiled by Karen F. Beall. p. 4. Baltimore: The Library of Congress, The Johns Hopkins Press, 1970.

1971   Gemini, G. E. L. *Josef Albers: White Embossings on Gray*. Los Angeles, Cal., 1971.

1973   Jane Haslem Gallery. *The Innovators: Renaissance in American Printmaking*. Washington, D.C., 1973.

1973   Miller, J. *Josef Albers Prints 1915–1970*. New York: Brooklyn Museum, 1973.

ALBRIGHT, IVAN LE LORRAINE (1897–   )

1949   Reese, Albert. *American Prize Prints of the 20th Century*. p. 4. New York: American Artists Group, 1949.

1969   Associated American Artists. *American Master Prints I*. p. 5. New York, 1969.

1970   Library of Congress. *American Prints in the Library of Congress: A Catalog of the Collection*. Compiled by Karen F. Beall. p. 6. Baltimore: The Library of Congress, The Johns Hopkins Press, 1970.

1971   Associated American Artists. *American Master Prints II*. p. 3. New York, 1971.

ALBRIGHT, MALVIN MARR (ZSISSLY) (1897–   )

1970   Library of Congress. *American Prints in the Library of Congress: A Catalog of the Collection*. Compiled by Karen F. Beall. p. 6. Baltimore: The Library of Congress, The Johns Hopkins Press, 1970.

ALCALAY, ALBERT (1917–   )

1968   De Cordova Museum. *Albert Alcalay: Paintings, Prints, Drawings*. Lincoln, Mass., 1968.

ALECHINSKY, PIERRE (1927–   )

1967   Galerie van de Loo. *Pierre Alechinsky: 20 Jahre Impressionen: Oeuvre–Katalog Druckgraphik*. Munich, 1967.

1896 Delignières, Emile. *Catalogue raisonné de l'oeuvre gravé de Jacques Aliamet, d'Abbéville.* Paris: Rapilly, 1896.

ALKEN, HENRY (1784–1851)

1923 Kendall, George. "New Light on the Alkens and their Sporting Prints." *Bookman's Journal* 8 (1923): 112.

1927 Sparrow, Walter Shaw. *Henry Alken.* London: Williams and Norgate Ltd.; New York: C. Scribner's Sons, 1927.

ALLAN, DAVID (1744–1796)

1927 Murdoch, W. G. Blaikie. "The Prints of David Allan." *Print Collector's Quarterly* 14 (1927): 347–361.

ALLEBÉ, AUGUST (1838–1927)

1929 Stuers, Charles Hubert de. *Het lithografisch werk von August Allebé.* Utrecht: De Ploeg, 1929.

ALLEN, JAMES E. (1894–1964)

1949 Reese, Albert. *American Prize Prints of the 20th Century.* p. 3. New York: American Artists Group, 1949.

1970 Library of Congress. *American Prints in the Library of Congress: A Catalog of the Collection.* Compiled by Karen F. Beall. p. 6. Baltimore: The Library of Congress, The Johns Hopkins Press, 1970.

ALTOON, JOHN (1925–1969)

1971 Whitney Museum of American Art. *John Altoon: Drawings and Prints.* New York, 1971.

AMAN-JEAN, EDMOND FRANÇOIS (1860–1936)

1944 Johnson, Una E. *Ambroise Vollard, Éditeur.* New York: Wittenborn and Co., 1944.

AMEN, IRVING (1918–   )

1968 Amen Galleries, Inc. *Amen: 1964–1968.* New York, 1968.

1970 Library of Congress. *American Prints in the Library of Congress: A Catalog of the Collection.* Compiled by Karen F. Beall. p. 8. Baltimore: The Library of Congress, The Johns Hopkins Press, 1970.

4   **AMSTEL, CORNELIS PLOOS VAN (1726–1798)**

1926   Bye, Arthur Edwin. "Ploos van Amstel." *Print Collector's Quarterly* 13 (1926): 305–321.

ANDERSEN, NIELS YDE (1888–   )

1949   Reese, Albert. *American Prize Prints of the 20th Century.* p. 5. New York: American Artists Group, 1949.

ANDERSON, ALEXANDER (1775–1870)

1970   Library of Congress. *American Prints in the Library of Congress: A Catalog of the Collection.* Compiled by Karen F. Beall. p. 9. Baltimore: The Library of Congress, The Johns Hopkins Press, 1970.

ANDERSON, STANLEY, R.E. (1884–1966)

1926   Salomon, M. C. "Etchings and Engravings of Stanley Anderson, R.E." *The Studio* [London] 91 (1926): 258.

1943   Hardie, Martin. "The Etchings and Engravings of Stanley Anderson." *Print Collector's Quarterly* 20 (1943): 226–246.

ANDRUS, VERA (1896–   )

1970   Library of Congress. *American Prints in the Library of Congress: A Catalog of the Collection.* Compiled by Karen F. Beall. p. 10. Baltimore: The Library of Congress, The Johns Hopkins Press, 1970.

ANQUETIN, LOUIS (1861–1932)

1970   Kovler Gallery. *The Graphic Art of Valloton and the Nabis.* pp. 36–37. Chicago, Ill., 1970.

1970   Stein, Donna and Karshan, Donald. *L'Estampe Originale: A Catalogue Raisonné.* New York: The Museum of Graphic Art, 1970.

ANTES, HORST (1936–   )

1968   Gercken, Günther. *Horst Antes: Catalog of Engravings 1962–1966.* Munich: Galerie Stangl, 1968.

1972   Sotriffer, Kristian. *Expressionism and Fauvism.* New York: McGraw-Hill Book Co., 1972.

1970   Library of Congress. *American Prints in the Library of Congress: A Catalog of the Collection*. Compiled by Karen F. Beall. p. 10. Baltimore: The Library of Congress, The Johns Hopkins Press, 1970.

1973   University of New Mexico Art Museum. *Garo Antreasian: A Retrospective Exhibition of Lithographs*. Albuquerque, N. Mex., 1973.

APPEL, KAREL (1921–   )

1962   Claus, H. *Karel Appel*. New York: Abrams, 1962.

1972   Associated American Artists. *Personages '70: Karel Appel, Exhibition Catalogue*. New York, 1972.

APPIAN, ADOLF (1818–1898)

1925   Jennings, H. H. "Adolf Appian." *Print Collector's Quarterly* 12 (1925): 94–117.

1967   Kovler Gallery. *Forgotten Printmakers of the 19th Century*. Chicago, 1967.

1968   Curtis, Atherton. *Adolphe Appian: son oeuvre gravé et lithographié*. Paris: P. Prouté, 1968.

ARCHIPENKO, ALEXANDER (1887–1964)

1957   Peters, H., ed. *Die Bauhaus Mappen: Neue Europäische Graphik 1921–1923*. Cologne: Czwiklitzer, 1957.

1965   Wingler, H. M. *Graphic Work from the Bauhaus*. Greenwich, Conn.: New York Graphic Society, 1965.

1967   Karshan, Donald. *Alexander Archipenko—A Memorial Exhibition 1967–1969*. Los Angeles, Cal.: UCLA Art Galleries, 1967.

ARMINGTON, FRANK M. (1876–1941)

1910   "Some Etchings by Frank Armington." *The Studio* [London] 51 (1910): 129.

1912   Chauvet, P. "Frank Armington." *Gazette des Beaux Arts* 8 (1912).

1970   Library of Congress. *American Prints in the Library of Congress: A Catalog of the Collection*. Compiled by Karen F. Beall. p. 12. Baltimore: The Library of Congress, The Johns Hopkins Press, 1970.

ARMS, JOHN TAYLOR (1887–1953)

1920 Truesdell, W. P. "Catalogue Raisonné of the Aquatints of John Taylor Arms." *The Print Connoisseur* 1 (1920): 112–121.

1925 "List of the Etchings of John Taylor Arms." *The Print Connoisseur* 5 (1925): 292–304.

1925 Whitmore, Elizabeth. "John Taylor Arms." *The Print Connoisseur* 5 (1925): 267.

1930 *John Taylor Arms*. American Etchers Series. Vol. 5. New York: The Crafton Collection, Inc.; London: P. and D. Colnaghi and Co., 1930.

1934 Arms, Dorothy Noyes. "John Taylor Arms: Modern Mediaevalist." *Print Collector's Quarterly* 21 (1934): 127–141.

1942 Zigrosser, Carl. *The Artist in America: 24 Close–ups of Contemporary Printmakers*. New York: Alfred Knopf, 1942.

1949 Reese, Albert. *American Prize Prints of the 20th Century*. p. 6. New York: American Artists Group, 1949.

1962 New York. New York Public Library. Chronological list of the prints of John Taylor Arms, from the studio of John Taylor Arms, Greenfield Hill, Fairfield, Conn. Unpublished manuscript. Catalog of the artist's published plates. Typescript. 1962.

1970 Library of Congress. *American Prints in the Library of Congress: A Catalog of the Collection*. Compiled by Karen F. Beall. pp. 12–34. Baltimore: The Library of Congress, The Johns Hopkins Press, 1970.

ARNOLD, GRANT (1904–   )

1949 Reese, Albert. *American Prize Prints of the 20th Century*. p. 7. New York: American Artists Group, 1949.

1970 Library of Congress. *American Prints in the Library of Congress: A Catalog of the Collection*. Compiled by Karen F. Beall. p. 35. Baltimore: The Library of Congress, The Johns Hopkins Press, 1970.

ARNOLD, JAMES IRZA (1887–   )

1934 Freund, Frank E. W. "A New Etcher: James Irza Arnold." *Prints* 5 (1934): 54–61.

ARP, HANS (JEAN) (1887–1966)

1957 Welcker–Giedon, C. *Hans Arp*. Stuttgart: Hatje, 1957.

1959   Klipstein and Kornfeld. *Hans Arp: Graphik 1912–1915*. Berne, 1959.

1968–69 Verlag Gertrud Arntz–Winter. "Hans (Jean) Arp." *Arntz–Bulletin* [Haag/Oberbayern, Germany] Vol. 1, parts 3–10, 1968–1969.

1970   Gimpel and Weitzenhoffer. *Original Prints of the Surrealists*. New York, 1970.

ATLAN, JEAN–MICHEL (1913–1960)

1962   Dorival, B. *Atlan*. Paris: P. Tisne, 1962.

AUBRY–LECOMTE, HYACINTHE (1797–1858)

1860   Galimard, Auguste. *Les grands artistes contemporains: Aubry–Lecomte, Hyacinthe-Louis–Victor–Jean–Baptiste, dessinateur–lithographe, 1797–1858*. Paris: E. Dentu, 1860.

AUDUBON, JOHN JAMES (1785–1851)

1966   Toledano, Roulhac. *Audubon in Louisiana*. New Orleans, La.: Louisiana State Museum, 1966.

See also HAVELL, ROBERT, Jr.

AUERBACH–LEVY, WILLIAM (1889–1964)

1914   Taylor, E. A. "William Auerbach–Levy." *The Studio* [London] 61 (1914): 66.

1949   Reese, Albert. *American Prize Prints of the 20th Century*. p. 8. New York: American Artists Group, 1949.

1970   Library of Congress. *American Prints in the Library of Congress: A Catalog of the Collection*. Compiled by Karen F. Beall. p. 36. Baltimore: The Library of Congress, The Johns Hopkins Press, 1970.

AURIOL, GEORGES (1863–1938)

1944   Johnson, Una E. *Ambroise Vollard, Éditeur*. New York: Wittenborn and Co., 1944.

1970   Stein, Donna and Karshan, Donald. *L'Estampe Originale: A Catalogue Raisonné*. New York: The Museum of Graphic Art, 1970.

AUSTEN, WINIFRED, R.E. (MRS. O. O. FRICK) (20th C.)

1923   "Catalogue Raisonné of Etchings by Winifred Austen." *Print Connoisseur* 3 (1923): 51.

8   1923   Sturges, Lucy Hale. "Winifred Austen; an Etcher of Animals."
Print Connoisseur 3 (1923): 43.

1927   "Catalogue of the Etchings and Drypoints of Winifred Austen."
Bookman's Journal 15 (1927): 30.

AUSTIN, ROBERT, R. E. (1895–   )

1927   "Three Etchings by Robert Austin, A.R.E." *The Studio* [London]
93(1927): 243.

1929   Dodgson, Campbell. "Robert Austin, Etcher and Engraver." *Print
Collector's Quarterly* 16 (1929): 327–352.

1930   Dodgson, Campbell. *A Catalogue of Etchings and Engravings by
Robert Austin.* London: The Twenty One Gallery, 1930.

1930   Salaman, Malcolm. *Robert Austin.* Modern Masters of Etching
Series, no. 25. London: The Studio, Ltd., 1930.

AVATI, MARIO (1921–   )

1967   Grunwald Graphic Arts Foundation. *Avati: Prints from 1957–1967.*
Los Angeles: Dickson Art Center, University of California, 1967.

1968   Hirsch, R. *En Manière Noire: Prints by Mario Avati.* Allentown,
N.J.: Allentown Art Museum, 1968.

1971   Associated American Artists. *Avati: Black and Color Mezzotints
from 1955 to 1970.* New York, 1971.

1973   Passeron, R. *L'oeuvre gravé de Mario Avati.* vol. 1. Paris: La
Bibliothèque des Arts, 1973.

AVERY, MILTON (1893–1965)

1966   Johnson, Una and Miller, Jo. *Milton Avery: Prints and Drawings,
1930–1964.* American graphic artists of the 20th century Series,
monograph no. 4. New York: Brooklyn Institute of Arts and
Sciences, Shorewood Publishers, 1966.

1970   Library of Congress. *American Prints in the Library of Congress: A
Catalog of the Collection.* Compiled by Karen F. Beall. p. 36.
Baltimore: The Library of Congress, The Johns Hopkins Press,
1970.

1973   Lunn, Harry H., Jr. *Milton Avery: Prints 1933–1955.* Introduction
by Frank Getlein. Note by Alan Fern. Washington, D.C.: Graphics
International Ltd., 1973.

1942 Sieben–Morgen, Ruth. "Samuel Putnam Avery (1822–1904), Engraver on Wood." Thesis, Columbia University, 1942.

BABBERGER, AUGUST (1885–1936)

1954 Würtenberger, Franzsepp. *Das Graphische Werk von August Babberger*. Karlsruhe: Staâtliche kunsthalle, 1954.

BACHER, OTTO H. (1856–1909)

1881 Koehler, S. R. *American Art Review* 2 (1881): 51,231.

1970 Library of Congress. *American Prints in the Library of Congress: A Catalog of the Collection*. Compiled by Karen F. Beall. p. 38. Baltimore: The Library of Congress, The Johns Hopkins Press, 1970.

BACON, PEGGY (1895–   )

1923 Brook, Alexander. *The Arts* 3 (1923): 68.

1931 Rosenfeld, P. "Caricature and Peggy Bacon." *Nation,* June 1931, pp. 617–618.

1949 Reese, Albert. *American Prize Prints of the 20th Century*. p. 9. New York: American Artists Group, 1949.

1970 Library of Congress. *American Prints in the Library of Congress: A Catalog of the Collection*. Compiled by Karen F. Beall. p. 39. Baltimore: The Library of Congress, The Johns Hopkins Press, 1970.

1973 Mount Holyoke College Art Museum and the Weyhe Gallery. *14 American Women Printmakers of the 30's and 40's*. South Hadley, Mass. and New York, 1973.

BADODI, ARNALDO (1913–1942)

1973 Bellini, Paolo. "Arnaldo Badodi: Complete Catalogue of his Engravings." *Print Collector* [Milan: Grafica Sipiel, s.r.] 2 (1973): 32–43.

BAJ, ENRICO (1924–   )

1970 Petit, Jean. *Baj; catalogue de l'oeuvre gravé et lithographié*. Geneva: Rousseau, 1970.

BALDRIDGE, CYRUS LEROY (1889–   )

1939 Singer, Caroline. "Cyrus Leroy Baldridge." *The Print Collector's Chronicle* 1 (May 1939): 21–23, 32, 34.

BALECHOU, J.–J. (1716–1764)

1908   Belleudy, Jules. *J.–J. Balechou, graveur du roi, 1716–1764.* Avignon: Editions de L'Académie de Vaucluse, 1908.

BALL, WILFRED, R.E. (1853–1917)

1899   "Wilfred Ball, Etcher and Water-colour Painter." *The Studio* [London] 16 (1899): 3.

1905   Cundall, H. M. "Wilfred Ball, R.E., Painter and Etcher." *Art Journal* (1905): 219.

BALLINGER, MAXIL (1914–)

1949   Reese, Albert. *American Prize Prints of the 20th Century.* p. 10. New York: American Artists Group, 1949.

1970   Library of Congress. *American Prints in the Library of Congress: A Catalog of the Collection.* Compiled by Karen F. Beall. p. 41. Baltimore: The Library of Congress, The Johns Hopkins Press, 1970.

BANGEMANN, OSKAR (1882–)

1931   Waldmann, Emil. "Oskar Bangemann." *Print Collector's Quarterly* 18 (1931): 79–98.

BARGHEER, EDUARD (1901–)

1966   Man, Felix H., ed. *Europäische Graphik.* Vol. 4. Munich: Galerie Wolfgang Ketterer, 1966.

1967   Man, Felix H., ed. *Europäische Graphik.* Vol. 5. Munich: Galerie Wolfgang Ketterer, 1967.

BARKER, ALBERT WINSLOW (1874–1947)

1934   Mechlin, Leila. "Albert Barker's Lithographs." *Prints* 5 (1934): 44–52.

1940   Whitmore, Elizabeth. "Albert Winslow Barker: Poet and Lithographer." *Print Collector's Quarterly* 27 (1940): 275–299.

1949   Reese, Albert. *American Prize Prints of the 20th Century.* p. 11. New York: American Artists Group, 1949.

1970   Library of Congress. *American Prints in the Library of Congress: A Catalog of the Collection.* Compiled by Karen F. Beall. p. 41. Baltimore: The Library of Congress, The Johns Hopkins Press, 1970.

1931   Carls, Carl Dietrich. *Ernst Barlach: das plastische, graphische und dichterische Werk*. Berlin: Rembrandt, 1931.

1958   Schult, Friedrich. *Ernst Barlach Werkverzeichnis: Das Graphische Werk*. Vol. 2. Hamburg: Dr. Ernst Hauswedell and Co., 1958.

1961   Stubbe, Wolfe. *Ernst Barlach; Zeichnungen*. Munich: Piper, 1961.

1966   Werner, Alfred. *Ernst Barlach*. New York: McGraw–Hill, 1966.

1968   Kunsthalle. *Barlach, Ernst: das druckgraphische Werk*. Bremen, 1968.

1972   Grunwald Graphic Arts Foundation. *Ernst Barlach*. Los Angeles, 1972.

1972   Sotriffer, Kristian. *Expressionism and Fauvism*. New York: McGraw–Hill Book Co., 1972.

BARNET, WILL (1911–   )

1949   Reese, Albert. *American Prize Prints of the 20th Century*. p. 12. New York: American Artists Group, 1949.

1965   Johnson, Una E. and Miller, Jo. *Will Barnet: Prints, 1932–1964*. American Graphic Artists of the Twentieth Century Series, monograph no. 3. New York: Brooklyn Institute of Arts and Sciences, Shorewood Publishers, 1965.

1970   Library of Congress. *American Prints in the Library of Congress: A Catalog of the Collection*. Compiled by Karen F. Beall. p. 42. Baltimore: The Library of Congress, The Johns Hopkins Press, 1970.

1972   Associated American Artists. *Will Barnet: Etchings, Lithographs, Woodcuts, Serigraphs: 1932–1972*. New York, 1972.

BAROOSHIAN, MARTIN (1929–   )

1970   Library of Congress. *American Prints in the Library of Congress: A Catalog of the Collection*. Compiled by Karen F. Beall. p. 42. Baltimore: The Library of Congress, The Johns Hopkins Press, 1970.

1971   Agbu Art Gallery. *Martin Barooshian: Exhibition of Paintings and Prints*. Watertown, Mass., 1971.

1971   Port Washington Public Library. *Martin Barooshian: Paintings and Prints*. Port Washington, N.Y., 1971.

12   1974   Prestige Gallery. *An Exhibition of Oils and Prints by Martin Barooshian*. Peabody, Mass., 1974.

BARRAUD, MAURICE (1889–1954)

1944   *Catalogue illustré de l'oeuvre gravé et lithographié de Maurice Barraud*. Geneva: Skira, 1944.

BARRETT, LAWRENCE (1897–   )

1970   Library of Congress. *American Prints in the Library of Congress: A Catalog of the Collection*. Compiled by Karen F. Beall. p. 42. Baltimore: The Library of Congress, The Johns Hopkins Press, 1970.

BARTOLINI, LUIGI (1892–1963)

1936   Bartolini, Luigi. *Luigi Bartolini. 30 tavole*. Milan: U. Hoepli, 1936.

1952   *Bartolini, Luigi: Gli esemplari unici o rari. 96 riproduzioni di acqueforti*. Rome: G. Casini, 1952.

BARTOLOZZI, FRANCESCO (1728–1815)

1883   *Catalogue of a Loan Collection of Engravings and Etchings*. London: E. B. Nash, 1883.

1885   Tuer, Andrew. *Bartolozzi and his Works*. London: Field and Tuer, 1885.

1904   Brinton, Selwyn. *Bartolozzi and his Pupils in England: With an Abridged List of his More Important Prints in Line and Stipple*. The Langham Series, an illustrated collection of monographs. London: Siegle, Hill and Co., 1904.

1912   Hind, Arthur. *Bartolozzi, and Other Stipple Engravers Working in England at the End of the Eighteenth Century*. London: Heinemann, 1912.

1927   Calabi, Augusto. "Francesco Bartolozzi." *Print Collector's Quarterly* 14 (1927): 137–162.

1928   Baudi di Vesmes, Alessandro. *Francesco Bartolozzi: Catalogue des estampes et notice biographiques d'après les manuscrits de A. de Vesme*. Milan: G. Modiano, 1928.

1934   Balken, E. D. "Holbein Drawings Engraved by Bartolozzi." *Carnegie Magazine* Vol. 8. November 1934, pp. 163–166.

BARYE, ANTOINE–LOUIS (1796–1870)

1910   Delteil, Loys. *Le Peintre-Graveur Illustré: Rude, Barye, Carpeaux, Rodin*. Vol. 6. Paris: Chez l'auteur, 1910.

1969   Delteil, Loys. *Le Peintre-Graveur Illustré: Rude, Barye, Carpeaux,*   **13**
           Rodin. Vol. 6. 1910. Reprint. New York: Da Capo Press, 1969.

BASKETT, CHARLES HENRY, R.E. (1893–1927)

1924   Allhusen, E. L. "The Aquatints of C. H. Baskett, R.E." *Print
           Connoisseur* 4 (1924): 325.

1924   "Catalogue Raisonné of the Works of C. H. Baskett." *Print
           Connoisseur* 4 (1924): 332.

BASKIN, LEONARD (1922–   )

1957   Worcester Art Museum. *Leonard Baskin: Sculpture, Drawings,
           Woodcuts.* Worcester, Mass., 1957.

1962   The Royal Watercolour Society Galleries. *Leonard Baskin: Wood-
           cuts and Wood Engravings—A Catalogue.* London, 1962.

1970   Library of Congress. *American Prints in the Library of Congress: A
           Catalog of the Collection.* Compiled by Karen F. Beall. p. 44.
           Baltimore: The Library of Congress, The Johns Hopkins Press,
           1970.

1970   Roylance, Dale. *Leonard Baskin: The Graphic Work 1950–1970.*
           New York: FAR Gallery, 1970.

1972   Sotriffer, Kristian. *Expressionism and Fauvism.* New York:
           McGraw-Hill Book Co., 1972.

1973   Jane Haslem Gallery. *The Innovators: Renaissance in American
           Printmaking.* Washington, D.C., 1973.

BAUDOUIN, P. A. (1723–1769)

1928   Francis, Eric C. "P. A. Baudouin." *Print Collector's Quarterly* 15
           (1928): 339–359.

BAUER, MARIUS A. (1867–1932)

1914   Sadler, M. T. H. "Some Recent Drawings by Mari Bauer." *Print
           Collector's Quarterly* 4 (1914): 363–380.

1925   Bloemkolk, W. "The Etched Work of M. A. J. Bauer." *Print
           Collector's Quarterly* 12 (1925): 393–418.

1926   *M. A. J. Bauer: Illustrated Catalogue of his Etchings.* Amsterdam:
           Wisselingh and Co., 1926.

1926   Salaman, Malcolm. *Marius Bauer.* Modern Masters of Etching
           Series, no. 8. London: The Studio, Ltd., 1926.

BAUER, RUDOLF (1889-1953)

1957 Peters, H., ed. *Die Bauhaus Mappen: Neue Europäische Graphik 1921–1923.* Cologne: C. Czwiklitzer, 1957.

1965 Wingler, H. M. *Graphic Work from the Bauhaus.* Greenwich, Conn.: New York Graphic Society, 1965.

BAUMEISTER, WILLI (1889–1955)

1957 Peters, H., ed. *Die Bauhaus-Mappen: Neue Europäische Graphik 1921–23.* Cologne: C. Czwiklitzer, 1957.

1963 Spielmann, H. "Willi Baumeister, das Graphische Werk." *Jahrbuch der Hamburger Kunstammlungen* 8 (1963).

1965 Spielmann, H. "Willi Baumeister, das Graphische Werk." *Jahrbuch der Hamburger Kunstammlungen* 10 (1965).

1965 Wingler, H. M. *Graphic Work from the Bauhaus.* Greenwich, Conn.: New York Graphic Society, 1965.

1966 Spielmann, H. "Willi Baumeister, das Graphische Werk." *Jahrbuch der Hamburger Kunstammlungen* 11 (1966).

n.d. Verlag, Gertrud Arnzt-Winter. "Willi Baumeister." *Arnzt-Bulletin* Haag, Oberbayern, n.d.

BAUMONT, LEONARD (1891–   )

1933 Dodgson, Campbell. "Leonard Baumont." *Print Collector's Quarterly* 20 (1933): 159–167.

BAUSE, JOHANN FRIEDRICH (1738–1814)

1849 Keil, George. *Catalog des Kupferstichwerkes von Johann Friedrich Bause.* Leipzig: R. Weigel, 1849.

BAWDEN, EDWARD (1903–   )

1950 Harling, Robert. *Edward Bawden.* English Masters of Black-and-White Series. London: Art and Technics, 1950.

BAXTER, GEORGE WILLIAM (1856–1888)

1938 Thorpe, James. "A Great Comic Draughtsman, George William Baxter." *Print Collector's Quarterly* 25 (1938): 59–79.

BEAL, GIFFORD (1879–1956)

1931 "Gifford Beal's Black and Whites." *Prints* 1 (1931): 28–31.

1949   Reese, Albert. *American Prize Prints of the 20th Century*. p. 13. New York: American Artists Group, 1949.

1970   Library of Congress. *American Prints in the Library of Congress: A Catalog of the Collection*. Compiled by Karen F. Beall. p. 46. Baltimore: The Library of Congress, The Johns Hopkins Press, 1970.

BEALE, (MRS. A. M.) *See* ELLIOTT, AILEEN MARY

BEARDSLEY, AUBREY (1872–1898)

1966   Reade, Brian and Dickinson, Frank. *Aubrey Beardsley: Exhibition at the Victoria and Albert Museum*. London: Her Majesty's Stationary Office, 1966.

BEAUFRÈRE, ADOLFE MARIE TIMOTHÉE (1876–1960)

1926   Dodgson, Campbell. "Adolfe Beaufrère." *Print Collector's Quarterly* 13 (1926): 157–175.

1930   Laran, Jean. *Bibliothèque Nationale: Inventaire du Fonds Français après 1800*. Vol. 1, pp. 468–481. Paris: Le Garree, 1930.

1967   Kovler Gallery. *Forgotten Printmakers of the 19th Century*. Chicago, 1967.

BECKMANN, MAX (1884–1950)

1924   Glaser, Curt. *Max Beckmann: mit Oeuvre-Katalog der Graphik bis 1923*. Munich, 1924.

1954   Buchheim, Lothar Günther. *Max Beckmann: Holzschnitte, Radierungen, Lithographien*. Feldafing, 1954.

1962   Gallwitz, Klaus. *Max Beckmann: Katalog der Druckgraphik: Radierungen, Lithographien, Holzschnitte, 1901–1948*. Karlsruhe: Badischer Kunstverein, 1962.

1965   Wingler, H. M. *Graphic Work from the Bauhaus*. Greenwich, Conn.: New York Graphic Society, 1965.

1970   Stedelijk Museum. *Catalogue 493: Beckmann*. Amsterdam, 1970.

1972   Sotriffer, Kristian. *Expressionism and Fauvism*. New York: McGraw-Hill Book Co., 1972.

1973   Tucson Art Center. *Max Beckmann: Graphics*. Tucson, Ariz., 1973.

BEHMER, MARCUS (1879–   )

1932   Birnbaum, Martin. "Marcus Behmer." *Print Collector's Quarterly* 19 (1932): 159–179.

16 BÉJOT, EUGÈNE (1867–1931)

1931 Roger-Marx, Claude. "Eugène Béjot." *Print Collector's Quarterly* 18 (1931): 245–269.

1937 Laran, Jean. *L'oeuvre gravé d'Eugène Béjot*. Paris: Editions des Bibliothèque Nationale de France, 1937.

BELCHER, GEORGE (1875–1947)

1923 Salaman, M. C. "Mr. George Belcher's Portrait Prints." *The Studio* [London] 86 (1923): 41.

BELLING, RUDOLF (1886–   )

1969 Man, Felix H., ed. *Europäische Graphik*. Vol. 6. Munich: Galerie Wolfgang Ketterer, 1969.

BELLMER, HANS (1902–   )

1970 Gimpel and Weitzenhoffer Ltd. *Original Prints of the Surrealists*. New York, 1970.

n.d. Grall, Alex, ed. *Hans Bellmer*. New York: St. Martin's Press, n.d.

BELLOWS, ALBERT F. (1829–1883)

1880 Koehler, S. R. "Albert F. Bellows." *American Art Review* 1 (1880): 293.

BELLOWS, GEORGE W. (1882–1925)

1924 "List of the Lithographs of George W. Bellows." *Print Connoisseur* 4 (1924): 236–244.

1924 Weitenkampf, Frank. "George W. Bellows, Lithographer." *Print Connoisseur* 4 (1924): 225.

1927 Bellows, Emma S. *George W. Bellows: His Lithographs*. New York and London: A. A. Knopf, 1927.

1938 Wunderlich, Silvia. "The Hag and the Young Man: A Drawing by George Bellows." *Print Collector's Quarterly* 25 (1938): 235.

1940 Francis, Henry Sayles. "The Lithographs of George Wesley Bellows." *Print Collector's Quarterly* 27 (1940): 139–165.

1949 Reese, Albert. *American Prize Prints of the 20th Century*. p. 220. New York: American Artists Group, 1949.

1970 Library of Congress. *American Prints in the Library of Congress: A Catalog of the Collection.* Compiled by Karen F. Beall. pp. 48–52. Baltimore: The Library of Congress, The Johns Hopkins Press, 1970.

BENDINER, ALFRED (1899–   )

1965 Philadelphia Museum of Art. *Alfred Bendiner: Lithographs, Complete Catalogue.* Philadelphia, 1965.

BENSON, FRANK WESTON (1862–1951)

1917 Paff, A. E. M. *Etchings and Dry Points by Frank W. Benson.* Boston and New York: Houghton Mifflin Co., 1917.

1921 Salaman, M. C. "Etchings and Drypoints of Frank W. Benson." *The Studio* 82 (1921):95.

1921–22 Rihani, Ameen. "Etchings of Frank W. Benson." *Print Connoisseur* 2 (1921–22): 257.

1925 Salaman, M. C. *Frank W. Benson.* Modern Masters of Etching Series, no. 6. London: The Studio Ltd., 1925.

1931 *Frank W. Benson, N.A.* American Etchers Series. Vol. 12. New York: The Crafton Collection, Inc., and London: P. and D. Colnaghi and Co., 1931.

1938 Chamberlain, Samuel. "Frank W. Benson—the Etcher." *Print Collector's Quarterly* 25 (1938): 167–183.

1949 Reese, Albert. *American Prize Prints of the 20th Century.* p. 15. New York: American Artists Group, 1949.

1959 Paff, A. E. M. *Etchings and Drypoints by Frank W. Benson.* 1917. Reprint. Boston and New York: Houghton Mifflin Co., 1959.

1970 Library of Congress. *American Prints in the Library of Congress: A Catalog of the Collection.* Compiled by Karen F. Beall. pp. 52–63. Baltimore: The Library of Congress, The Johns Hopkins Press, 1970.

BENTON, THOMAS HART (1889–   )

1942 Zigrosser, Carl. *The Artist in America: 24 Close-ups of Contemporary Printmakers.* New York: Alfred Knopf, 1942.

1949 Reese, Albert. *American Prize Prints of the 20th Century.* p. 16. New York: American Artists Group, 1949.

1969 Fath, Creekmore. *The Lithographs of Thomas Hart Benton.* Austin, Texas and London: University of Texas Press, 1969.

18   1970   Library of Congress. *American Prints in the Library of Congress: A Catalog of the Collection.* Compiled by Karen F. Beall. pp. 63–65. Baltimore: The Library of Congress, The Johns Hopkins Press, 1970.

BERG, WERNER (1904–   )

1964   Berg, Werner. *Woodcuts.* Vienna: Gruberner & Hierchammer, 1964.

1972   Sotriffer, Kristian. *Expressionism and Fauvism.* New York: McGraw-Hill Book Co., 1972.

BERGMAN, ANNA EVA (1909–   )

1967   *Catalogue of the Exhibition at the Galleria Civica d'Arte Moderna.* Turin: L. Mallé, 1967.

BERKMAN-HUNTER, BERNECE (1911–   )

1949   Reese, Albert. *American Prize Prints of the 20th Century.* p. 17. New York: American Artists Group, 1949.

BERMAN, EUGENE (1899-1972)

1970   Library of Congress. *American Prints in the Library of Congress: A Catalog of the Collection.* Compiled by Karen F. Beall. p. 65. Baltimore: The Library of Congress, The Johns Hopkins Press, 1970.

1971   *The Graphic Work of Eugene Berman.* Preface and notes by Eugene Berman. Foreword by Russell Lynes. New York: Potter, 1971.

BERNARD, EMILE (1868–1941)

1944   Johnson, Una E. *Ambroise Vollard, Éditeur.* New York: Wittenborn and Co., 1944.

1967   Bibliothèque Nationale, Cabinet des Estampes. *Emile Bernard: Catalogue of an Exhibition at Kunsthalle, Bremen.* Paris, 1967.

1970   Kovler Gallery. *The Graphic Art of Valloton and the Nabis.* pp. 38–39. Chicago, Ill., 1970.

1970   Stein, Donna and Karshan, Donald. *L'Estampe Originale: A Catalogue Raisonné.* New York: The Museum of Graphic Art, 1970.

BERNI, ANTONIO (1905–   )

1963   Galerie du Passeur. *Antonio Berni.* Introduction by Michel Ragon. Paris, 1963.

1963   Ragon, Michel. "Antonio Berni and the Adventures of Ramona Montiel." *Artist's Proof* 5 (1963): 18.

BERNIK, JANEZ (1933–   )

1966   *Kunst unserer Zeit.* Cologne: Du Mont Schauberg, 1966.

BESNARD, ALBERT (1849–1934)

1921   Clément-Janin. "Albert Besnard." *Print Collector's Quarterly* 8 (1921): 247–266.

1926   Delteil, Loys. *Le Peintre-Graveur Illustré: Besnard.* Vol. 30. Paris: Chez l'auteur, 1926.

1929   Godefroy, L. *L'oeuvre gravé de Besnard.* Paris, 1929.

1944   Johnson, Una E. *Ambroise Vollard, Éditeur.* New York: Wittenborn and Co., 1944.

1949   Bibliothèque Nationale. *Albert Besnard: l'oeuvre gravé, peintures, dessins, pastels-centenaire de sa naissance.* Paris, 1949.

1967   Kovler Gallery. *Forgotten Printmakers of the 19th Century.* Chicago, 1967.

1969   Delteil, Loys. *Le Peintre-Graveur Illustré: Besnard.* Vol. 30. 1926. Reprint. New York: Da Capo Press, 1969.

1970   Stein, Donna and Karshan, Donald. *L'Estampe Originale: A Catalogue Raisonné.* New York: The Museum of Graphic Art, 1970.

BETHERS, RAY (1902–   )

1949   Reese, Albert. *American Prize Prints of the 20th Century.* p. 18. New York: American Artists Group, 1949.

1970   Library of Congress. *American Prints in the Library of Congress: A Catalog of the Collection.* Compiled by Karen F. Beall. p. 67. Baltimore: The Library of Congress, The Johns Hopkins Press, 1970.

BETTELHEIM, (JOLAN) GROSS (1900-   )

1970   Library of Congress. *American Prints in the Library of Congress: A Catalog of the Collection.* Compiled by Karen F. Beall. p. 67. Baltimore: The Library of Congress, The Johns Hopkins Press, 1970.

BEVAN, ROBERT (1865–1925)

1968   Dry, Graham. *Robert Bevan: Catalogue Raisonné of the Lithographs and Other Prints*. London: Maltzahn Gallery, Ltd., 1968.

1972   William Weston Gallery. *Lithographs by Robert Bevan 1865–1925*. London, 1972.

1974   *Robert Bevan 1865–1925*. London: P. & D. Colnaghi and Co. Ltd., 1974.

BEWICK, THOMAS (1753–1828)

1866   Hugo, Thomas. *The Bewick Collector*. London: L. Reeve and Co., 1866.

1868   Hugo, Thomas. *The Bewick Collector: A Supplement to a Descriptive Catalogue of the Works of Thomas and John Bewick*. London: L. Reeve and Co., 1868.

1904   Anderton, Basil. *Catalogue of the Bewick Collection*. Newcastle-on-Tyne: R. Ward and Sons, 1904.

1925   Image, Selwyn. "Bewick the Wood Engraver." *Print Collector's Quarterly* 12 (1925): 183–203.

1949   Reynolds, Graham. *Thomas Bewick: a Resumé of his Life and Work*. London: Art and Technics, 1949.

1962   Cirker, B. *1800 Woodcuts by Thomas Bewick and His School*. New York: Dover Publications, 1962.

BIANCO, PAMELA (RUBY; MRS. G. T. HARTMAN) (1906–)

1970   Library of Congress. *American Prints in the Library of Congress: A Catalog of the Collection*. Compiled by Karen F. Beall. p. 67. Baltimore: The Library of Congress, The Johns Hopkins Press, 1970.

BIDDLE, GEORGE (1885–1973)

1939   Biddle, George. *An American Artist's Story*. Boston: Little Brown and Co., 1939.

1942   Zigrosser, Carl. *The Artist in America: 24 Close-ups of Contemporary Printmakers*. New York: Alfred Knopf, 1942.

1949   Reese, Albert. *American Prize Prints of the 20th Century*. p. 19. New York: American Artists Group, 1949.

1951   "Catalogue of the Lithographs of George Biddle." *The Bulletin of the New York Public Library* 55 (1951).

1970   Library of Congress. *American Prints in the Library of Congress: A Catalog of the Collection.* Compiled by Karen F. Beall. pp. 68–72. Baltimore: The Library of Congress, The Johns Hopkins Press, 1970.

BILL, MAX (1908–   )

1968   Kunsthalle Nürnberg. *Max Bill: Das druckgraphische Werk bis 1968.* Nürnberg: Albrecht Dürer Gesellschaft, 1968.

1969   Man, Felix H., ed. *Europäische Graphik.* Vol. 6. Munich: Galerie Wolfgang Ketterer, 1969.

1971   Victoria and Albert Museum. *Homage to Senefelder.* Introduction by Felix H. Man. London, 1971.

BINGHAM, GEORGE CALEB (1811–1879)

1940   Bender, J. H. "Catalogue of Engravings and Lithographs after George C. Bingham." *Print Collector's Quarterly* 27 (1940): 106–108.

1940   Christ-Janer, Albert. *George Caleb Bingham of Missouri.* New York: Dodd, Mead and Co., 1940.

1940   Hall, Virginius C. "George Caleb Bingham: The Missouri Artist." *Print Collector's Quarterly* 27 (1940): 9–25.

BISHOP, ISABEL (1902–   )

1949   Reese, Albert. *American Prize Prints of the 20th Century.* p. 20. New York: American Artists Group, 1949.

1964   Johnson, Una E. *Isabel Bishop: Prints and Drawings, 1925–1964.* American Graphic Artists of the Twentieth Century Series, monograph no. 2. New York: Brooklyn Institute of Arts and Sciences, Shorewood Publishers, 1964.

1970   Library of Congress. *American Prints in the Library of Congress: A Catalog of the Collection.* Compiled by Karen F. Beall. p. 72. Baltimore: The Library of Congress, The Johns Hopkins Press, 1970.

1973   Mount Holyoke College Art Museum, and the Weyhe Gallery. *14 American Women Printmakers of the 30's and 40's.* South Hadley, Mass. and New York, 1973.

BISHOP, RICHARD EVETT (1887–   )

1924 Crawford, A. W. "A New Etcher (Richard E. Bishop)." *American Magazine of Art* 15 (1924): 375.

1936 Bishop, Richard Evett. *Bishop's Birds; Etchings of Waterfowl and Upland Game Birds*. Philadelphia: J. B. Lippincott Company, 1936.

1970 Library of Congress. *American Prints in the Library of Congress: A Catalog of the Collection*. Compiled by Karen F. Beall. p. 73. Baltimore: The Library of Congress, The Johns Hopkins Press, 1970.

BISSIER, JULIUS (1893–1965)

1964 Man, Felix H. *Europäische Graphik*. Vol. 2. Munich: Galerie Wolfgang Ketterer, 1964.

BLACHE, PHILIPPE-CHARLES (19th C.)

1970 Stein, Donna and Karshan, Donald. *L'Estampe Originale: A Catalogue Raisonné*. New York: The Museum of Graphic Art, 1970.

BLAKE, WILLIAM (1757–1827)

1912 Russell, Archibald. *The Engravings of William Blake*. Boston: Houghton Mifflin Co., 1912.

1915 Cary, Elisabeth Luther. "William Blake and his Watercolor Drawings in the Museum of Fine Arts, Boston." *Print Collector's Quarterly* 5 (1915): 39–57.

1917 Binyon, Laurence. "The Engravings of William Blake and Edward Calvert." *Print Collector's Quarterly* 7 (1917): 307–332.

1921 Keynes, G. L. *A Bibliography of William Blake*. New York: The Grolier Club of New York, 1921.

1922 Binyon, L. *The Drawings and Engravings of William Blake*. London: The Studio Ltd., 1922.

1926 Binyon, L. *The Engraved Designs of William Blake*. London: The Studio Ltd., 1926.

1938 McDonald, Robert. "William Blake's Canterbury Pilgrims." *Print Collector's Quarterly* 25 (1938): 185–199.

1938 Newberry, John S. "William Blake's Original Line Engravings in the Philadelphia Exhibition." *Print Collector's Quarterly* 25 (1938): 67–81.

1942   Hellman, George S. " 'The Judgement of Solomon' by William
        Blake." *Print Collector's Quarterly* 29 (1942): 105–118.

1948   Todd, Ruthven. "The Techniques of William Blake's Illuminated
        Painting." *Print Collector's Quarterly* 29 (1948): 25–37.

1956   Keynes, G. L. *Engravings by William Blake.* Dublin: Walker, 1956.

1965   Cornell University. *William Blake; an Annotated Catalogue.* Ithaca,
        New York: Andrew D. White Museum of Art, 1965.

1966   Damon, S. Foster. *Blake's Job.* Providence: Brown University
        Press, 1966.

1967   Binyon, L. *The Engraved Designs of William Blake.* 1926. Reprint.
        New York: Da Capo Press, 1967.

BLAMPIED, EDMUND, R.E. (1886–1966)

1922   Salaman, Malcolm C. "Edmund Blampied's Etchings." *Bookman's
        Journal* 6 (1922): 140.

1926   Allhusen, E. L. "Etchings of Edmund Blampied." *Print Collector's
        Quarterly* 13 (1926): 69–96.

1926   Dodgson, Campbell. *A Complete Catalogue of the Etchings and
        Drypoints of Edmund Blampied, R.E.* London: Halton and Truscott
        Smith, 1926.

1926   Salaman, Malcolm C. *Edmund Blampied.* Modern Masters of
        Etching Series, no. 10. London: The Studio Ltd., 1926.

1932   Salaman, Malcolm C. "The Lithographs of Edmund Blampied."
        Print Collector's Quarterly 19 (1932): 299–319.

1937   Baily, Harold J. "Blampied: Artist and Philosopher." *Print Col-
        lector's Quarterly* 24 (1937): 363–393.

BLANCH, ARNOLD (1896–1968)

1949   Reese, Albert. *American Prize Prints of the 20th Century.* p. 21. New
        York: American Artists Group, 1949.

1970   Library of Congress. *American Prints in the Library of Congress: A
        Catalog of the Collection.* Compiled by Karen F. Beall. p. 74.
        Baltimore: The Library of Congress, The Johns Hopkins Press,
        1970.

BLANCH, LUCILLE (1895–   )

1949   Reese, Albert. *American Prize Prints of the 20th Century.* p. 22. New
        York: American Artists Group, 1949.

24   **BLANCHE, JACQUES-EMILE (1861–1942)**

1944   Johnson, Una E. *Ambroise Vollard, Éditeur.* New York: Witten-
       born and Co., 1944.

BLOCH, JULIUS THIENGEN (1888–1966)

1949   Reese, Albert. *American Prize Prints of the 20th Century.* p. 23. New
       York: American Artists Group, 1949.

1970   Library of Congress. *American Prints in the Library of Congress: A
       Catalog of the Collection.* Compiled by Karen F. Beall. p. 75.
       Baltimore: The Library of Congress, The Johns Hopkins Press,
       1970.

BLONDEL, GEORGES-FRANÇOIS (1730–after 1791)

1922   Dodgson, Campbell. "The Mezzotints of G. F. Blondel." *Print
       Collector's Quarterly* 9 (1922): 303–314.

1936   Lejeaux, Jeanne. "Georges-François Blondel: Engraver and
       Draughtsman." *Print Collector's Quarterly* 23 (1936): 261–277.

BO, LARS (1924–   )

1965   Madsen, F. and Giraud, R. *L'Oeuvre gravé de Lars Bo.* Copen-
       hagen: Galerie Carit Andersen, 1965.

1969   Avati, M. *Album des Peintres-Graveurs Français, 80ᵉ anniversaire.*
       Paris, 1969.

BOCCIONI, UMBERTO (1882–1916)

1957   Peters, H., ed. *Die Bauhaus-Mappen: Neue Europäische Graphik
       1921–1923.* Cologne: C. Czwiklitzer, 1957.

1961   Taylor, J. C. *The Graphic Work of Umberto Boccioni.* New York:
       Museum of Modern Art, 1961.

1965   Wingler, H. M. *Graphic Work from the Bauhaus.* Greenwich,
       Conn.: New York Graphic Society, 1965.

1972   Bellini, Paolo. *Umberto Boccioni: Catalogo completo dell-opera
       grafica.* I classici dell' Incisione series, vol. 2. Milan: Salamon e
       Agustoni, 1972.

1973   Calvesi, Maurizio. *Umberto Boccioni: Incisioni e Disegni.* 1973.

BOEHLE, FRITZ (1873–1916)

1914   Schrey, Rudolf. *Das Graphische Werk: Fritz Boehle.* Frankfurt:
       Schneider, 1914.

1949   Reese, Albert. *American Prize Prints of the 20th Century*. p. 24. New York: American Artists Group, 1949.

1970   Library of Congress. *American Prints in the Library of Congress: A Catalog of the Collection*. Compiled by Karen F. Beall. p. 76. Baltimore: The Library of Congress, The Johns Hopkins Press, 1970.

BOILLY, LOUIS LÉOPOLD (1761–1845)

1898   Harrisse, H. *L. L. Boilly, Peintre, Dessinateur et Lithographé; sa vie et son oeuvre*. Paris: Société des livres d'art, 1898.

BOLDINI, GIOVANNI (1845–1931)

1967   Kovler Gallery. *Forgotten Printmakers of the 19th Century*. Chicago, 1967.

BOLOTOWSKY, ILYA (1907–   )

1972   Heckscher Museum. *Artists of Suffolk County: Part 6, Contemporary Prints*. Huntington, N.Y., 1972.

BONE, MUIRHEAD (1876–1953)

1909   Dodgson, Campbell. *Etchings and Drypoints by Muirhead Bone*. London: Orbach & Co., 1909.

1912   Biermann, G. "Der Schotte Muirhead Bone." *Kunstwelt* (1912): 383.

1922   Dodgson, Campbell. "Later Drypoints of Muirhead Bone." *Print Collector's Quarterly* 9 (1922): 173–200.

1932   Knoedler and Co. *Drypoints by Muirhead Bone*. New York, 1932.

BONINGTON, RICHARD PARKES (1802–1828)

1873   Bouvenne, A. *Catalogue de l'oeuvre gravé et lithographié de Richard Parkes Bonington*. Paris: J. Claye, 1873.

1876   Mantz, P. "Bonington." *Gazette des Beaux Arts* 14 (1876): 288.

1890   Hédiard, Germain. *Les lithographies de Bonington*. Le Mans: E. Monnoyer, 1890.

1924   Dubuisson, A. and Hughes, C. E. *Richard Parkes Bonington, his Life and Work*. London, 1924.

26 1939 Curtis, A. *Catalogue de l'oeuvre lithographié et gravé de Richard Parkes Bonington*. Paris: Prouté, 1939.

BONNARD, PIERRE (1867–1947)

1923 Floury, J. *Catalogue de l'oeuvre gravé*, in *Bonnard*, by C. Terrasse. Paris, 1923.

1944 Johnson, Una E. *Ambroise Vollard, Éditeur*. New York: Wittenborn and Co., 1944.

1947 Roger-Marx, Claude. "Bonnard Illustrateur de La Fontaine." *Portique* [Paris] 5 (1947).

1950 Werth, L. "Bonnard Illustrateur." *Portique* [Paris] 7 (1950).

1952 Roger-Marx, Claude. *Bonnard Lithographe*. Monte Carlo: Sauret, 1952.

1968 Rouir, E. "Quelques Remarques sur les Lithographies de P. Bonnard." *Le Livre et L'Estampe*. (1968): 53–54.

1970 Kovler Gallery. *The Graphic Art of Valloton and the Nabis*. pp. 40–43. Chicago, Ill., 1970

1970 Stein, Donna and Karshan, Donald. *L'Estampe Originale: A Catalogue Raisonné*. New York: The Museum of Graphic Art, 1970.

1973 Rouir, Eugène. "Lithographs by Bonnard." *Print Collector* [Milan: Grafica Sipiel, s.r.] 3 (1973): 8–23.

BONNET, LOUIS-MARIN (1736–1793)

1935 Hérold, Jacques. *Louis-Marin Bonnet, Catalogue de l'oeuvre gravé*. Paris: la Société pour l'étude de la gravure Française, 1935.

BONTECOU, LEE (1931–   )

1971 Towle, Tony. "Two Conversations with Lee Bontecou." *Print Collector's Newletter* 2 (1971): 25–28.

BONVIN, FRANÇOIS SAINT (1817–1887)

1924 Roux, Alphonse. "François Bonvin: Graveur." *L'Amateur d'Estampes,* May 1924, pp. 80–87.

1927 Moreau-Nelaton, Étienne. *Bonvin raconté par lui-même*. Paris: H. Laurens, 1927.

1970   Library of Congress. *American Prints in the Library of Congress: A Catalog of the Collection.* Compiled by Karen F. Beall. p. 76. Baltimore: The Library of Congress, The Johns Hopkins Press, 1970.

1971   Galvin, J. *The Etchings of Edward Borein, a Catalogue of his Work.* San Francisco: John Howell, 1971.

BORNE, MORTIMER (1902–   )

1949   Reese, Albert. *American Prize Prints of the 20th Century.* p. 25. New York: American Artists Group, 1949.

1970   Library of Congress. *American Prints in the Library of Congress: A Catalog of the Collection.* Compiled by Karen F. Beall. p. 77. Baltimore: The Library of Congress, The Johns Hopkins Press, 1970.

BOTKE, CORNELIS (1887–1954)

1949   Reese, Albert. *American Prize Prints of the 20th Century.* p. 26. New York: American Artists Group, 1949.

1970   Library of Congress. *American Prints in the Library of Congress: A Catalog of the Collection.* Compiled by Karen F. Beall. p. 77. Baltimore: The Library of Congress, The Johns Hopkins Press, 1970.

BOUCHER, FRANÇOIS (1703–1770)

1971   Musée du Louvre. *Gravures et dessins provenant du cabinet des dessins et de la collection Edmond de Rothschild.* Paris, 1971.

BOUCHOT, HENRI FRANCOIS XAVIER MARIE (1849–1906)

1895   *Henri Bouchot: Cabinet des Estampes de la Bibliothèque Nationale.* Paris: E. Dentu, 1895.

BOUTET, HENRI (1851–1919)

1970   Stein, Donna and Karshan, Donald. *L'Estampe Originale: A Catalogue Raisonné.* New York: The Museum of Graphic Art, 1970.

BOUVY, EUGÈNE (1859–   )

1932   Bibliothèque Nationale. *L'Inventaire du Fonds Français au Cabinet des estampes de la Bibliothèque Nationale.* Paris, 1932.

28   **BOYD, ARTHUR MERRIL BLOOMFIELD (1920–   )**

1971   von Maltzahn, I. *Arthur Boyd, Etchings and Lithographs, 1962–1969.*
London, 1971.

1972   Victoria and Albert Museum. *Australian Prints.* London, 1972.

BOYD, FISKE (1895–   )

1949   Reese, Albert. *American Prize Prints of the 20th Century.* p. 27. New
York: American Artists Group, 1949.

1970   Library of Congress. *American Prints in the Library of Congress: A
Catalog of the Collection.* Compiled by Karen F. Beall. p. 79.
Baltimore: The Library of Congress, The Johns Hopkins Press,
1970.

BOYER, LOUISE MILLER (RIVE-KING; MILLER) (1890–   )

1949   Reese, Albert. *American Prize Prints of the 20th Century.* p. 28. New
York: American Artists Group, 1949.

1970   Library of Congress. *American Prints in the Library of Congress: A
Catalog of the Collection.* Compiled by Karen F. Beall. p. 80.
Baltimore: The Library of Congress, The Johns Hopkins Press,
1970.

BOYER, RALPH (1879–1952)

1931   "List of Plates by Ralph Boyer." *Print Connoisseur* 11–12 (1931):
133.

BOYS, SHOTTER (1803–1874)

1962   Groschwitz, Gustave von. "The Prints of Thomas Shotter Boys."
Prints. Edited by Carl Zigrosser. New York: Holt, Rinehart and
Winston, 1962.

1971   Victoria and Albert Museum. *Homage to Senefelder.* Introduction
by Felix H. Man. London, 1971.

BRACQUEMOND, FÉLIX (1833–1914)

1885   Béraldi, Henri. *Les Graveurs du XIXe Siècle.* Vol. 3. Paris, 1885.

1897   Bénédite, Léonce. *Catalogue des oeuvres exposées de Bracquemond.*
Paris: Librairies-Imprimeries réunies, 1897.

1907   Vaillat, Léandre. *Catalogue: Oeuvres de Bracquemond.* Paris: Société Nationale des Beaux-Arts, 1907.

1912   Weitenkampf, Frank. "Félix Bracquemond: An Etcher of Birds." *Print Collector's Quarterly* 2 (1912): 209–224.

1923   Delteil, Loys. "Félix Bracquemond." *Print Connoisseur* 8 (1923): 131.

1967   Kovler Gallery. *Forgotten Printmakers of the 19th Century*. Chicago, 1967.

1970   Stein, Donna and Karshan, Donald. *L'Estampe Originale: A Catalogue Raisonné*. New York: The Museum of Graphic Art, 1970.

BRAEKELEER, HENRI DE (1840–1888)

1925   Delteil, Loys. *Le Peintre-Graveur Illustré: Leys, Braekeleer, Ensor*. Vol. 19. Paris: Chez l'auteur, 1925.

1969   Delteil, Loys. *Le Peintre-Graveur Illustré: Leys, Braekeleer, Ensor*. Vol. 19. 1925. Reprint. New York: Da Capo Press, 1969.

BRANGWYN, FRANK WILLIAM, R.A. (1867–1956)

1908   Newbolt, Frank. *Etched Work of Frank Brangwyn*. London, 1908.

1912   *Catalogue of the Etched Work of Frank Brangwyn*. London: The Fine Art Society, 1912.

1912   Roger-Marx, Claude. "L'oeuvre gravé de Frank Brangwyn." *Gazette des Beaux-Arts* 7 (1912): 31.

1924   Salaman, Malcolm C. *Frank Brangwyn*. Modern Masters of Etching Series, no. 1. London: The Studio Ltd., 1924.

1926   Gaunt, W. *Etchings of Frank Brangwyn, R.A., Catalogue Raisonné*. London: The Studio, Ltd., 1926.

1932   Salaman, Malcolm C. *Frank Brangwyn*. Modern Masters of Etching Series, no. 30. London: The Studio, Ltd., 1932.

BRAQUE, GEORGES (1882–1963)

1944   Johnson, Una E. *Ambroise Vollard, Éditeur*. New York: Wittenborn and Co., 1944.

1953   Musée des Beaux-Arts. *L'oeuvre graphique de Braque*. Liège, 1953.

1958   Engelberts, E. *Georges Braque, Oeuvre graphique Originale,* Genève: Musée d'art et d'histoire, et Galerie Nicolas Rauch, 1958.

1960   Adhémar, J. and Lethène, G. *Georges Braque: Oeuvre graphique*. Paris: Bibliothèque Nationale, 1960.

30   1961   Hoffman, W. *Georges Braque: His Graphic Work*. New York: Abrams, 1961.

1962   Hoffman, W. *Georges Braque: His Graphic Work*. London, 1962 and Lausanne: Clairefontaine, 1962.

1963   Mourlot, Fernand. *Braque Lithographe*. Monte Carlo: Sauret, 1963.

1971   Rheinischen Landesmuseum. *Georges Braque: das Lithographische Werk*. Foreword by Edwin Engelberts. Bonn: Herman Wünsche, 1971.

1973   Daniele, Silvano. "Georges Braque." *Print Collector* [Milan: Grafica Sipiel, s.r.] 4 (1973): 59–61.

BRENNAN, ALFRED LAURENS (1853–1921)

1880   Koehler, S. R. "Alfred Laurens Brennan." *American Art Review* 1 (1880): 330.

BRENSON, THÉODORE (1893–1959)

1942   Focillon, Henri. "Théodore Brenson." *Print Collector's Quarterly* 29 (1942): 9–25.

1949   Reese, Albert. *American Prize Prints of the 20th Century*. p. 29. New York: American Artists Group, 1949.

1970   Library of Congress. *American Prints in the Library of Congress: A Catalog of the Collection*. Compiled by Karen F. Beall. p. 81. Baltimore: The Library of Congress, The Johns Hopkins Press, 1970.

BRESDIN, RODOLPHE (1822–1885)

1927   Roger-Marx, C. "Rodolphe Bresdin, Called 'Chien-Caillou'." *Print Collector's Quarterly* 14 (1927): 251–270.

1929   Neumann, J. B. *Rodolphe Bresdin*. The Art Lover Library, Vol. 1. New York, 1929.

1930   van Gelder, H. E. "Drawings by Rodolphe Bresdin." *Print Collector's Quarterly* 17 (1930): 363-374.

1931   Art Institute of Chicago. *Exhibition of Etchings, Lithographs and Drawings by Rodolphe Bresdin*. Essay by Mildred J. Prentiss. Chicago, 1931.

1963   Adhémar, J. and Gambier, A. *Rodolphe Bresdin, 1822–1885*. Paris: Bibliothèque Nationale, 1963.

1970   Cain, Fred. "Rodolphe Bresdin: A Drawing and a Print." *Print Collector's Newsletter* 1 (1970): 53–54.

1973   Brion, Marcel. *Quatre Siècles de Surréalisme: L'Art Fantastique dans la Gravure.* Paris: Pierre Belford, 1973. [American distributor: New York: Wittenborn and Co.]

BRISCOE, ARTHUR (1873–)

1926   Laver, James. "The Etchings of Arthur Briscoe." *Bookman's Journal* 13 (1926): 165.

1926   Salaman, Malcolm C. "Etchings of Arthur Briscoe." *The Studio* 91 (1926): 91.

1930   Salaman, Malcolm C. *Arthur Briscoe.* Modern Masters of Etching Series, no. 23. London: The Studio, Ltd., 1930.

1938   Wright, Harold J. L. "Arthur Briscoe: A Chronological List of his Later Etchings." *Print Collector's Quarterly* 25 (1938): 97–103.

1938   Wright, Harold J. L. "The Etchings of Arthur Briscoe." *Print Collector's Quarterly* 25 (1938): 285–311.

BROCKHURST, GERALD L., A.R.A., R.E. (1890–)

1924   Stokes, Hugh. "Etchings of G. L. Brockhurst." *Print Collector's Quarterly* 11 (1924): 409–443.

1928   Salaman, Malcolm C. *G.L. Brockhurst, A.R.A., R.E.* Modern Masters of Etching Series, no. 19. London: The Studio, Ltd., 1928.

1934   Wright, Harold J. L. "The Later Etchings of Gerald L. Brockhurst, A.R.A." *Print Collector's Quarterly* 21 (1934): 317–336.

1935   Wright, Harold J. L. "Catalogue of the Etchings of G. L. Brockhurst, A.R.A., R.E." *Print Collector's Quarterly* 22 (1935): 63–77.

BROOK, ALEXANDER (1898–)

1970   Library of Congress. *American Prints in the Library of Congress: A Catalog of the Collection.* Compiled by Karen F. Beall. p. 82. Baltimore: The Library of Congress, The Johns Hopkins Press, 1970.

BROOKS, JAMES (1906–)

1972   Heckscher Museum. *Artists of Suffolk County: Part 6, Contemporary Prints.* Huntington, N.Y., 1972.

BROUET, AUGUSTE (1872-1941)

1923   Geffroy, G. *Auguste Brouet, Catalogue de Son Oeuvre Gravé.* 2 vols. Paris, 1923.

1967   Kovler Gallery. *Forgotten Printmakers of the 19th Century.* Chicago, 1967.

BROWN, BOLTON COIT (1865–1936)

1938   Kleeman Galleries. *Catalogue of Lithographs by Bolton Brown.* New York, 1938.

1949   Reese, Albert. *American Prize Prints of the 20th Century.* p. 221. New York: American Artists Group, 1949.

1970   Library of Congress. *American Prints in the Library of Congress: A Catalogue of the Collection.* Compiled by Karen F. Beall. p. 82. Baltimore: The Library of Congress, The Johns Hopkins Press, 1970.

BROWN, HENRY STUART (1871–1941)

1927   Walker, R. A. "The Etchings of Henry Stuart Brown." *Print Collector's Quarterly* 14 (1927): 363–392.

BROWNE, SYD (1907–)

1949   Reese, Albert. *American Prize Prints of the 20th Century.* p. 30. New York: American Artists Group, 1949.

1970   Library of Congress. *American Prints in the Library of Congress: A Catalog of the Collection.* Compiled by Karen F. Beall. p. 87. Baltimore: The Library of Congress, The Johns Hopkins Press, 1970.

BRUSSEL-SMITH, BERNARD (1914–)

1949   Reese, Albert. *American Prize Prints of the 20th Century.* p. 31. New York: American Artists Group, 1949.

1970   Library of Congress. *American Prints in the Library of Congress: A Catalog of the Collection.* Compiled by Karen F. Beall. p. 88. Baltimore: The Library of Congress, The Johns Hopkins Press, 1970.

BRUYCKER, JULES de (1870–1945)

1923   Sturges, Lucy Hale. "An Etcher of Flanders." *Print Connoisseur* 3 (1923): 157.

1933 *Catalogue de l'oeuvre gravé de Bruycker*. Brussels: Nouvelle Société   **33**
d'Editions, 1933.

1934 Walker, R. A. "Jules de Bruycker." *Print Collector's Quarterly* 21
(1934): 37–58.

BUFF, CONRAD (1886–)

1949 Reese, Albert. *American Prize Prints of the 20th Century*. p. 32. New
York: American Artists Group, 1949.

BUFFET, BERNARD (1928–)

1967 Mourlot, Fernand and Simenon, Georges. *Bernard Buffet: Ouevre
gravé: Lithographies 1952–1966*. Paris: Mazo, 1967.

1967 Mourlot, Fernand and Simenon, Georges. *Werkverzeichnis Lithographien 1952–1966*. Cologne, Orangerie, 1967.

1968 Mourlot, Fernand and Simenon, Georges. *Bernard Buffet: Lithographs 1952–1966*. New York: Tudor Publishing Co., 1968.

1968 Reinz, Gerhard F. *Bernard Buffet: Engravings, 1948–1967*. New
York: Tudor Publishing Co., 1968.

1968 Reinz, Gerhard. *Bernard Buffet: Gravures: Engravings: Radierungen*. Cologne, Orangerie, 1968.

1969 Avati, M. *Album des Peintres-Graveurs français, 80ᵉ anniversaire*.
Paris, 1969.

BUHOT, FÉLIX HILAIRE (1847–1898)

1899 Bourcard, G. *Félix Buhot, Catalogue Descriptif de Son Oeuvre
Gravé*. Paris: H. Floury, 1899.

1938 Bender, J. H. "Félix Buhot's Cab Stand." *Print Collector's Quarterly* 25 (1938): 201–208.

1938 Filsinger, Catherine. "Félix Buhot's Cab Stand: A Recently
Discovered Ninth State." *Print Collector's Quarterly* 25 (1938): 481.

1967 Kovler Gallery. *Forgotten Printmakers of the 19th Century*. Chicago,
1967.

BULLER, CECIL (MRS. C. T. MURPHY) (1890–)

1930 Fletcher, John Gould. "The Woodcuts of Cecil Buller." *Print
Collector's Quarterly* 17 (1930): 93–105.

1949 Reese, Albert. *American Prize Prints of the 20th Century*. p. 33. New
York: American Artists Group, 1949.

34   1970   Library of Congress. *American Prints in the Library of Congress: A Catalog of the Collection.* Compiled by Karen F. Beall. p. 88. Baltimore: The Library of Congress, The Johns Hopkins Press, 1970.

BURCHARTZ, MAX (1887–1961)

1957   Peters, H., ed. *Die Bauhaus-Mappen: Neue Europäische Graphik 1921–1923.* Cologne: C. Czwiklitzer, 1957.

1965   Wingler, H. M. *Graphic Work from the Bauhaus.* Greenwich, Conn.: New York Graphic Society, 1965.

BURCHFIELD, CHARLES EPHRAIM (1893–1967)

1970   Library of Congress. *American Prints in the Library of Congress: A Catalog of the Collection.* Compiled by Karen F. Beall. p. 89. Baltimore: The Library of Congress, The Johns Hopkins Press, 1970.

1970   Munson-Williams-Proctor Institute. *The Nature of Charles Burchfield.* Utica, N. Y., 1970.

BURR, GEORGE ELBERT (1859–1939)

1921   Powell, Edith. "George Elbert Burr: An Etcher of the Desert." *Print Connoisseur* 1 (1921): 311–321.

1923   Austen, Winifred. "Catalogue Raisonné of the Etchings of George Elbert Burr." *Print Connoisseur* 3 (1923): 81–86.

1923   McCauley, L. M. *George Elbert Burr, Painter, Etcher.* Privately printed, 1923.

1928   Allhusen, E. L. "Recent Etchings by George Elbert Burr." *The Studio* (1928): 168.

1928   Allhusen, E. L. "The Etchings of George Elbert Burr." *Print Collector's Qurterly.* 15 (1928): 360–378.

1930   *George Elbert Burr.* American Etchers Series. Vol. 7. New York: Crafton Collection Inc., and London: P. and D. Colnaghi and Co., 1930.

1970   Library of Congress. *American Prints in the Library of Congress: A Catalog of the Collection.* Compiled by Karen F. Beall. pp. 90-94. Baltimore: The Library of Congress, The Johns Hopkins Press, 1970.

1971   Seeber, Louise Combes. *George Elbert Burr (1859–1939): Catalogue Raisonné and Guide to the Etched Works with Biographical and Critical Notes.* Flagstaff, Ariz.: Northland Press, 1971.

1908   Newbolt, F. "Etchings of F. V. Burridge." *The Studio* 42 (1908): 279.

BURT, CHARLES (1823–1892)

1924   Thomas, Thomas H. "Charles Burt; Bank Note Engraver." *Print Connoisseur* 4 (1924): 115.

BUTLER, REG (1913–)

1969   Man, Felix H., ed. *Europäische Graphik*. Vol. 6. Munich: Galerie Wolfgang Ketterer, 1969.

CADMUS, PAUL (1904–)

1935   Morrow, B. F. "Highlights of Copper: Paul Cadmus." *Prints* 6 (1935): 15–19.

1949   Reese, Albert. *American Prize Prints of the 20th Century*. p. 34. New York: American Artists Group, 1949.

1968   Johnson, Una and Miller, Jo. *Paul Cadmus: Prints and Drawings, 1922–1967*. American Graphic Artists of the Twentieth Century Series, monograph no. 6. New York: Brooklyn Institute of Arts and Sciences, Shorewood Publishers, 1968.

1970   Library of Congress. *American Prints in the Library of Congress: A Catalog of the Collection*. Compiled by Karen F. Beall. p. 95. Baltimore: The Library of Congress, The Johns Hopkins Press, 1970.

CADY, W. HARRISON (1877–)

1934   Morrow, B. F. "Highlights of Copper: Harrison Cady." *Prints* 4 (1934): 44–48.

1949   Reese, Albert. *American Prize Prints of the 20th Century*. p. 35. New York: American Artists Group, 1949.

1970   Library of Congress. *American Prints in the Library of Congress: A Catalog of the Collection*. Compiled by Karen F. Beall. p. 95. Baltimore: The Library of Congress, The Johns Hopkins Press, 1970.

CAIN, CHARLES WILLIAM (1893–)

1923   Brown, Warren Wilmer. "Charles W. Cain and his Orientalia." *Print Connoisseur* 3 (1923): 99.

36   1927   Greig, James. *Charles W. Cain: Catalogue of Drypoints*. London, 1927.

CALAME, ALEXANDRE (1810–1864)

1937   Calabi, Auguste. "Les eaux-fortes et les lithographies d'Alexandre Calame." *Die Graphischen Künste*. Baden bei Wien: Verlag Rohrer, 1937.

1966   Schreiber-Favre, A. *La Lithographie Artistique en Suisse au XIXe Siècle: Alexandre Calame, le Paysage*. Neuchâtel, Switzerland: Les Editions de la Baconnière, 1966.

1967   Kovler Galleries. *Forgotten Printmakers of the 19th Century*. Chicago, 1967.

CALAPAI, LETTERIO (1902–   )

1949   Reese, Albert. *American Prize Prints of the 20th Century*. p. 36. New York: American Artists Group, 1949.

1970   Library of Congress. *American Prints in the Library of Congress: A Catalog of the Collection*. Compiled by Karen F. Beall. p. 96. Baltimore: The Library of Congress, The Johns Hopkins Press, 1970.

CALVERT, EDWARD (1799–1883)

1917   Binyon, Laurence. "The Engravings of William Blake and Edward Calvert." *Print Collector's Quarterly* 7 (1917): 307–332.

1930   Finberg, A. J. "Edward Calvert's Engravings." *Print Collector's Quarterly* 17 (1930): 139–153.

CAMERON, DAVID YOUNG (1865–1945)

1908   *Etchings and Drypoints by D. Y. Cameron*. New York: The Grolier Club of New York, 1908.

1911   "David Young Cameron." *Print Collector's Quarterly* 1 (1911): 74.

1911   "List of Etchings by Cameron from the Tracy Dows Collection." *Print Collector's Quarterly* 1 (1911): 77–85.

1912   Rinder, Frank. *D. Y. Cameron: An Illustrated Catalogue of his Etched Work*. Glasgow: J. Mackhose and Sons, 1912.

1924   Hind, Arthur M. *The Etchings of D. Y. Cameron*. London: Halton and Truscott Smith, 1924.

1924   Rinder, Frank. "Cameron Etchings: A Supplement." *Print Collector's Quarterly* 11 (1924): 45–68.

1925   Salaman, M. C. *Sir D. Y. Cameron.* Modern Masters of Etching Series, no. 7. London: The Studio, Ltd. 1925.

CAMERON, KATHERINE, A.R.E. (MRS. KATHERINE KAY)

1922   Wright, Helen. "Etchings of Katherine Cameron." *International Studio* 75 (1922): 401.

CAMPENDONK, HEINRICH (1889–1957)

1922   Mayer, W. "Heinrich Campendonk." Published in *Deutsche Graphik Des Westens.* Edited by H. von Wedderkop. Weimar, 1922.

1958   Engels, Mathias Toni. *Heinrich Campendonk.* Recklinghausen, 1958.

1959   Engels, Mathias Toni. *Heinrich Campendonk: Holzschitte.* Stuttgart: Kohlhammer, 1959.

1965   Wingler, H. M. *Graphic Work from the Bauhaus.* Greenwich, Conn.: The New York Graphic Society, 1965.

1972   Sotriffer, Kristian. *Expressionism and Fauvism.* New York: McGraw-Hill Book Co., 1972.

CAMPIGLI, MASSIMO (1895–1971)

1964   Man, Felix H. *Europäische Graphik.* Vol. 2. Munich: Galerie Wolfgang Ketterer, 1964.

1965   Russoli, F. *Campigli.* Milan: Ed. del Milione, 1965.

CANADÉ, VINCENT (1879–   )

1963   Zigrosser, Carl. "The Lithographs of Vincent Canadé." *Artist's Proof* 5 (1963): 32–33.

1970   Library of Congress. *American Prints in the Library of Congress: A Catalog of the Collection.* Compiled by Karen F. Beall. p. 97. Baltimore: The Library of Congress, The Johns Hopkins Press, 1970.

CANALETTO (ANTONIO CANALE) (1697–1768)

1913   Metcalfe, Louis R. "The Etchings of Antonio Canale, Called Canaletto (1697–1768)." *Print Collector's Quarterly* 3 (1913): 31–60.

38   CAPOGROSSI, GIUSEPPE (1890–1972)

1962   Dorfles, G. *L'Alfabeto di Capogrossi*. Milan: Scheiwiller, 1962.

CARABIN, FRANÇOIS-RUPERT (1862–   )

1944   Johnson, Una E. *Ambroise Vollard, Éditeur*. New York: Wittenborn and Co., 1944.

CARPEAUX, JEAN-BAPTISTE (1827–1875)

1886   Béraldi, Henri. *Les Graveurs du XIXᵉ Siècle*. Vol. 4. Paris: L.
Conquet, 1886.

1910   Delteil, Loys. *Le Peintre-Graveur Illustré: Rude, Barye, Carpeaux,
Rodin*. Vol. 6. Paris: Chez l'auteur, 1910.

1969   Delteil, Loys. *Le Peintre-Graveur Illustré: Rude, Barye, Carpeaux,
Rodin*. Vol. 6. 1910. Reprint. New York: Da Capo Press, 1969.

CARRA, CARLO (1881–1966)

1957   Peters, H., ed. *Die Bauhaus-Mappen: Neue Europäische Graphik
1921–1923*. Cologne, C. Czwiklitzer, 1957.

1965   Wingler, H. M. *Graphic Work from the Bauhaus*. Greenwich,
Conn.: New York Graphic Society, 1965.

CARRIÈRE, EUGÈNE (1849–1906)

1908   Fauré, Élie. *Eugène Carrière: Peintre et Lithographe*. Paris: Floury,
1908.

1913   Delteil, Loys. *Le Peintre-Graveur Illustré: Carrière*. Vol. 8. Paris:
Chez l'auteur, 1913.

1944   Johnson, Una E. *Ambroise Vollard, Éditeur*. New York: Wittenborn and Co., 1944.

1969   Delteil, Loys. *Le Peintre-Graveur Illustré: Carrière*. Vol. 8. 1913.
Reprint. New York: Da Capo Press, 1969.

1970   Kovler Gallery. *The Graphic Art of Valloton and the Nabis*. pp.
44–47. Chicago, 1970.

1970   Stein, Donna and Karshan, Donald. *L'Estampe Originale: A
Catalogue Raisonné*. New York: The Museum of Graphic Art,
1970.

CARTER, FREDERICK (1885–   )

1933   Furst, Herbert. "Frederick Carter." *Print Collector's Quarterly* 20 (1933): 347–361.

CARZOU, JEAN (1907–   )

1962   *Carzou: Catalogue raisonné de l'oeuvre gravé et lithographié.* Geneva: P. Cailler, 1962

1971   Furhange, Maguy. *Carzou: Graveur et Lithographe; Catalogue raisonné et commente de l'oeuvre gravé.* Preface by Roger Caillois. Vol. 1. (1948–1962). Nice: Editions d'Art de Francony, 1971.

CASSATT, MARY (1845–1926)

1916   Weitenkampf, Frank. "The Dry-Points of Mary Cassatt." *Print Collector's Quarterly* 6 (1916): 397–409.

1936   Breeskin, Adelyn. "The Graphic Works of Mary Cassatt." *Prints* 7 (1936): 63–71.

1948   Breeskin, Adelyn Dohme. *The Graphic Work of Mary Cassatt: A Catalogue Raisonné.* New York: H. Bittner, 1948.

1967   Karshan, D. *The Graphic Art of Mary Cassatt.* Washington, D. C.: Smithsonian Institution Press, 1967.

1970   Library of Congress. *American Prints in the Library of Congress: A Catalog of the Collection.* Compiled by Karen F. Beall. pp. 98–101. Baltimore: The Library of Congress, The Johns Hopkins Press, 1970.

CASTELLON, FEDERICO (1914–1971)

1942   Zigrosser, Carl. *The Artist in America: 24 Close-ups of Contemporary Printmakers.* New York: Alfred Knopf, 1942.

1949   Reese, Albert. *American Prize Prints of the 20th Century.* p. 37. New York: American Artists Group, 1949.

1966   Associated American Artists. *Recent Etchings and Lithographs by Frederico Castellon.* New York, 1966.

1970   Library of Congress. *American Prints in the Library of Congress: A Catalog of the Collection.* Compiled by Karen F. Beall. pp. 102–103. Baltimore: The Library of Congress, The Johns Hopkins Press, 1970.

1972   The American Academy of Arts and Letters. *Memorial Exhibition.* New York, 1972.

40　　　　CÉZANNE, PAUL (1839–1906)

1923　　Vollard, Ambroise. *Paul Cézanne: His Life and Art*. Translated by H. L. Van Doren. New York: Brown, 1923.

1925　　Delteil, Loys. *Manuel de L'amateur d'estampes*. Vol. 2. Paris, 1925.

1936　　Venturi, L. *Cézanne: son Art, son Oeuvre*. 2 vols. Paris: P. Rosenberg, 1936.

1944　　Johnson, Una. *Ambroise Vollard: Éditeur*. New York: Wittenborn and Co., 1944.

1949　　Adhémar, Jean. *Inventaire du Fond Français du Cabinet des Estampes de la Bibliothèque Nationale, Gravures après 1800*. Vol. 4. Paris, 1949.

1972　　Cherpin, Jean. *L'Oeuvre Gravé de Cézanne*. Marseilles: Arts et Livres de Provence, 1972.

1972　　Leymarie, Jean and Melot, Michel. *The Graphic Works of the Impressionists: the Complete Prints of Manet, Pissarro, Renoir, Cézanne and Sisley*. New York: Abrams, 1972.

1973　　Salamon, Harry. "Paul Cézanne: Critical Notes and Catalogue of his Engravings." *Print Collector* [Milan: Grafica Sipiel, s.r.l.] 4 (1973): 36–45.

CHAGALL, MARC (1887–　　)

1944　　Johnson, Una E. *Ambroise Vollard: Éditeur*. New York: Wittenborn and Co., 1944.

1960　　Mourlot, Fernand. *Chagall Lithographe: 1922–1957*. Vol. 1. Monte Carlo: Sauret, 1960.

1963　　Mourlot, Fernand. *Chagall Lithographe: 1957–1962*. Vol. 2. Monte Carlo: Sauret, 1963.

1966　　Leymarie, J. *Marc Chagall, Monotypes: 1961–1965*. Geneva: Cramer Gallery, 1966.

1969　　Mourlot, Fernand. *Chagall Lithographe: 1962–1968*. Vol. 3. Monte Carlo: Sauret, 1969 and Boston: Boston Book and Art Shop, Inc., 1969.

1969　　Wingler, Hans M. *Graphic Work from the Bauhaus*. Greenwich, Conn.: New York Graphic Society, 1969.

1970　　Bibliothèque Nationale. *Marc Chagall: l'oeuvre gravé*. Paris, 1970.

1970   Kornfeld, E. W. *Verzeichnis der Kupferstiche, Radierungen und*   **41**
       Holzschnitte von Marc Chagall: Vol. 1: Werke 1922–1966. Berne:
       Kornfeld and Klipstein, 1970.

CHAHINE, EDGAR (1874–1947)

1949   Adhémar, Jean *Bibliothèque Nationale: Inventaire du Fonds Français Après 1800.* Vol. 4., pp. 202–216. Paris: Bibliothèque Nationale, 1949.

1967   Kovler Gallery. *Forgotten Printmakers of the 19th Century.* Chicago, 1967.

CHAMBERLAIN, SAMUEL (1895–   )

1926   Childs, Charles D. "Etchings and Lithographs of Samuel Chamberlain." *Print Connoisseur* 6 (1926): 9–28.

1927   Childs, Charles D. *Samuel Chamberlain: Etcher and Lithographer.* Boston: C. E. Goodspeed & Co., 1927.

1949   Reese, Albert. *American Prize Prints of the 20th Century.* p. 38. New York: American Artists Group, 1949.

1968   Chamberlain, Samuel. *Etched in Sunlight.* Boston: Boston Public Library, 1968.

1970   Library of Congress. *American Prints in the Library of Congress: A Catalog of the Collection.* Compiled by Karen F. Beall. pp. 104–105. Baltimore: The Library of Congress, The Johns Hopkins Press, 1970.

1974   Hitchings, Sinclair. *Samuel Chamberlain: "Etched in Sunlight"—A Quarter Century of Printmaking in Retrospect (1924–1949).* Washington, D.C.: June 1 Gallery of Fine Art, 1974.

CHARDIN, JEAN BAPTISTE SIMEON (1699–1779)

1934   Francis, Eric C. "Chardin and his Engravers." *Print Collector's Quarterly* 21 (1934): 229.

CHARLET, NICOLAS TOUSSAINT (1792–1845)

1856   Combe, J. F. de la. *Charlet: Description raisonné de son oeuvre lithographique.* Paris, 1856.

1967   Kovler Gallery. *Forgotten Printmakers of the 19th Century.* Chicago, 1967.

1971   Victoria and Albert Museum. *Homage to Senefelder.* Introduction by Felix H. Man. London, 1971.

CHARLOT, JEAN (1898–   )

1949   Reese, Albert. *American Prize Prints of the 20th Century*. p. 39. New York: American Artists Group, 1949.

1970   Library of Congress. *American Prints in the Library of Congress: A Catalog of the Collection*. Compiled by Karen F. Beall. p. 107. Baltimore: The Library of Congress, The Johns Hopkins Press, 1970.

Morse, Peter. Work in progress.

CHARLTON, EDWARD WILLIAM, R.E. (1859–   )

1896   "Etchings of E. W. Charlton." *Studio* 7 (1896): 219.

CHARPENTIER, ALEXANDRE (1856–1909)

1970   Stein, Donna and Karshan, Donald. *L'Estampe Originale: A Catalogue Raisonné*. New York: The Museum of Graphic Art, 1970.

CHASSÉRIAU, THÉODORE (1819–1856)

1886   Béraldi, Henri. *Les Graveurs du XIXᵉ Siècle*. Vol. 4. Paris: L. Conquet, 1886.

1971   Victoria and Albert Museum. *Homage to Senefelder*. Introduction by Felix H. Man. London, 1971.

CHAVANNES, PIERRE PUVIS de *See* PUVIS de CHAVANNES, PIERRE

CHEFFETZ, ASA (1896–1965)

1949   Reese, Albert. *American Prize Prints of the 20th Century*. p. 40. New York: American Artists Group, 1949.

1970   Library of Congress. *American Prints in the Library of Congress: A Catalog of the Collection*. Compiled by Karen F. Beall. pp. 107–108. Baltimore: The Library of Congress, The Johns Hopkins Press, 1970.

CHENEY, PHILIP (1897–   )

1949   Reese, Albert. *American Prize Prints of the 20th Century*. p. 41. New York: American Artists Group, 1949.

1970   Library of Congress. *American Prints in the Library of Congress: A Catalog of the Collection*. Compiled by Karen F. Beall. p. 108. Baltimore: The Library of Congress, The Johns Hopkins Press, 1970.

1896   Maindron, E. *Les Affiches Illustrées: 1886–1895.* Paris, 1896.

1967   Kovler Gallery. *Forgotten Printmakers of the 19th Century.* Chicago, 1967.

1970   Stein, Donna and Karshan, Donald. *L'Estampe Originale: A Catalogue Raisonné.* New York: The Museum of Graphic Art, 1970.

CHESTON, CHARLES SUDNEY (1882–   )

1929   Laver, James. "The Etchings of Charles S. Cheston." *Print Collector's Quarterly* 16 (1929): 287–301.

CHILLIDA, EDUARDO (1924–   )

1969   Man, Felix H., ed. *Europäische Graphik.* Vol. 6. Munich: Galerie Wolfgang Ketterer, 1969.

CHIRICO, GIORGIO DE (1888–   )

1965   Wingler, H. M. *Graphic Work from the Bauhaus.* Greenwich, Conn.: New York Graphic Society, 1965

1969   Ciranna, A. *Giorgio de Chirico: catalogo delle opere grafice; incisioni; e litografie, 1921–1969.* Milan, 1969.

1970   Gimpel and Weitzenhoffer, Ltd. *Original Prints of the Surrealists.* New York, 1970.

1971   Victoria and Albert Museum. *Homage to Senefelder.* Introduction by Felix H. Man. London, 1971.

CHRIST-JANER, ALBERT WILLIAM (1910-1973)

1970   Library of Congress. *American Prints in the Library of Congress: A Catalog of the Collection.* Compiled by Karen F. Beall. p. 108. Baltimore: The Library of Congress, The Johns Hopkins Press, 1970.

CHURCH, FREDERICK STUART (1842–1924)

1881   Koehler, S. R. *American Art Review* 2 (1881): 143.

1970   Library of Congress. *American Prints in the Library of Congress: A Catalog of the Collection.* Compiled by Karen F. Beall. p. 109. Baltimore: The Library of Congress, The Johns Hopkins Press, 1970.

44   **CIRY, MICHEL (1919–   )**

1953   Heintzelman, A. W. "Prints of Michel Ciry." *The Boston Public Library Quarterly,* 1953.

1968   Passeron, R. *Michel Ciry: L'oeuvre gravé 1949–1954.* La Bibliothèque des Arts. Vol. 1. Paris, 1968.

1969   Passeron, R. *Michel Ciry: L'Oeuvre gravé 1955–1968.* La Bibliothèque des Arts. Vol. 2. Paris, 1969.

Passeron, R. *Michel Ciry: L'Oeuvre gravé 1935–1948.* In preparation.

CITRON, MINNA (1896–   )

1949   Reese, Albert. *American Prize Prints of the 20th Century.* p. 42. New York: American Artists Group, 1949.

1970   Library of Congress. *American Prints in the Library of Congress: A Catalog of the Collection.* Compiled by Karen F. Beall. p. 109. Baltimore: The Library of Congress, The Johns Hopkins Press, 1970.

CLAUSEN, GEORGE, R.A. (1852–1944)

1921   Gibson, F. "Etchings and Lithographs of George Clausen, R.A." *Print Collector's Quarterly* 8 (1921): 203–227.

1921   "Notes to Catalogue of Etchings by George Clausen, R.A." *Print Collector's Quarterly* 8 (1921): 433.

CLAVÉ, ANTONI (1913–   )

1960   Cassou, J. *Antoni Clavé* Barcelona: Rauter, 1960.

1969   Avati, M. *Album des Peintres-Graveurs français, 80ᵉ anniversaire.* Paris, 1969.

1974   Weintraub Gallery. *Clavé: Paintings, Sculpture, Graphics.* New York, 1974.

CLERK, JOHN (JOHN CLERK of ELDIN) (1728–1812)

1925   Lumsden, E. S. "Etchings of John Clerk of Eldin." *Print Collector's Quarterly* 12 (1925): 15–39.

1926   Lumsden, E. S. "A Supplement to the Catalogue of Etchings by John Clerk of Eldin." *Print Collector's Quarterly* 13 (1926): 97.

1933 Hardie, Martin. "Letters from Paul Sandby to John Clerk of Eldin." *Print Collector's Quarterly* 20 (1933): 362–364.

CLIFT, JOHN RUSSEL (1925–   )

1952 De Cordova Museum. *John Russel Clift: Serigraphs*. Lincoln, Mass., 1952.

1956 De Cordova Museum. *John Clift: Printmaker*. Lincoln, Mass., 1956.

CLOAR, CARROLL (1913–   )

1970 Library of Congress. *American Prints in the Library of Congress: A Catalog of the Collection*. Compiled by Karen F. Beall. p. 110. Baltimore: The Library of Congress, The Johns Hopkins Press, 1970.

COBB, VICTOR

1916–17 Lindsay, Lionel. "Victor Cobb." *Art in Australia* (1916–17): 17.

COCHIN, CHARLES-NICOLAS, FILS (1715-1790)

1927 Rocheblave, S. *Charles-Nicolas Cochin: Graveur et Dessinateur*. Paris and Brusells: G. Vanoest, 1927.

1928 Goncourt, E. and J. A. H. de. *L'Art du dix-huitième siècle*. pp. 272–396. Paris, 1928.

COLE, ERNEST (1890-   )

1924 Dodgson, Campbell. "Drypoints of Ernest Cole." *Print Collector's Quarterly* 11 (1924): 485.

1925 Dodgson, Campbell. "Catalogue of the Dry-Points of Ernest Cole." *Print Collector's Quarterly* 12 (1925): 7–13.

COLE, J. FOXCROFT (1837–1892)

1880 Koehler, S. R. *American Art Review* 1 (1880): 191.

COLE, TIMOTHY (1852–1931)

1911 Cole, Timothy. "Some Difficulties of Wood-Engraving." *Print Collector's Quarterly* 1 (1911): 335–343.

1911 "Timothy Cole: A Biographical Note." *Print Collector's Quarterly* 1 (1911): 344–347.

46 1970 Library of Congress. *American Prints in the Library of Congress: A Catalog of the Collection*. Compiled by Karen F. Beall. p. 111. Baltimore: The Library of Congress, The Johns Hopkins Press, 1970.

COLEMAN, GLENN O. (1887–1932)

1949 Reese, Albert. *American Prize Prints of the 20th Century*. p. 222. New York: American Artists Group, 1949.

COLEMAN, THOMAS (1935–   )

1970 Library of Congress. *American Prints in the Library of Congress: A Catalog of the Collection*. Compiled by Karen F. Beall. p. 112. Baltimore: The Library of Congress, The Johns Hopkins Press, 1970.

1972 Sheldon Art Gallery. *Thomas Coleman: Printmaker*. Monographs on American Art, no. 3. Lincoln, Neb.: University of Nebraska, 1972.

COLESCOTT, WARRINGTON (1921–   )

1968 Taylor, John Lloyd. *Warrington Colescott: Graphics*. Milwaukee: Milwaukee Art Center, 1968.

1970 Library of Congress. *American Prints in the Library of Congress: A Catalog of the Collection*. Compiled by Karen F. Beall. p. 112. Baltimore: The Library of Congress, The Johns Hopkins Press, 1970.

1972 Canaday, John. *Warrington Colescott*. Madison, Wis.: Madison Art Center, 1972.

COLMAN, SAMUEL (1832–1920)

1880 Koehler, S. R. *American Art Review* 1 (1880): 387.

CONDENHOVE, (MRS.) E. M. *See* HENDERSON, ELSIE

CONDER, CHARLES (1868–1909)

1913 Gibson, F. and Dodgson, Campbell. *Charles Conder: With a Catalogue of Lithographs and Etchings*. London, 1913.

CONSTANT, GEORGE (1892–   )

1970 Library of Congress. *American Prints in the Library of Congress: A Catalog of the Collection*. Compiled by Karen F. Beall. p. 113. Baltimore: The Library of Congress, The Johns Hopkins Press, 1970.

1972   Heckscher Museum. *Artists of Suffolk County: Part 6, Contemporary*
       Prints. Huntington, N.Y., 1972

COOK, HOWARD (1901–   )

1931   Weyhe Gallery. *The Checkerboard: Cook Number.* New York, 1931.

1942   Zigrosser, Carl. *The Artist in America: 24 Close-ups of Contemporary Printmakers.* New York: Alfred Knopf, 1942.

1949   Reese, Albert. *American Prize Prints of the 20th Century.* p. 43. New York: American Artists Group, 1949.

1970   Library of Congress. *American Prints in the Library of Congress: A Catalog of the Collection.* Compiled by Karen F. Beall. p. 114. Baltimore: The Library of Congress, The Johns Hopkins Press, 1970.

COPLEY, JOHN (1875–1950)

1924   Wright, H. J. L. *The Lithographs of John Copley and Ethel Gabain.* Chicago: A. Roullier's Art Galleries, 1924.

1926   Walker, R. A. "The Lithographs of John Copley." *Print Collector's Quarterly* 13 (1926): 273–296.

COPLEY, MRS. JOHN *See* GABAIN, ETHEL

CORINTH, LOVIS (1858–1925)

1921   Schwarz, Karl. *Das Graphische Werk von Lovis Corinth.* Berlin: Fritz Gurlitt, 1921.

1960   Müller, Heinrich. *Die Späte Graphik von Lovis Corinth.* Hamburg, 1960.

1965   Miller, Jo. "The Dry-Points of Lovis Corinth." *Artist's Proof* 8 (1965): 34–37.

       Smithsonian Institution. *Prints and Drawings by Lovis Corinth.* Washington, D.C.

CORNELL, THOMAS (1937–   )

1970   Library of Congress. *American Prints in the Library of Congress: A Catalog of the Collection.* Compiled by Karen F. Beall. p. 115. Baltimore: The Library of Congress, The Johns Hopkins Press, 1970.

1971   Bowdoin College Museum of Art. *Thomas Cornell: Drawings and Prints.* Brunswick, Me., 1971.

COROT, JEAN-BAPTISTE CAMILLE (1796–1875)

1905   Robaut, A. *L'Oeuvre de Corot*. Paris, 1905.

1910   Delteil, Loys. *Le Peintre-Graveur Illustré: Corot*. Vol. 5. Paris: Chez
        l'auteur, 1910.

1912   Wickenden, R. F. "Le Père Corot." *Print Collector's Quarterly* 2
        (1912): 365–385.

1916   Bradley, William Aspenwall. "Corot as a Lithographer." *Print
        Collector's Quarterly* 6 (1916): 281–298.

1969   Delteil, Loys. *Le Peintre-Graveur Illustré: Corot. Vol. 5. 1910.
        Reprint. New York: Da Capo Press, 1969.*

COSTA, GIANFRANCESCO (1711–1772)

1940   Mauroner, Fabio. "Gianfrancesco Costa." *Print Collector's Quar-
        terly* 27 (1940): 471–485.

1940   Mauroner, Fabio. "Catalogue of the Etchings of Gianfrancesco
        Costa." *Print Collector's Quarterly* 27 (1940): 487–495.

COSTIGAN, JOHN E. (1888–1972)

1949   Reese, Albert. *American Prize Prints of the 20th Century*. p. 44. New
        York: American Artists Group, 1949.

1970   Library of Congress. *American Prints in the Library of Congress: A
        Catalog of the Collection*. Compiled by Karen F. Beall. p. 115.
        Baltimore: The Library of Congress, The Johns Hopkins Press,
        1970.

COTMAN, JOHN JOSEPH (1814–1878)

1972   William Weston Gallery. *Etchings by John Sell Cotman and his
        Sons*. London, 1972.

COTMAN, JOHN SELL (1782–1842)

1905   Dickes, W. F. *The Norwich School of Painting*. Chap. 13. London,
        1905.

1922   Popham, A. E. "Etchings of John Sell Cotman." *Print Collector's
        Quarterly* 9 (1922): 237–273.

1926   Smith, S. C. K. *Cotman*. New York: Stokes, 1926.

1972   William Weston Gallery. *Etchings by John Sell Cotman and his
        Sons*. London, 1972.

1972   William Weston Gallery. *Etchings by John Sell Cotman and his Sons*. London, 1972.

COUBINE, OTHON (1883–   )

1957   Peters, H., ed. *Die Bauhaus Mappen: Neue Europäische Graphik 1921–23*. Cologne: Czwiklitzer, 1957.

1965   Wingler, H. M. *Graphic Work from the Bauhaus*. Greenwich, Conn.: New York Graphic Society, 1965.

COURTIN, PIERRE (1921–   )

1959   *Pierre Courtin: Gravures*. Paris: Berggruen and Co., 1959.

1961   Boudaille, Georges. "Pierre Courtin: 'Engraving is a Tactile Art. ... ' " *Artists Proof* 2 (1961): 2–5.

1973   Putnam, Jacques and Meiller, Daniel, eds. *Pierre Courtin: L'Oeuvre gravé, 1944–1972*. Paris, 1973.

COUSINS, SAMUEL (1801–1887)

1904   Whitman, A. *Nineteenth Century Mezzotinters: Samuel Cousins*. London: George Bell & Sons, 1904.

COZENS, ALEXANDER (c.1700–1786)

1921   Oppe, A. P. "Fresh Light on Alexander Cozens." *Print Collector's Quarterly* 8 (1921): 61–90.

CRAIG, EDWARD GORDON (1872–1966)

1908   *Catalogue of Etchings: Being Designs for Motions by Gordon Craig*. Florence, 1908.

1922   MacFall, Haldane. "Concerning the Woodcuts of E. Gordon Craig." *Print Collector's Quarterly* 9 (1922): 407–432.

CRANE, ALAN H. (1901–1969)

1949   Reese, Albert. *American Prize Prints of the 20th Century*. p. 45. New York: American Artists Group, 1949.

1970   Library of Congress. *American Prints in the Library of Congress: A Catalog of the Collection*. Compiled by Karen F. Beall. p. 116. Baltimore: The Library of Congress, The Johns Hopkins Press, 1970.

CRANE, WALTER (1845–1915)

1970   Stein, Donna and Karshan, Donald. *L'Estampe Originale: A Catalogue Raisonné.* New York: The Museum of Graphic Art, 1970.

CRAWFORD, RALSTON (1906–   )

1949   Reese, Albert. *American Prize Prints of the 20th Century.* p. 46. New York: American Artists Group, 1949.

1953   Freeman, Richard B. *Ralston Crawford.* Tuscaloosa: U. of Alabama Press, 1953.

1970   Library of Congress. *American Prints in the Library of Congress: A Catalog of the Collection.* Compiled by Karen F. Beall. p. 117. Baltimore: The Library of Congress, The Johns Hopkins Press, 1970.

1973   Freeman, R. B. *Graphics '73: Ralston Crawford.* Lexington, Ky.: University of Kentucky, 1973.

CRODEL, CARL (1894–   )

1972   Sotriffer, Kristian. *Expressionism and Fauvism.* New York: McGraw-Hill Book Co., 1972.

CROME, JOHN (1768–1821)

1905   Dickes, W. F. *The Norwich School of Painting.* Chap. 4. London and Norwich, 1905.

1907   Theobold, H. S. *Crome's Etching: A Catalogue.* London, 1907.

1968   Clifford, Derek, and Timothy. *John Crome.* London: Faber and Faber, 1968.

1971   William Weston Gallery. *An Exhibition of the Published Etchings of John Crome.* London, 1971.

CROSS, HENRI-EDMOND (1856–1910)

1944   Johnson, Una E. *Ambroise Vollard, Éditeur.* New York: Wittenborn and Co., 1944.

1964   Compin, Isabelle. *Henri-Edmond Cross.* Preface by Bernard Dorival. Paris: Quatre Chemins, 1964.

1971   Victoria and Albert Museum. *Homage to Senefelder.* Introduction by Felix H. Man. London, 1971.

1897   Marchmont, F. *The Three Cruikshanks: A Bibliography Describing More Than 500 Works*. London: W. T. Spencer, 1897.

1903   Douglas, Richard John Hardy. *The Works of George Cruikshank: Classified and Arranged with References to Reid's Catalogue*. London, 1903.

1924   Cohn, Albert. *George Cruikshank: A Catalogue Raisonné*. London, 1924.

1972   Bates, William. *George Cruikshank: The Artist, the Humorist, and the Man*. 1879. Reprint. London, 1972.

CRUIKSHANK, ISAAC (1756–1810)

1897   Marchmont, F. *The Three Cruikshanks: A Bibliography Describing More Than 500 Works*. London: W. T. Spencer, 1897.

1966   Krumbharr, E. B. *Isaac Cruikshank: A Catalogue Raisonné*. Philadelphia: University of Pennsylvania Press, 1966.

CRUIKSHANK, ROBERT (1789–1856)

1897   Marchmont, F. *The Three Cruikshanks: A Bibliography Describing More Than 500 Works*. London: W. T. Spencer, 1897.

CSOKA, STEPHAN (1897–   )

1949   Reese, Albert. *American Prize Prints of the 20th Century*. p. 47. New York: American Artists Group, 1949.

1970   Library of Congress. *American Prints in the Library of Congress: A Catalog of the Collection*. Compiled by Karen F. Beall. p. 118. Baltimore: The Library of Congress, The Johns Hopkins Press, 1970.

CURRY, JOHN STEUART (1897–1946)

1943   Schmeckebier, L. E. *John Steuart Curry's Pageant of America*. New York: American Artists Group, 1943.

1949   Reese, Albert. *American Prize Prints of the 20th Century*. p. 223. New York: American Artists Group, 1949.

1970   Library of Congress. *American Prints in the Library of Congress: A Catalog of the Collection*. Compiled by Karen F. Beall. p. 120. Baltimore: The Library of Congress, The Johns Hopkins Press, 1970.

52   DAGLISH, ERIC FITCH (1892–   )

1930   Bliss, Douglas Percy. "The Wood Engravings of Eric Fitch
        Daglish." *Print Collector's Quarterly* 17 (1930): 279–298.

DALI, SALVADOR (1904–   )

1941   Soby, James Thrall. *Paintings, Drawings, Prints: Salvador Dali.*
        New York: Museum of Modern Art, 1941.

1962   Descharnes, R. *The World of Salvador Dali.* Lausanne: Edita, 1962.

1964   Tsunetaka, Veda. *Exposition Salvador Dali.* Tokyo, 1964.

1970   Gimpel and Weitzenhoffer Ltd. *Original Prints of the Surrealists.*
        New York, 1970.

1972   Morse, A. Reynolds. "Who's Dali's Publisher?" *Print Collector's
        Newsletter* 3 (1972): 54.

DANCE, GEORGE (1741–1825)

1929   Stokes, Hugh. "George Dance's 'Heads'." *Print Collector's Quar-
        terly* 16 (1929): 9–32.

DANIEL, LEWIS C. (1901–1952)

1934   Morrow, B. F. "Highlights of Copper: Lewis C. Daniel." *Prints* 5
        (1934): 10–13.

1949   Reese, Albert. *American Prize Prints of the 20th Century.* p. 48. New
        York: American Artists Group, 1949.

1970   Library of Congress. *American Prints in the Library of Congress: A
        Catalog of the Collection.* Compiled by Karen F. Beall. p. 121.
        Baltimore: The Library of Congress, The Johns Hopkins Press,
        1970.

DANIELL, REV. EDWARD THOMAS (1804–1842)

1899   Binyon, L. "Edward Thomas Daniell, Painter and Etcher." *The
        Dome,* New Series 4 (1899): 209.

1905   Dickes, W. F. *Norwich School of Painting.* Chap. 21. London and
        Norwich, 1905.

DANIELL, SAMUEL (1775–1811)

1928   Sutton, Major I. "The Daniell Aquatints." *Print Collector's Quar-
        terly* 15 (1928): 51–64.

1954   Sutton, Thomas. *The Daniells: Artists and Travellers*. London: Bodley Head, 1954.

DANIELL, THOMAS (1749–1840)

1928   Sutton, Major I. "The Daniell Aquatints." *Print Collector's Quarterly* 15 (1928): 51–64.

1954   Sutton, Thomas. *The Daniells: Artists and Travellers*. London: Bodley Head, 1954.

DANIELL, WILLIAM (1769–1837)

1928   Sutton, Major I. "The Daniell Aquatints." *Print Collector's Quarterly* 15 (1928): 51–64.

1954   Sutton, Thomas. *The Daniells: Artists and Travellers*. London: Bodley Head, 1954.

DARLEY, FELIX O.C. (1822–1888)

1971   Ewers, John C. "Not Quite Redmen: The Plains Indian Illustrations of Felix O. C. Darley." *The American Art Journal* 3 (1971): 88–98.

DASH, ROBERT (1934–   )

1972   Heckscher Museum. *Artists of Suffolk County: Part 6, Contemporary Prints*. Huntington, N.Y., 1972.

DAUBIGNY, CHARLES FRANÇOIS (1817–1878)

1875   Henriet, Frédéric. *Charles Daubigny et Son Ouevre Gravé*. Paris: A. Lévy, 1875.

1913   Wickenden, R. F. "Charles François Daubigny; Painter and Etcher." *Print Collector's Quarterly* 3 (1913): 177–206.

1921   Delteil, Loys. *Le Peintre-Graveur Illustré: Charles Daubigny*. Vol. 13. Paris: Chez l'auteur, 1921.

1922   Barnard, O. H. "The 'Cliches-verre' of the Barbizon School." *Print Collector's Quarterly* 9 (1922) 149–172.

1967   Kovler Gallery. *Forgotten Printmakers of the 19th Century*. Chicago, 1967.

1969   Delteil, Loys. *Le Peintre-Graveur Illustré: Charles Daubigny*. Vol. 13. 1921. Reprint. New York: Da Capo Press, 1969.

DAUMIER, HONORÉ (1808–1879)

1914   Seaver, Henry L. "Daumier's Lithographs." *Print Collector's Quarterly* 1 (1914): 63–82.

1914   Thackeray, William Makepeace. "Daumier's 'Robert Macaire'." *Print Collector's Quarterly* 4 (1914): 83–100.

1916   Delteil, Loys. "Honoré Daumier." *Print Collector's Quarterly* 6 (1916): 3–36.

1926   Delteil, Loys. *Le Peintre-Graveur Illustré: Honoré Daumier.* Vols. 20–29. Paris: Chez l'auteur, 1926–1930.

1933   Bouvy, Eugène. *Daumier.* 1933.

1934   Bibliothèque Nationale. *Daumier: lithographies, gravures sur bois, sculptures.* Paris, 1934.

1958   Bibliothèque Nationale. *Daumier: le peintre-graveur.* Paris, 1958.

1969   Delteil, Loys. *Le Peintre-Graveur Illustré: Honoré Daumier.* Vols. 20–29. 1926–1930. Reprint. New York: Da Capo Press, 1969.

1970   Mayor, A. Hyatt. "Daumier." *Print Collector's Newsletter* 1 (1970): 1–4.

DAVIEL, LÉON (1867–1932)

1938   Fell, H. Granville. "Léon Daviel: Engraver and Painter." *Print Collector's Quarterly* 20 (1938): 57–64.

DAVIES, ARTHUR BOWEN (1862–1928)

1923   Burroughs, Alan. "The Art of Arthur B. Davies." *Print Connoisseur* 3 (1923): 195.

1925   Burroughs, Alan. *Art of Arthur B. Davies.* New York, 1925.

1929   Price, Frederic Newlin. *The Etchings and Lithographs of Arthur B. Davies.* New York: M. Kennerly; London: M. and M. Kennerly, Jr., 1929.

1949   Reese, Albert. *American Prize Prints of the 20th Century.* p. 224. New York: American Artists Group, 1949.

1956   Rueppel, Merrill Clement. *The Graphic Art of Arthur Bowen Davies and John Sloan.* Ann Arbor, Michigan: University Microfilms, 1956.

1972   Harbor Gallery. *Arthur B. Davies: An Exhibition of Etchings, Aquatints, Woodcuts and Lithographs.* Foreword by Elke Solomon. Cold Spring Harbor, N.Y., 1972.

DAVIS, HUBERT (1902–   )

1970   Library of Congress. *American Prints in the Library of Congress: A Catalog of the Collection.* Compiled by Karen F. Beall. p. 125. Baltimore: The Library of Congress, The Johns Hopkins Press, 1970.

DAVIS, STUART (1894–1964)

1945   Johnson, J. *Stuart Davis.* New York: Museum of Modern Art, 1945.

1965   National Collection of Fine Arts. *Stuart Davis Memorial Exhibition.* Washington, D.C.: Smithsonian Institution, 1965.

1965   Ross, John. "A Salute to the Fine Arts and Stuart Davis." *Artist's Proof* 8 (1965): 2–3.

1970   Library of Congress. *American Prints in the Library of Congress: A Catalog of the Collection.* Compiled by Karen F. Beall. p. 125. Baltimore: The Library of Congress, The Johns Hopkins Press, 1970.

1971   Kainen, Jacob. "Prints of the Thirties: Reflections on the Federal Art Project." *Artist's Proof* 11 (1971): 34–41.

DAWSON, NELSON, R. E. (20th C.)

1913   Salaman, M. C. "Soft-ground Etchings of Nelson Dawson." *The Studio* 59 (1913): 194.

DEBENJAK, RIKO (1908–   )

1961   Krzhishnik, R. *Riko Debenjak: Catalogue of the Exhibition.* Ljubljana, Yugoslavia, 1961.

DEBUCOURT, PHILIBERT-LOUIS (1755–1832)

1880   Portalis, R. and Béraldi, H. *Les Graveurs du 18ᵉ Siècle.* Vol. 1. Paris, 1880.

1899   Fenaille, M. *L'Oeuvre Gravé de Philibert-Louis Debucourt.* Paris, 1899.

1923   Dacier, Emile. "Philbert-Louis Debucourt." *Print Connoisseur* 3 (1923): 237.

56   **DECAMPS, ALEXANDRE GABRIEL (1803–1860)**

1879   Moreau, A. *Decamps et son Oeuvre*. Paris, 1879.

1886   Béraldi, Henri. *Les Graveurs du XIXᵉ Siècle*. Vol. 5. Paris, 1886.

1967   Kovler Gallery. *Forgotten Printmakers of the 19th Century*. Chicago, 1967.

DEGAS, EDGAR (1834–1917)

1919   Delteil, Loys. *Le Peintre-Graveur Illustré: Edgar Degas*. Vol. 9. Paris: Chez l'auteur, 1919.

1944   Johnson, Una E. *Ambroise Vollard, Éditeur*. New York: Wittenborn and Co., 1944.

1958   Lefevre Gallery. *Edgar Degas: Monotypes, Drawings, Sculpture*. Foreword by Douglas Cooper. London, 1958.

1967   Janis, E. Parry. "The Role of the Monotype in the Working Method of Degas." *The Burlington Magazine*. Vol. 109. part 1, no. 766, pp. 20–27. part 2, no. 767, pp. 71–81. London, 1967.

1968   Janis, E. Parry. *Degas: Monotypes, Essay, Catalogue and Checklist*. Cambridge, Mass.: Fogg Art Museum, Harvard University, 1968.

1969   Delteil, Loys. *Le Peintre-Graveur Illustré: Edgar Degas*. Vol. 9. 1919. Reprint. New York: Da Capo Press, 1969.

1973   Adhémar, Jean and Cachin, F. *Degas: Gravures et Monotypes*. Paris, 1973.

DEHN, ADOLF (1895–1968)

1942   Zigrosser, Carl. *The Artist in America: 24 Close-ups of Contemporary Printmakers*. New York: Alfred Knopf, 1942.

1949   Reese, Albert. *American Prize Prints of the 20th Century*. p. 49. New York: American Artists Group, 1949.

1950   Dehn, Adolf and Barrett, Lawrence. *How to Draw and Print Lithographs*. New York: American Artists Group, 1950.

1970   Library of Congress. *American Prints in the Library of Congress: A Catalog of the Collection*. Compiled by Karen F. Beall. p. 128. Baltimore: The Library of Congress, The Johns Hopkins Press, 1970.

1972   June 1 Gallery. *The Many Faces of Adolf Dehn*. Washington, D.C., 1972.

DEINES, HUBERT E. (1894–1967)

1949   Reese, Albert. *American Prize Prints of the 20th Century.* p. 50. New York: American Artists Group, 1949.

1970   Library of Congress. *American Prints in the Library of Congress: A Catalog of the Collection.* Compiled by Karen F. Beall. p. 129. Baltimore: The Library of Congress, The Johns Hopkins Press, 1970.

DE KOONING, WILLEM (1904–)

1972   Heckscher Museum. *Artists of Suffolk County: Part 6, Contemporary Prints.* Huntington, N.Y., 1972.

1974   Larson, Philip. "Willem de Kooning: The Lithographs." *Print Collector's Newsletter* 5 (1974): 6–7.

DELACROIX, EUGÈNE (1798–1863)

1908   Delteil, Loys. *Le Peintre-Graveur Illustré: Ingres and Delacroix.* Vol. 3. Paris: Chez l'auteur, 1908.

1917   Weitenkampf, Frank. "The Lithographs of Eugène Delacroix." *Print Collector's Quarterly* 7 (1917): 271–287.

1926–29 Escholier, R. *Delacroix: peintre, graveur, é crivain.* 2 vols. Paris: H. Floury, 1926–29.

1969   Delteil, Loys. *Le Peintre-Graveur Illustré: Ingres and Delacroix.* Vol. 3. 1908. Reprint. New York: Da Capo Press, 1969.

DE LATENAY, GERARD *See* LATENAY, GERARD DE

DELÂTRE, AUGUSTE (1822–1907)

1906   Delâtre, A. "Erinnerungen eines Künstlerdruckers." *Zeitschrift für bildende Kunst* 17 (1906): 1.

DELÂTRE, EUGÈNE (1864–)

1905   Béraldi, H. "Eugène Delâtre, peintre-graveur et imprimeur." *Revue de l'art ancien et moderne* 17 (1905): 442.

1970   Stein, Donna and Karshan, Donald. *L'Estampe Originale: A Catalogue Raisonné.* New York: The Museum of Graphic Art, 1970.

DELAUNAY, NICOLAS (1739–1792)

1880   Béraldi, Henri and Portalis, R. *Les Graveurs du XVIIIe Siècle.* Vol. 2. Paris: Damascène Morgand et Charles Fatout, 1880.

58   1910   Lawrence, H. W. and Dighton, Basil. *French Line Engravings of the 18th Century*. London: Lawrence and Jellicoe, Ltd., 1910.

DELAUNEY, ROBERT (1885–1941)

1926   Waldemar, George. "Lithographs of Robert Delauney." *Amour de l'Art* pp. 329–332. Paris, 1926.

1970   Goldman, Judith. "Robert Delauney; Restrikes . . . " *Print Collector's Newsletter* 1 (1970): 8.

1970   Goldman, Judith. "Delauney Lithographs? Photo Reproductions." *Print Collector's Newsletter* 1 (1970): 32–33.

DELAUNEY, SONIA (1885–   )

1962   *Huit eaux-fortes originales en couleurs par Sonia Delauney*. Paris, 1962.

DELOTZ, GEORGE (1819–1879)

1928   Dodgson, Campbell. "The Etchings and Aquatints of George Delotz." *Print Collector's Quarterly* 15 (1928): 71–79.

DE MARTELLY, JOHN S. (1903–   )

1949   Reese, Albert. *American Prize Prints of the 20th Century*. p. 51. New York: American Artists Group, 1949.

1970   Library of Congress. *American Prints in the Library of Congress: A Catalog of the Collection*. Compiled by Karen F. Beall. p. 131. Baltimore: The Library of Congress, The Johns Hopkins Press, 1970.

DENIS, MAURICE (1870–1943)

1944   Johnson, Una. *Ambroise Vollard, Éditeur*. New York: Wittenborn and Co., 1944.

1968   Cailler, P. *Catalogue raisonné de l'oeuvre gravé et lithographie de Maurice Denis*. Geneva: Editions Pierre Cailler, 1968.

1970   Kovler Gallery. *The Graphic Art of Valloton and the Nabis*. pp. 48–53. Chicago, Ill., 1970.

1970   Stein, Donna and Karshan, Donald. *L'Estampe Originale: A Catalogue Raisonné*. New York: The Museum of Graphic Art, 1970.

1971   Kunsthalle, Bremen. *Gemalde, Handzeichnungen, Druckgraphik: From the Collection of the Artist's Family*. Bremen, 1971.

1944 Johnson, Una E. *Ambroise Vollard, Éditeur*. New York: Witten-born and Co., 1944.

1955 Adhémar, J. *Derain: Peintre-Graveur: Catalogue de l'Exposition*. Paris: Bibliothèque Nationale, 1955.

1957 Rauch, N. *Les Peintres et le livre*. Geneva, 1957.

1958 Hugues, J. *50 Ans d'Edition de D. H. Kahnweiler, Galerie Louise Leiris*. Paris, 1958.

1972 Sotriffer, Kristian. *Expressionism and Fauvism*. New York: McGraw-Hill Book Co., 1972.

DE RUTH JAN (1922–   )

1967 Associated American Artists. *The Nude by Jan De Ruth: A Suite of Six Sepia and White Lithographs*. New York, 1967.

DESBOUTIN, MARCELLIN (1822–1902)

1936 Clément-Janin. "Marcellin Desboutin." *Print Collector's Quarterly* 23 (1936): 45–63.

DESPREZ, LOUIS-JEAN (1743–1804)

1933 Wollin, Dr. Nils. *Gravures originales de Desprez*. Malmö, Sweden: John Kroon, 1933.

DETMOLD, EDWARD (1883–   )

1911 Wood, T. M. "A Note on Edward Detmold." *The Studio* 51 (1911): 289.

1922 Dodgson, Campbell. "Maurice and Edward Detmold." *Print Collector's Quarterly* 9 (1922): 373–405.

DETMOLD, MAURICE (1883–1908)

1910 Dodgson, Campbell. "Maurice Detmold." *Die Graphischen Kunste (1910)*.

1922 Dodgson, Campbell. "Maurice and Edward Detmold." *Print Collector's Quarterly* 9 (1922): 373–405.

DETWILLER, FREDERICK KNECHT (1882–1953)

1949 Reese, Albert. *American Prize Prints of the 20th Century*. p. 52. New York: American Artists Group, 1949.

60   1970   Library of Congress. *American Prints in the Library of Congress: A Catalog of the Collection.* Compiled by Karen F. Beall. p. 132. Baltimore: The Library of Congress, The Johns Hopkins Press, 1970.

DEVÉRIA, ACHILLE (1800–1857)

1887   Béraldi, H. *Les Graveurs du XIXᵉ Siècle.* Vol. 5. Paris: L. Conquet, 1887.

1967   Kovler Gallery. *Forgotten Printmakers of the 19th Century.* Chicago, 1967.

DEXEL, WALTER (1890–   )

1957   Peters, H., ed. *Die Bauhaus-Mappen: Neue Europäische Graphik 1921–1923.* Cologne: C. Czwiklitzer, 1957.

1965   Wingler, H. M. *Graphic Work from the Bauhaus.* Greenwich, Conn.: New York Graphic Society, 1965.

DEY, MUKUL CHANDRA (1895–   )

1938   Bender, J. H. "The Graphic Art of Mukul Dey." *Print Collector's Quarterly* 25 (1938): 51–65.

DICKSON, JENNIFER (20th C)

1972   Colescott, Warrington. *Jennifer Dickson: Sweet Death and other Pleasures.* Madison, Wis.: Madison Print Club, 1972.

DIGHTON, RICHARD (1795–   )

1906   Calthorp, O. C. "Robert and Richard Dighton." *Connoisseur* (1906): 231.

DIGHTON, ROBERT (1752–1812)

1906   Calthrop, O. C. "Robert and Richard Dighton." *Connoisseur* (1906): 231.

1926   Hake, H. M. "Dighton Caricatures." *Print Collector's Quarterly* 13 (1926): 137, 237.

DILLON, HENRI-PATRICE (1851–1909)

1970   Stein, Donna and Karshan, Donald. *L'Estampe Originale: A Catalogue Raisonné.* New York: The Museum of Graphic Art, 1970.

1970   Galerie Mikro. *Jim Dine: Complete Graphics*. Berlin, 1970.

1970   Library of Congress. *American Prints in the Library of Congress: A Catalog of the Collection*. Compiled by Karen F. Beall. p. 136. Baltimore: The Library of Congress, The Johns Hopkins Press, 1970.

DISERTORI, BENVENUTO (1887–1969)

1935   Calabi, Augusto. "The Etchings of Benvenuto Disertori." *Print Collector's Quarterly* 22 (1935): 41–61.

1973   Bellini, Paolo. "Benvenuto Disertori: a Complete Catalogue of his Engravings." *Print Collector* [Milan: Grafica Sipiel, s.r.] 3 (1973): 24–41.

DIX, OTTO (1891–1969)

1961   Nierendorf Gallery. *Otto Dix: Exhibition Catalogue*. Berlin, 1961.

1966–67 Man, Felix H., ed. *Europäische Graphik*. Vols. 4, 5. Munich: Galerie Wolfgang Ketterer, 1966, 1967.

1970   Karsch, Florian. *Otto Dix: das Graphische Werk 1913–1960*. Hannover, 1970.

1972   Sotriffer, Kristian. *Expressionism and Fauvism*. New York: McGraw-Hill Book Co., 1972.

DOBKIN, ALEXANDER (1908–   )

1968   Associated American Artists. *Alexander Dobkin: Lithographs 1961–68*. New York, 1968.

1970   Library of Congress. *American Prints in the Library of Congress: A Catalog of the Collection*. Compiled by Karen F. Beall. p. 136. Baltimore: The Library of Congress, The Johns Hopkins Press, 1970.

DODD, FRANCIS, A.R.A. (1874–1949)

1926   Schwabe, Randolph. "Francis Dodd." *Print Collector's Quarterly* 13 (1926): 249–272.

1926   Schwabe, Randolph. "List of Plates by Francis Dodd." *Print Collector's Quarterly* 13 (1926): 369–375.

DORÉ, GUSTAVE (1832–1883)

1931   Leblanc, Henri. *Catalogue de l'oeuvre complet de Gustave Doré.* Paris: C. Bosse, 1931.

1969   Gropper Art Gallery. *Gustave Doré: Catalogue of all Works on Display.* Cambridge, Mass., 1969.

1970   Stevens, James, ed. *A Doré Treasury.* New York: Bounty Books Division of Crown Publishers, 1970.

DOW, ARTHUR WESLEY (1857–1922)

1895   Boston Museum of Fine Arts. *Special Exhibition of Color Prints, Designed, Engraved, and Printed by Arthur Wesley Dow.* Boston, 1895.

DOWELL, JOHN E., JR. (1941–   )

1971   Stein, Donna. *John E. Dowell, Jr.: Prints and Drawings.* Washington, D.C.: Corcoran Gallery of Art, 1971.

DREWES, WERNER (1899–   )

1961   Cleveland Museum of Art. *Catalogue of an Exhibition of Prints and Drawings by Werner Drewes.* Cleveland, Ohio: The Print Club, 1961.

1969   National Collection of Fine Arts. *Werner Drewes Woodcuts.* Washington, D. C.: Smithsonian Institution Press, 1969.

1970   Library of Congress. *American Prints in the Library of Congress: A Catalog of the Collection.* Compiled by Karen F. Beall. p. 138. Baltimore: The Library of Congress, The Johns Hopkins Press, 1970.

DRURY, PAUL (1903–   )

1929   Ogg, David. "The Etchings of Graham Sutherland and Paul Drury." *Print Collector's Quarterly* 16 (1929): 77–100.

1929   Walker, R. A. "A Chronological List of the Etchings and Drypoints of Graham Sutherland and Paul Drury." *Print Collector's Quarterly* 16 (1929): 97–100.

DUBUFFET, JEAN (1901–   )

1953   Limbourg, G. *L'Art brut de Jean Dubuffet.* Paris, 1953.

1961   Arthaud, N. *Jean Dubuffet: Gravures et Lithographies.* Silkeborg, Denmark: Musée de Silkeborg, 1961.

1962   Johnson, Elaine. "The 'Phenomena' of Jean Dubuffet." *Artist's Proof* 3 (1962): 26–29.

1964   Loreau, Max. *Catalogue des travaux.* 20 vols. Paris: J. J. Pauvert, 1964.

1964   McNulty, Kneeland et. al. *The Lithographs of Jean Dubuffet.* Philadelphia: Philadelphia Museum of Art, 1964.

1972   Sotriffer, Kristian. *Expressionism and Fauvism.* New York: McGraw-Hill Book Co., 1972.

DUCHAMP, GASTON *see* VILLON, JACQUES

DUCHAMP, MARCEL (1887–1968)

1970   Gimpel and Weitzenhoffer Ltd. *Original Prints of the Surrealists.* New York, 1970.

1973   D'Harnoncourt, A. and McShine, K., eds. *Marcel Duchamp.* New York: Museum of Modern Art, and Philadelphia: Philadelphia Museum of Art, 1973.

DUEZ, ERNEST-ANGE (1843–1896)

1970   Stein, Donna and Karshan, Donald. *L'Estampe Originale: A Catalogue Raisonné.* New York: The Museum of Graphic Art, 1970.

DUFRESNE, CHARLES GEORGES (1876–1938)

1972   Sotriffer, Kristian. *Expressionism and Fauvism.* New York: McGraw-Hill Book Co., 1972.

DUFY, RAOUL (1877–1953)

1938   Roger-Marx, C. "Dufy Illustrateur." *Renaissance* 3 (1938): 40–42.

1944   Johnson, Una E. *Ambroise Vollard, Éditeur.* New York: Wittenborn and Co., 1944.

1946   Camo, P. "Dans l'Atelier de Dufy: Bibliographie des ouvrages illustrés." *Portique* 4 (1946).

1951   Courthion, P. *Raoul Dufy.* Geneva: Cailler, 1951.

1953   Bresson, G. *Raoul Dufy.* Paris, 1953.

1957   Rauch, N. *Les Peintres et le Livre, 1867–1957.* Geneva, 1957.

64   1972   Sotriffer, Kristian. *Expressionism and Fauvism.* New York: McGraw-Hill Book Co., 1972.

DULAC, CHARLES-MARIE (1865–1898)

1970   Stein, Donna and Karshan, Donald. *L'Estampe Originale: A Catalogue Raisonné.* New York: The Museum of Graphic Art, 1970.

DUNOYER DE SEGONZAC, ANDRÉ (1884–1974)

1929   Roger-Marx, Claude. "Etched Work of Dunoyer de Segonzac." *Print Collector's Quarterly* 16 (1929): 33–55.

1937   Bibliothèque Nationale. *Oeuvre gravé de Dunoyer de Segonzac.* Paris, 1937.

1937   Rollins, Lloyd La Page. "Segonzac." *Prints* 7 (1937): 185–193.

1944   Johnson, Una. *Ambroise Vollard Éditeur.* New York: Wittenborn and Co., 1944.

1951   Roger-Marx, Claude. *Dunoyer de Segonzac.* Geneva: Cailler, 1951.

1958   Bibliothèque Nationale. *Oeuvre gravé de Dunoyer de Segonzac: 2nd exhibition.* Paris, 1958.

1958–   Lioré, A. and Cailler, P. *Catalogue de l'Oeuvre gravé de Dunoyer de Segonzac, 1919–1927.* Vol. 1. Geneva: Cailler, 1958.

———. *Catalogue de l'Oeuvre gravé de Dunoyer de Segonzac.* Vol. 2. 1928–1930. Geneva: Cailler, 1959.

———. *Catalogue de l'Oeuvre gravé de Dunoyer de Segonzac.* Vol. 3. 1930–1932. Geneva: Cailler, 1963.

———. *Catalogue de l'Oeuvre gravé de Dunoyer de Segonzac.* Vol. 4. 1933–1935. Geneva: Cailler, 1964.

———. *Catalogue de l'Oeuvre gravé de Dunoyer de Segonzac.* Vol. 5. 1937–1947. Geneva: Cailler, 1965.

———. *Catalogue de l'Oeuvre gravé de Dunoyer de Segonzac.* Vol. 6. 1948–1952. Geneva: Cailler, 1966.

———. *Catalogue de l'Oeuvre gravé de Dunoyer de Segonzac.* Vol. 7. 1953–1956. Geneva: Cailler, 1968.

———. *Catalogue de l'Oeuvre gravé de Dunoyer de Segonzac.* Vol. 8. [in preparation.]

DUPRÉ, JULES (1811–1889)

1906   Delteil, Loys. *Le Peintre-Graveur Illustré: Millet, Rousseau, Dupré.* Vol. 1. Paris: Chez l'auteur, 1906.

1969   Delteil, Loys. *Le Peintre-Graveur Illustré: Millet, Rousseau, Dupré.*   **65**
         Vol. 1. 1906. Reprint. New York: Da Capo Press, 1969.

DURAND, ASHER B. (1796–1886)

1895   Grolier Club. *Catalogue of the Engraved Work of Asher B. Durand.*
         New York, 1895.

1971   Craven, Wayne. "Asher B. Durand's Career as an Engraver." *The
         American Art Journal* 3 (1971): 39–57.

1971   Hendricks, Gordon. "Durand, Maverick and The 'Declaration'."
         The American Art Journal 3 (1971): 58–71.

1971   Jaffe, Irma B. "Trumbull's 'The Declaration of Independence':
         Keys and Dates." *The American Art Journal* 3 (1971): 41–49.

DURIEUX, CAROLINE (1896–   )

1942   Zigrosser, Carl. *The Artist in America: 24 Close-ups of Contemporary
         Printmakers.* New York: Alfred Knopf, 1942.

1949   *Caroline Durieux: 43 Lithographs and Drawings.* Foreword by Carl
         Zigrosser. Louisiana State University Press, 1949.

1949   Reese, Albert. *American Prize Prints of the 20th Century.* p. 53. New
         York: American Artists Group, 1949.

1970   Library of Congress. *American Prints in the Library of Congress: A
         Catalog of the Collection.* Compiled by Karen F. Beall. p. 139.
         Baltimore: The Library of Congress, The Johns Hopkins Press,
         1970.

DUVENECK, FRANK (1848–1919)

1918   Hurmann, Norbert. *Frank Duveneck.* Boston and New York, 1918.

1938   Poole, Emily. "The Etchings of Frank Duveneck." *Print Collector's
         Quarterly* 25 (1938): 313–331.

1938   Poole, Emily. "Catalogue of the Etchings of Frank Duveneck."
         Print Collector's Quarterly 25 (1938): 447–463.

1970   Library of Congress. *American Prints in the Library of Congress: A
         Catalog of the Collection.* Compiled by Karen F. Beall. p. 140.
         Baltimore: The Library of Congress, The Johns Hopkins Press,
         1970.

DWIGHT, MABEL (1876–1955)

1942   Zigrosser, Carl. *The Artist in America: 24 Close-ups of Contemporary
         Printmakers.* New York: Alfred Knopf, 1942.

66   1949   Reese, Albert. *American Prize Prints of the 20th Century*. p. 54. New York: American Artists Group, 1949.

1949   Zigrosser, Carl. "Mabel Dwight: Master of Comedie Humaine." *American Artist* 13 (1949): 42–45.

1970   Library of Congress. *American Prints in the Library of Congress: A Catalog of the Collection*. Compiled by Karen F. Beall. p. 141. Baltimore: The Library of Congress, The Johns Hopkins Press, 1970.

1973   Mount Holyoke College Art Museum, and the Weyhe Gallery. *14 American Women Printmakers of the 30's and 40's*. South Hadley, Mass., and New York, 1973.

DYSON, WILL (1883–1938)

1934   "Will Dyson: Artist—Economist." *Prints* 4 (1934): 14-18.

EAST, ALFRED, R.A. (1849–1913)

1905   Newbolt, F. "Etchings of Alfred East." *Studio* 34 (1905): 124.

1913   Hind, A. M. *Graphischen Kunst*. (1913): 12.

EBY, KERR (1890–1946)

1924   "List of Plates by Kerr Eby." *Print Connoisseur* 4 (1924): 50–55.

1924   Weitenkampf, Frank. "Kerr Eby: Artist in Black and White." *Print Connoisseur* 4 (1924): 37.

1930   *Kerr Eby, A.N.A.* American Etchers Series. Vol. 8. New York: The Crafton Collection and London: P. & D. Colnaghi and Co., 1930.

1938   Keppel, Dorothy. "Kerr Eby." *Print Collector's Quarterly* 25 (1938): 83.

1949   Reese, Albert. *American Prize Prints of the 20th Century*. p. 225. New York: American Artists Group, 1949.

1970   Library of Congress. *American Prints in the Library of Congress: A Catalog of the Collection*. Compiled by Karen F. Beall. pp. 142–143. Baltimore: The Library of Congress, The Johns Hopkins Press, 1970.

EDWARDS, EDWIN (1823–1879)

1879   Burty, P. "Edwin Edwards, Peintre de Paysages et Aquafortiste." *L' Art* 19 (1879): 109.

1906   Butler, Daniel and Co. *List of Mezzotint Engravings by S. Arlent Edwards*. New York: D. B. Butler and Co., 1906.

1910   Knoedler, E. L. *List of Mezzotint Engravings by S. Arlent Edwards*. New York, 1910.

1921   Minneapolis Institute of Arts. *Mezzotints in Color after Famous Paintings: an Exhibition of S. Arlent Edwards*. Minneapolis, Minn., 1921.

EICHENBERG, FRITZ (1901–   )

1949   Reese, Albert. *American Prize Prints of the 20th Century*. p. 55. New York: American Artists Group, 1949.

1967   Associated American Artists. *Fritz Eichenberg: 47 Years of Prints and Illustrated Books*. Introduction by Alan Fern. New York, 1967.

1970   Library of Congress. *American Prints in the Library of Congress: A Catalog of the Collection*. Compiled by Karen F. Beall. pp. 144–145. Baltimore: The Library of Congress, The Johns Hopkins Press, 1970.

1973   Jane Haslem Gallery. *The Innovators: Renaissance in American Printmaking*. Washington, D.C., 1973.

EISEN, CHARLES DOMINIQUE JOSEPH (1720–1778)

1972   Salomons, Vera. *Charles Eisen: Eighteenth Century French Book Illustrator and Engraver*. Amsterdam: G. W. Hissink and Co., and New York: Abner Schram, 1972.

ELIOT, MAURICE (1864–   )

1944   Johnson, Una E. *Ambroise Vollard, Éditeur*. New York: Wittenborn and Co., 1944.

ELLIOTT, AILEEN MARY (MRS. A. M. BEALE) (1896–   )

1926   Laver, James. "A New Etcher: Miss A. M. Elliott." *Bookman's Journal* 14 (1926): 18.

ELTEN, H. KRUSEMAN VAN (1829–1904)

1880   Koehler, S. R. *American Art Review* 1 (1880): 475.

ENSOR, JAMES (1860–1949)

1925   Delteil, Loys. *Le Peintre-Graveur Illustré: Leys, Braekeleer, Ensor*. Vol. 19. Paris: Chez l'auteur, 1925.

68   1935   Croquez, A. *L'Oeuvre Gravé de James Ensor*. Paris: M. Le Garrac, 1935.

1947   Croquez, A. *L'Oeuvre Gravé de James Ensor*. Geneva and Brussels: Editions Pierre Cailler, 1947.

1966   Damase, J. *L'Oeuvre Gravé de James Ensor*. Geneva: Motte, 1966.

1969   Albert Loeb and Krugier Gallery, Inc. *James Ensor: The Complete Graphic Works*. New York, 1969.

1969   Delteil, Loys. *Le Peintre-Graveur Illustré: Leys, Braekeleer, Ensor*. Vol. 19. 1925. Reprint. New York: Da Capo Press, 1969.

1971   H. Shickman Gallery. *The Prints of James Ensor*. New York: Da Capo Press, 1971.

1972   Sotriffer, Kristian. *Expressionism and Fauvism*. New York: McGraw-Hill Book Co., 1972.

1973   Brion, Marcel. *Quatres Siècles de Surréalisme: L'Art Fantastique dans la Gravure*. Paris: Pierre Belfond, 1973. [American distributor: New York: Wittenborn and Co.]

ENTERS, ANGNA (1907–   )

1958   Enters, Angna. *Artist's Life*. New York: Coward, McCann Inc., 1958.

1973   Mount Holyoke College Art Museum and the Weyhe Gallery. *14 American Women Printmakers of the 30's and 40's*. South Hadley, Mass., and New York, 1973.

ERNI, HANS (1909–   )

1969   Cailler, Pierre. *Catalogue Raisonné de L'Oeuvre Lithographié et Gravé de Hans Erni: 1930–1957*. Vol. 1. Geneva: Editions Pierre Cailler, 1969.

ERNST, JIMMY (1920–   )

1972   Heckscher Museum. *Artists of Suffolk County: Part 6, Contemporary Prints*. Huntington, N.Y. 1972.

ERNST, MAX (1891–   )

1951   *Max Ernst. Gemalde u. Graphik 1920–1950*. Brülh, Germany, 1951.

1963   Hugues and Poupard-Lieussou. *Max Ernst: Ecrits et Oeuvre gravé*. Tours: Bibliothèque Municipale and Paris: Point Cardinal, 1963.

1970   Gimpel and Weitzenhoffer Ltd. *Original Prints of the Surrealists.*
New York, 1970.

1970   Goerg, Charles. *Max Ernst: Oeuvre Gravé.* Geneva: Musée d'art et
d'Histoire, 1970.

1972   Brusberg. *Dokumente 3: Max Ernst, Jenseits der Malerei, das
graphische Oeuvre.* Hanover, 1972.

ESCHER, MAURITS (1898–1972)

1961   Escher, M. C. *The Graphic Work of M. C. Escher.* New York:
Hawthorne, 1961.

1963–4 Nemerov, Howard. "The Miraculous Transformations of Maurits
Cornelis Escher." *Artist's Proof* 6 (1963–64): 32–39.

1964   De Cordova Museum. *Prints by Maurits Escher.* Lincoln, Mass.,
1964.

1967   Escher, M. C. *The Graphic Work of M. C. Escher.* 2nd ed. New
York: Hawthorne, 1967.

1971   Escher, M. C. *The Graphic Work of M. C. Escher.* 2nd ed. 1967. 2nd
printing. New York: Ballantine Books, 1971.

1972   Locher, J. L., ed. *The World of M. C. Escher.* New York: Harry N.
Abrams, 1972.

ESTÈVE, MAURICE (1904–   )

1961   Muller, J. E. *Maurice Estève.* Paris: Hazan, 1961.

EVANS, MERLYN (1910–   )

1972   Victoria and Albert Museum. *The Graphic Work of Merlyn Evans.*
London, 1972.

EVERGOOD, PHILIP HOWARD FRANCIS (1901–1973)

1946   ACA Gallery. *20 Years of Evergood.* New York: Simon and
Schuster, 1946.

1949   Reese, Albert. *American Prize Prints of the 20th Century.* p. 56. New
York: American Artists Group, 1949.

1966   Lippard, Lucy. *The Graphic Work of Philip Evergood.* New York:
Crown Publishers, 1966.

70 1970 Library of Congress. *American Prints in the Library of Congress: A Catalog of the Collection.* Compiled by Karen F. Beall. p. 147. Baltimore: The Library of Congress,The Johns Hopkins Press, 1970.

FABRI, RALPH (1894–   )

1949 Reese, Albert. *American Prize Prints of the 20th Century.* p. 57. New York: American Artists Group, 1949.

1970 Library of Congress. *American Prints in the Library of Congress: A Catalog of the Collection.* Compiled by Karen F. Beall. p. 148. Baltimore: The Library of Congress, The Johns Hopkins Press, 1970.

FALCONER, JOHN M. (1820–1903)

1880 Koehler, S. R. *American Art Review* 1 (1880): 190.

FANTIN-LATOUR, IGNACE HENRI (1836–1904)

1906 Hédiard, Germain. *Les Maîtres de la lithographie: Fantin-Latour, catalogue de l'oeuvre lithographique.* Paris: Librairie de l'art ancien et moderne, 1906.

1907 Bénédite, L. *L'Oeuvre lithographique de Fantin-Latour.* Paris: Delteil, 1907.

1916 Weitenkampf, Frank. "Fantin-Latour's Lithographs." *Print Collector's Quarterly* 6 (1916): 259–280.

1944 Johnson, Una E. *Ambroise Vollard, Éditeur.* New York: Wittenborn and Co., 1944.

1970 Stein, Donna and Karshan, Donald. *L'Estampe Originale: A Catalogue Raisonné.* New York: The Museum of Graphic Art, 1970.

FARRELL, FREDERICK ARTHUR (1882–1935)

1928 "Modern Etchers: Frederick Arthur Farrell." *Walker's Monthly* [London] July 1928, pp. 3–4.

FARRER, HENRY (1843–1903)

1880 Koehler, S. R.*American Art Review* 1 (1880): 55, 526.

FATTORI, GIOVANNI (1825–1908)

1935 De Witt, Antony. "The Etchings of Giovanni Fattori." *Print Collector's Quarterly* 22 (1935): 225–244.

1924   Clément-Janin. "The Etchings of Amédée Féau." *Print Connoisseur* 4 (1924): 21.

1924   "List of Etchings by Amédée Féau." *Print Connoisseur* 4 (1924): 30.

FEININGER, LYONEL (1871–1956)

1965   Wingler, H. M. *Graphic Work from the Bauhaus.* Greenwich, Conn.: New York Graphic Society, 1965.

1970   Library of Congress. *American Prints in the Library of Congress: A Catalog of the Collection.* Compiled by Karen F. Beall. pp. 149–151. Baltimore: The Library of Congress, The Johns Hopkins Press, 1965.

1972   Associated American Artists. *Feininger.* New York, 1972.

1972   Prasse, Leona E. *Lyonel Feininger: A Definitive Catalogue of his Graphic Work.* Cleveland: Cleveland Museum of Art, 1972.

1974   Associated American Artists. *Catalogue of Exhibition: Lyonel Feininger Woodcuts Used as Letterheads.* New York, 1974.

FELDMAN, EUGENE (1921–   )

1965   Philadelphia Museum of Art. *Eugene Feldman: Prints.* Philadelphia, Pa., 1965.

1970   Library of Congress. *American Prints in the Library of Congress: A Catalog of the Collection.* Compiled by Karen F. Beall. p. 151. Baltimore: The Library of Congress, The Johns Hopkins Press, 1970.

FELIXMÜLLER, CONRAD (1897–   )

1965   Nierendorf Gallery. *Catalogue of the Conrad Felixmüller Exhibition.* Berlin, 1965.

1972   Sotriffer, Kristian. *Expressionism and Fauvism.* New York: McGraw-Hill Book Co., 1972.

FERNE, HORTENSE (1885–   )

1973   June 1 Gallery of Fine Arts. *Prints and Pastels by Hortense Ferne: A Sampler.* Washington, D.C., 1973.

FERRIS, J. L. G. (1863–1930)

1924   Brown, Warren Wilmer. "J. L. G. Ferris: America's Painter-Historian." *Print Connoisseur* 4 (1924): 85.

72   1924   "List of the American Historical Paintings by J. L. G. Ferris." *Print Connoisseur* 4 (1924): 106.

1965   Heckscher Museum. *The Moran Family*. Huntington, N.Y., 1965.

FERRIS, STEPHEN JAMES (1835–1915)

1880   Koehler, S. R. *American Art Review* 1 (1880): 104.

FEURE, GEORGES DE (1868–1928)

1944   Johnson, Una E. *Ambroise Vollard, Éditeur*. New York: Wittenborn and Co., 1944.

1970   Stein, Donna and Karshan, Donald. *L'Estampe Originale: A Catalogue Raisonné*. New York: The Museum of Graphic Art, 1970.

FIENE, ERNEST (1894–1965)

1949   Reese, Albert. *American Prize Prints of the 20th Century*. p. 58. New York: American Artists Group, 1949.

1970   Library of Congress. *American Prints in the Library of Congress: A Catalog of the Collection*. Compiled by Karen F. Beall. p. 152. Baltimore: The Library of Congress, The Johns Hopkins Press, 1970.

FINCH, HENEAGE, 4th EARL OF AYLESFORD (1751–1812)

1924   Oppe, A. P. "The Fourth Earl of Aylesford." *Print Collector's Quarterly* 11 (1924): 263–292.

FINNIE, JOHN (1829–1906)

1907   *Memorial Exhibition Catalogue*. Liverpool, 1907.

FISCHER, HANS (1909–1958)

1968   Scheidegger, Alfred. *Hans Fischer: Das Druckgraphische Werk*. Berne: Stämpfli, 1968.

FISCHER, OSKAR (1892–1955)

1957   Peters, H., ed. *Die Bauhaus-Mappen: Neue Europäische Graphik 1921–23*. Cologne: C. Czwiklitzer, 1957.

1965   Wingler, H. M. *Graphic Work from the Bauhaus*. Greenwich, Conn.: New York Graphic Society, 1965.

1941   Whitmore, Elizabeth. "A. Hugh Fisher, A.R.E.: Enemy Bombs and a British Artist." *Print Collector's Quarterly* 28 (1941): 381.

FITTON, HEDLEY, R.E. (1859–1929)

1911   Dunthorne, R. *Catalogue of Etchings of Hedley Fitton, R.E.* London: Rembrandt Gallery, 1911.

FLINT, WILLIAM RUSSELL (1880–1969)

1931   Salaman, Malcolm. *W. Russell Flint.* Modern Masters of Etching Series. no. 27. London: The Studio, Ltd., 1931.

1957   Wright, Harold J. L. *Etchings and Drypoints by Sir William Russell Wright.* London: Colnaghi, 1957.

1973   Sotheby and Co. *The Arthur Mitchell Collection of Drypoints by Sir William Russell Flint.* London, 1973.

FLORSHEIM, RICHARD A. (1916–   )

1970   Library of Congress. *American Prints in the Library of Congress: A Catalog of the Collection.* Compiled by Karen F. Beall. p. 153. Baltimore: The Library of Congress, The Johns Hopkins Press, 1970.

1971   Associated American Artists. *Richard Florsheim: Recent Lithographs.* New York, 1971.

FONTANA, LUCIO (1899–1968)

1966   Cirlot, J. E. *Fontana.* Barcelona: G. Gili, 1966.

FORAIN, JEAN-LOUIS (1852–1931)

1910   Guérin, Marcel. *Jean-Louis Forain Lithographe.* Paris, 1910.

1912   Guérin, Marcel. *Jean-Louis Forain: Aquafortiste: 1873–1886.* Vol. 1. *1908–1910. Vol. 2.* Paris: H. Floury, 1912.

1921   Dodgson, Campbell. "The Etchings of Jean-Louis Forain." *Print Collector's Quarterly* 8 (1921): 3–36.

1925   Salaman, Malcolm. *Jean-Louis Forain.* Modern Masters of Etching Series, no. 4. London: The Studio, Ltd., 1925.

1931   Dodgson, Campbell. *Sixty Lithographs, Etchings and Drypoints by Jean-Louis Forain 1852–1931.* New York: M. Knoedler and Co., Inc., 1931.

74 1935 Dodgson, Campbell. *Forain: Aquafortiste et lithographe 1852–1931.* New York: M. Knoedler and Co., Inc., 1935.

1944 Johnson, Una E. *Ambroise Vollard, Éditeur.* New York: Wittenborn and Co., 1944.

1972 Denison University. *Jean-Louis Forain: The War Sketches.* Granville, Ohio, 1972.

FORBES, ELIZABETH ADELA (1859–1912)

1922 Sabin, A. K. "The Dry-Points of Elizabeth Adela Forbes." *Print Collector's Quarterly* 9 (1922): 75–101.

FORTESS, KARL (1907–   )

1973 Associated American Artists. *Karl Fortess Retrospective 1929–1971.* New York, 1973.

FORTUNY, CARBÓ MARIANO (1838–1874)

1887 Béraldi, Henri. *Les Graveurs du XIXᵉ Siècle.* Vol. 6. pp. 149–151. Paris, 1881.

1911 "A Catalogue by Fortuny" *Print Collector's Quarterly* 1 (1911): 248–250.

1911 "Bibliography of Fortuny." *Print Collector's Quarterly* 1 (1911): 251.

1911 Cortissoz, Royal. "The Etchings of Fortuny." *Print Collector's Quarterly* 1 (1911): 209–235.

FRANCIS, SAM (1923–   )

1961–63 Klipstein and Kornfeld. *Lithographies.* 3 vols. Berne, 1961–63.

1967 San Francisco Museum of Art. *Sam Francis: Exhibition of Drawings and Lithographs.* San Francisco, 1967.

1970 Library of Congress. *American Prints in the Library of Congress: A Catalog of the Collection.* Compiled by Karen F. Beall. p. 155. Baltimore: The Library of Congress, The Johns Hopkins Press, 1970.

FRASCONI, ANTONIO (1919–   )

1950 Johnson, Una. "The Woodcuts of Antonio Frasconi." *Print Collector's Quarterly* 30 (1950): 33–40.

1952   Cleveland Museum of Art. *The Work of Antonio Frasconi: Catalogue of an Exhibition.* Cleveland: Print Club of Cleveland, 1952.

1967   De Cordova Museum. *Antonio Frasconi: Prints.* Lincoln, Mass., 1967.

1970   Library of Congress. *American Prints in the Library of Congress: A Catalog of the Collection.* Compiled by Karen F. Beall. pp. 156–159. Baltimore: The Library of Congress, The Johns Hopkins Press, 1970.

1973   Jane Haslem Gallery. *The Innovators: Renaissance in American Printmaking.* Washington, D.C., 1973.

FREEMAN, DON (1908–   )

1949   Reese, Albert. *American Prize Prints of the 20th Century.* p. 59. New York: American Artists Group, 1949.

1970   Library of Congress. *American Prints in the Library of Congress: A Catalog of the Collection.* Compiled by Karen F. Beall. p. 160. Baltimore: The Library of Congress, The Johns Hopkins Press, 1970.

FRÉLAUT, JEAN (1879–1954)

1926   Delteil, Loys. *Le Peintre-Graveur Illustré: Frélaut.* Vol. 31. Paris: Chez l'auteur, 1926.

1955   Lethève, J. *Jean Frélaut: Catalogue of an Exhibition.* Paris: Bibliothèque Nationale, 1955.

1957   Ferry, M. *Jean Frélaut: Catalogue of an Exhibition.* Nice: Bibliothèque Municipale, 1957.

1958   Parcevaux, H. de. *Jean Frélaut: Catalogue of an Exhibition.* Vannes: Museum of Linuer, 1958.

1967   Kovler Gallery. *Forgotten Printmakers of the 19th Century.* Chicago, 1967.

1969   Delteil, Loys. *Le Peintre-Graveur Illustré: Frélaut.* Vol. 31. 1926. Reprint. New York: Da Capo Press, 1969.

FRICK, (MRS.) O. O. *See* AUSTEN, WINIFRED

FRIEDLAENDER, JOHNNY (1912–   )

1960   Schmücking, E. *Johnny Friedlaender: Katalog der Radierungen 1949–60.* Braunschweig: Schmücking, 1960.

1965   *Johnny Friedlaender: Oeuvre 1961–1965.* Introduction by Max-Pol Fouchet. New York: Touchstone Publishers Ltd., 1965.

1973   Schmücking, Rolf. *Johnny Friedlaender: Radierungen 1930–1972.* New York: Wittenborn and Co., 1973.

FRIEDLANDER, ISAAC (1890–1968)

1949   Reese, Albert. *American Prize Prints of the 20th Century.* p. 60. New York: American Artists Group, 1949.

FROOD, HESTER (1882–   ) (MRS. HESTER GWYNNE-EVANS)

1916   "Etchings by Hester Frood." *Studio* 66 (1916): 123.

FUCHS, ERNST (1930–   )

1967   Weis, Helmut. *Ernst Fuchs; Das Graphische Werk.* Vienna: Verlag für Jugend und Volk, 1967.

FULLER, SUE (1914–   )

1949   Reese, Albert. *American Prize Prints of the 20th Century.* p. 61. New York: American Artists Group, 1949.

1970   Library of Congress. *American Prints in the Library of Congress: A Catalog of the Collection.* Compiled by Karen F. Beall. p. 162. Baltimore: The Library of Congress, ThC Johns Hopkins Press, 1970.

GABAIN, ETHEL (MRS. JOHN COPLEY) (1883–1950)

1923   Wright, Harold J. L. "The Lithographs of Ethel Gabain." *Print Collector's Quarterly* 10 (1923): 225–287.

1924   Wright, Harold J. L. *The Lithographs of John Copley and Ethel Gabain.* Chicago: Albert Roullier's Art Galleries, 1924.

GACHET, DR. PAUL (PAUL VAN RYSSEL-*pseudonym*) (1828–1909)

1954   Gachet, Paul. *Paul van Ryssel: le Docteur Gachet Graveur.* Paris: Beaux Arts, 1954.

1970   Gropper Art Gallery. *Recent Acquisitions.* Cambridge, Mass., 1970.

GAG, WANDA (1893–1946)

1942   Zigrosser, Carl. *The Artist in America: 24 Close-ups of Contemporary Printmakers.* New York: Alfred Knopf, 1942.

1949   Reese, Albert. *American Prize Prints of the 20th Century*. p. 226.   **77**
New York: American Artists Group, 1949.

1970   Library of Congress. *American Prints in the Library of Congress: A Catalog of the Collection*. Compiled by Karen F. Beall. p. 163.
Baltimore: The Library of Congress, The Johns Hopkins Press, 1970.

1973   Mount Holyoke College Art Museum, and the Weyhe Gallery. *14 American Women Printmakers of the 30's and 40's*. South Hadley, Mass. and New York, 1973.

GAINSBOROUGH, THOMAS (1727–1788)

1891   Horne, Henry Percy. *Catalogue of Engraved Portraits Painted by Thomas Gainsborough, R.A.* 1891.

1922   Hall, Mark W. "George, Prince of Wales by J. R. Smith, after Thomas Gainsborough." *Print Collector's Quarterly* 9 (1922): 315–321. 1961–62

1972   Hayes, John. *Gainsborough as Printmaker*. New Haven: Yale University Press and London, 1972.

GALLAGHER, MICHAEL J. (1898–   )

1949   Reese, Albert. *American Prize Prints of the 20th Century*. p. 62. New York: American Artists Group, 1949.

1970   Library of Congress. *American Prints in the Library of Congress: A Catalog of the Collection*. Compiled by Karen F. Beall. pp. 163–164.
Baltimore: The Library of Congress, The Johns Hopkins Press, 1970.

GALLAGHER, SEARS (1869–1955)

1920   Holman, Louis Arthur. *Sears Gallagher's Etchings of Boston*. Boston: C. E. Goodspeed and Co., 1920.

1949   Reese, Albert. *American Prize Prints of the 20th Century*. p. 63. New York: American Artists Group, 1949.

1970   Library of Congress. *American Prints in the Library of Congress: A Catalog of the Collection*. Compiled by Karen F. Beall. p. 164.
Baltimore: The Library of Congress, The Johns Hopkins Press, 1970.

GANDARA, ANTONIO DE LA (1862–1917)

1970   Stein, Donna and Karshan, Donald. *L'Estampe Originale: A Catalogue Raisonné*. New York: The Museum of Graphic Art, 1970.

GANSO, EMIL (1895–1941)

1942   Zigrosser, Carl. *The Artist in America: 24 Close-ups of Contemporary Printmakers.* New York: Alfred Knopf, 1942.

1949   Reese, Albert. *American Prize Prints of the 20th Century.* p. 227. New York: American Artists Group, 1949.

1970   Library of Congress. *American Prints in the Library of Congress: A Catalog of the Collection.* Compiled by Karen F. Beall. pp. 164–165. Baltimore: The Library of Congress, The Johns Hopkins Press, 1970.

GARBER, DANIEL (1880–1959)

1926   "A Group of Unique and Distinguished Etchings by Daniel Garber." *International Studio* 84 (1926): 49.

GARRETT, EDMUND HENRY (1853–1929)

1881   Koehler, S. R. "Edmund Henry Garrett." *American Art Review* 2 (1881): 103.

GASKELL, PERCIVAL, R.E. (1868–1934)

1914   Salaman, M. C. "Prints of Percival Gaskell, R.E., R.B.A." *The Studio* 61 (1914): 283.

GAUGUIN, PAUL (1848–1903)

1927   Guérin, M. *L'oeuvre gravé de Gauguin.* Vols. 1 and 2. Paris: Floury, 1927.

1931   Petiet, H. M. *Catalogue de l'Exposition des Gravures de Gauguin.* Paris: Galerie de la Pléiade, 1931.

1935   Daragnès, G. *Les Bois gravés de Gauguin.* Paris, 1935.

1959   The Art Institute of Chicago. *Gauguin Prints.* Chicago, 1959.

1963   Sýkorová, Libuše. *Paul Gauguin: Unknown Woodcuts.* Prague, 1963.

1963   Sýkorová, Libuše. *Gauguin's Woodcuts.* London: Paul Hamlyn, 1963.

1968   Field, R. S. "Gauguin's Noa Noa." *Burlington Magazine* [London] (1968).

1970   Kovler Gallery. *The Graphic Art of Valloton and the Nabis.* pp. 54–55. Chicago, Ill., 1970.

1970   Stein, Donna and Karshan, Donald. *L'Estampe Originale: A Catalogue Raisonné.* New York: The Museum of Graphic Art, 1970.

1972   "An Unpublished Wood-engraving by Paul Gauguin." *Print Collector* [Milan: Grafica Sipiel, s.r.] (1972): 70–71.

1972   Sotriffer, Kristian. *Expressionism and Fauvism.* New York: McGraw-Hill Book Co., 1972.

GAVARNI, GUILLAUME SULPICE CHEVALIER (1804–1866)

1873   Armelhaut, J. and Bocher, E. *L'Oeuvre de Gavarni.* Paris, 1873.

1888   Béraldi, Henri. *Les Graveurs du XIXᵉ Siècle.* Vol. 7. Paris: L. Conquet, 1888.

1915   Wickenden, Robert J. "Gavarni." *Print Collector's Quarterly* 5 (1915): 59–83.

1924–28 Lemoisne, P.-A. *Gavarni: Peintre et Lithographe.* 2 vols. Paris, 1924–28.

1967   Kovler Gallery. *Forgotten Printmakers of the 19th Century.* Chicago, 1967.

1970   Fryberger, Betsy G. *Gavarni: Prints from the Collection of R.E. Lewis.* Stanford, Calif.: Stanford University Museum of Art, 1970.

GEDDES, ANDREW (1783–1844)

1875   Laing, D. *Etchings by Wilkie and Geddes.* Edinburgh, 1875.

1919   Dodgson, Campbell. "Etchings of Andrew Geddes." *Walpole Society* [London] 5 (1919).

1929   Sanderson, Kenneth. "Engravings after Andrew Geddes." *Print Collector's Quarterly* 16 (1929): 109–131.

GEERLINGS, GERALD KENNETH (1897–   )

1949   Reese, Albert. *American Prize Prints of the 20th Century.* p. 65. New York: American Artists Group, 1949.

1970   Library of Congress. *American Prints in the Library of Congress: A Catalog of the Collection.* Compiled by Karen F. Beall. p. 168. Baltimore: The Library of Congress, The Johns Hopkins Press, 1970.

80   **GEIKIE, WALTER, R.S.A. (1795–1837)**

1935   Morris, Roy. "The Etchings of Walter Geikie, R.S.A." *Print Collector's Quarterly* 22 (1935): 305–324.

GEISER, KARL (1898–1957)

1958   Naef, Hans. *Karl Geiser: das graphische Werk.* Zurich: Manesse, 1958.

GELLER, TODROS (1889–1949)

1949   Reese, Albert. *American Prize Prints of the 20th Century.* p. 65. New York: American Artists Group, 1949.

1970   Library of Congress. *American Prints in the Library of Congress: A Catalog of the Collection.* Compiled by Karen F. Beall. p. 169. Baltimore: The Library of Congress, The Johns Hopkins Press, 1970.

GEORGE, SIR ERNEST (1839–1922)

1875   Hamerton, P. G. "Etchings on the Loire by Mr. Ernest George." *Portfolio* 6 (1875): 60.

GÉRICAULT, JEAN-LOUIS-ANDRÉ-THÉODORE (1791–1824)

1924   Delteil, Loys. *Le Peintre-Graveur Illustré: Théodore Géricault.* Vol. 18. Paris: Chez l'auteur, 1924.

1969   Delteil, Loys. *Le Peintre-Graveur Illustré: Théodore Géricault.* Vol. 18. 1924. Reprint. New York: Da Capo Press, 1969.

1969   Spencer, Kate H. *The Graphic Art of Géricault.* New Haven, Conn.: Yale University Gallery, 1969.

GETHIN, PERCY FRANCIS (1874–1916)

1927   Wright, H. J. L. "Etchings and Lithographs of Percy Francis Gethin." *Print Collector's Quarterly* 14 (1927): 69–93.

GEYER, HAROLD CARL (1905–   )

1949   Reese, Albert. *American Prize Prints of the 20th Century.* p. 66. New York: American Artists Group, 1949.

GIACOMETTI, ALBERTO (1901–1966)

1967   Engelberts, E. *Alberto Giacometti.* Geneva, 1967.

1970   Lust, Herbert C. *Giacometti: The Complete Graphics and 15 Drawings.* New York: Tudor, 1970.

1949   Balston, Thomas. *Robert Gibbings*. London: Art and Technics, 1949.

1959   Empson, Patience. *Wood Engravings by Robert Gibbings* 1959.

GIFFORD, ROBERT SWAIN (1840–1905)

1880   Koehler, S. R. *American Art Review* 1 (1880): 5.

1970   Library of Congress. *American Prints in the Library of Congress: A Catalog of the Collection*. Compiled by Karen F. Beall. p. 170. Baltimore: The Libary of Congress, The Johns Hopkins Press, 1970.

GILKEY, GORDON WAVERLY (1912–   )

1939   Gilkey, Gordon W. "Etchings, New York World's Fair." *Building the World of Tomorrow*. London and New York: Charles Scribner's Sons, 1939.

1970   Library of Congress. *American Prints in the Library of Congress: A Catalog of the Collection*. Compiled by Karen F. Beall. pp. 171–174. Baltimore: The Library of Congress, The Johns Hopkins Press, 1970.

GILL, ERIC (1882–1940)

1928   Walker, R. A. "The Engravings of Eric Gill." *Print Collector's Quarterly* 15 (1928): 145–167.

1949   Pepler, H. D. C. "Gill in Ditchling." *Print Collector's Quarterly* 30 (1949): 48–59.

1963   Physick, John. *The Engraved Work of Eric Gill*. London: Victoria and Albert Museum, 1963.

1970   Physick, John. *The Engraved Work of Eric Gill*. 1963. Reprint. London: Victoria and Albert Museum, 1970.

1973   *Eric Gill and Modern British Wood Engravers*. London: Christopher Drake, Ltd., 1973.

GILLROY, JAMES (1757–1815)

1873   Grego, J. *Works of James Gillroy, the Caricaturist*. London, 1873.

1902   Nevill, R. "James Gillroy." *Connoisseur* 3 (1902): 24.

82 1911 Marcel, H. "La Caricatiere en Angleterre, James Gillroy." *Gazette des Beaux-Arts* 6 (1911): 467.

GIRTIN, THOMAS (1775–1802)

1900 Binyon, R. L. *Thomas Girtin, his Life and Works.* London, 1900.

GLACKENS, WILLIAM J. (1870–1938)

1956 De Gregorio, Vincent John. "The Life and Art of William J. Glackens." 2 Vols. Ph. D. dissertation, Ohio State University, 1955. Ann Arbor, Michigan: University Microfilms, 1956.

1970 Library of Congress. *American Prints in the Library of Congress: A Catalog of the Collection.* Compiled by Karen F. Beall. pp. 173–174. Baltimore: The Library of Congress, The Johns Hopkins Press, 1970.

GLARNER, FRITZ (1899–1972)

1972 Heckscher Museum. *Artists of Suffolk County: Part 6, Contemporary Prints.* Huntington, N.Y., 1972.

GLEICHMAN, OTTO (1887–1963)

1957 Peters, H., ed. *Die Bauhaus-Mappen: neue Europäische Graphik 1921–1923.* Cologne: C. Czwiklitzer, 1957.

1965 Wingler, H. M. *Graphic Work from the Bauhaus.* Greenwich, Conn.: New York Graphic Society, 1965.

GOBO, GOERGES (1876–   )

1924 Angoulvent, P. J. "Etchings of Georges Gobo." *Print Connoisseur* 4 (1924): 247.

1924 "Catalogue Raisonné, Georges Gobo." *Print Connoisseur* 4 (1924): 256.

GODEFROY, LOUIS (20th C.)

1923 "Catalogue of the Etchings of Louis Godefroy." *Print Connoisseur* 3 (1923): 123.

1923 Lemoisne, P. A. "Louis Godefroy, Painter-Etcher." *Print Connoisseur* 3 (1923): 111.

GOENEUTTE, NORBERT (1854–1894)

1970 Stein, Donna and Karshan, Donald. *L'Estampe Originale: A Catalogue Raisonné.* New York: The Museum of Graphic Art, 1970.

1953 Thieffry. *L'Oeuvre Gravé de Goerg: Catalogue*. Thesis, Ecole du Louvre, 1953.

1963 Bibliothèque Nationale. *Oeuvre Gravé de Goerg: Catalogue*. Paris, 1963.

1969 Avati, M. *Album des Peintres-Graveurs Français, 80ᵉ anniversaire*. Paris, 1969.

GOETHE, JOHANN WOLFGANG VON (1749–1832)

1932 *Goethe und die Graphischen Kunste*. Leipzig, 1932.

1949 Münz, Ludwig. *Goethe's Zeichnungen und Radierungen*. Vienna: Osterreichischen Staatsdruckerei, 1949.

1970 Eichenberg, Fritz. "Johann Wolfgang von Goethe: Graphic Artist." *Artist's Proof* 10 (1970): 80–83.

GOFF, (COLONEL) ROBERT CHARLES (1837–1922)

1893 "Etchings by Colonel Goff and Charles J. Watson." *Studio* 2 (1893): 41.

1903 "Colonel Robert Goff." *Magazine of Art* (1903–4): 318.

GOGH, VINCENT VAN (1853–1890)

1928 Faille, J. B. de la. *L'oeuvre de Vincent van Gogh: Catalogue Raisonné*. Paris: Van Oest, 1928.

1937 "Checklist of Van Gogh Lithographs." *Prints* 7 (1937): 133.

1937 Newhall, Bernard. "Van Gogh on Prints for the People." *Prints* 7 (1937): 123–133.

1944 Johnson, Una E. *Ambroise Vollard, Éditeur*. New York: Wittenborn and Co., 1944.

1958 Faille, J. B. de la. *Complete and Definitive, Illustrated and Classified Catalogue of the Work of Van Gogh*. The Hague, 1958.

1970 Faille, J. B. de la. *The Works of Vincent Van Gogh: His Paintings and Drawings*. New York: Reynal and Co., 1970.

1972 Sotriffer, Kristian. *Expressionism and Fauvism*. New York: McGraw-Hill Book Co., 1972.

1973 Bellini, Paolo. "Vincent van Gogh—Amsterdam 1973." *Print Collector* [Milan: Grafica Sipiel, s.r.] 5 (1973): 54–55.

GOLDTHWAITE, ANNE (1875–1944)

1970   Library of Congress. *American Prints in the Library of Congress: A Catalog of the Collection.* Compiled by Karen F. Beall. p. 175. Baltimore: The Library of Congress, The Johns Hopkins Press, 1970.

GONCOURT, JULES DE (1830–1870)

1916   Bradley, William Aspenwall. "The Goncourts and their Circle." *Print Collector's Quarterly* 6 (1916): 89–110.

GONTCHAROVA, NATHALIE (1881–1962)

1965   Wingler, H. M. *Graphic Work from the Bauhaus.* Greenwich, Conn.: New York Graphic Society, 1965.

GOOD, MINETTA (1895–1945)

1970   Library of Congress. *American Prints in the Library of Congress: A Catalog of the Collection.* Compiled by Karen F. Beall. p. 175. Baltimore: The Library of Congress, The Johns Hopkins Press, 1970.

GOODE, JOE (20th C.)

1973   Fort Worth Art Center Museum. *Joe Goode: Work Until Now.* Fort Worth, Tex., 1973.

GOODEN, STEPHEN (1892–   )

1941   Dodgson, Campbell. "The Engravings of Stephen Gooden." *Print Collector's Quarterly* 28 (1941): 141–163.

1941   Dodgson, Campbell. "Catalogue of Engravings of Stephen Gooden: 1923–June, 1941." *Print Collector's Quarterly* 28 (1941): 293–321.

1941   Dodgson, Campbell. "Catalogue of Engravings of Stephen Gooden, (continued.)" *Print Collector's Quarterly* 28 (1941): 479–495.

GORKY, ARSHILE (1904–1948)

1971   Kainen, Jacob. "Prints of the Thirties: Reflections on the Federal Art Project." *Artist's Proof* 11 (1971): 34–41.

GORSLINE, DOUGLAS WARNER (1913–   )

1949   Reese, Albert *American Prize Prints of the 20th Century.* p. 67. New York: American Artists Group, 1949.

1970   Library of Congress. *American Prints in the Library of Congress: A*   **85**
        Catalog of the Collection. Compiled by Karen F. Beall. p. 177.
        Baltimore: The Library of Congress, The Johns Hopkins Press,
        1970.

GOSSE, SYLVIA, A.R.E. (1881–   )

1925   Salaman, M. C. "Sylvia Gosse." *Apollo* 2 (1925): 293.

1925   Stokes, Hugh. "The Etchings of Sylvia Gosse." *Print Collector's*
        Quarterly 12 (1925): 315–338.

GOTTLIEB, ADOLF (1903–1974)

1970   Library of Congress. *American Prints in the Library of Congress: A*
        Catalog of the Collection. Compiled by Karen F. Beall. p. 178.
        Baltimore: The Library of Congress, The Johns Hopkins Press,
        1970.

1972   Heckscher Museum. *Artists of Suffolk County: Part 6, Contemporary*
        Prints. Huntington, N.Y., 1972.

GOTTLIEB, HARRY (1895–   )

1970   Library of Congress. *American Prints in the Library of Congress: A*
        Catalog of the Collection. Compiled by Karen F. Beall. p. 178.
        Baltimore: The Library of Congress, The Johns Hopkins Press,
        1970.

GOULDING, FREDERICK (1842–1909)

1910   Hardie, Martin. *Frederick Goulding, Master Printer of Copperplates:*
        with Catalogue of his Etched Works. Stirling, England, 1910.

GOYA Y LUCIENTES, FRANCISCO JOSÉ DE (1746–1828)

1911   "Bibliography of Goya." *Print Collector's Quarterly* 1 (1911): 236.

1911   Caffin, Charles H. "Francisco Goya y Lucientes." *Print Collector's*
        Quarterly 1 (1911): 191–203.

1911   " 'The Caprices': A List of Titles, Together with a Translation of
        Goya's Own Notes Upon the Etching Included in this Series."
        Print Collector's Quarterly 1 (1911): 209–235.

1911   Ivins, William M., Jr. "A Note on Goya." *Print Collector's*
        Quarterly 1 (1911): 204–208.

1915   Mather, Frank Jewett, Jr. "Goya and 'Los Desastres de la
        Guerra'." *Print Collector's Quarterly* 5 (1915): 171–190.

86   1922   Delteil, Loys. *Le Peintre-Graveur Illustré: Goya.* Vols. 14, 15. Paris: Chez l'auteur, 1922.

1923   Zigrosser, Carl. "A Note on Goya and Christophe Huet." *Print Collector's Quarterly* 10 (1923): 472–474.

1927   Dodgson, Campbell. "Some Undescribed States of Goya's Etchings." *Print Collector's Quarterly* 14 (1927): 31–45.

1927   Salaman, Malcolm. *Goya.* Modern Masters of Etching Series. Vol. 15. London: The Studio, Ltd., 1927.

1934   Dodgson, Campbell. "The First State of Goya's Self-portrait." *Print Collector's Quarterly* 21 (1934): 287–288.

1940   Hofer, Philip. "Goya's Aquatint Series 'La Tauromaquia'." *Print Collector's Quarterly* 27 (1940): 337–363.

1943   *The Complete Etchings of Goya.* New York: Crown Publishers, 1943.

1964   Harris, Tomás. *Goya: Engravings and Lithographs.* 2 vols. Oxford, 1964.

1967   Hofer, Philip. *The Disasters of War by Francisco Goya y Lucientes.* New York: Dover Publications, 1967.

1969   Delteil, Loys. *Le Peintre-Graveur Illustré: Goya.* Vols. 14, 15. 1922. Reprint. New York: Da Capo Press, 1969.

1973   Robison, Andrew. "The Disasters of War." *Print Collector's Newsletter* 6 (1973): 121–125.

GRANT, GORDON HOPE (1875–1962)

1949   Reese, Albert. *American Prize Prints of the 20th Century.* p. 68. New York: American Artists Group, 1949.

1970   Library of Congress. *American Prints in the Library of Congress: A Catalog of the Collection.* Compiled by Karen F. Beall. p. 179. Baltimore: The Library of Congress, The Johns Hopkins Press, 1970.

GRASSET, EUGÈNE SAMUEL (1841–1917)

1944   Johnson, Una E. *Ambroise Vollard, Éditeur.* New York: Wittenborn and Co., 1944.

1970   Stein, Donna and Karshan, Donald. *L'Estampe Originale: A Catalogue Raisonné.* New York: The Museum of Graphic Art, 1970.

1950   Wolf, Edwin, II. "Gravelot as Designer of Engraved Portrait Frames." *Print Collector's Quarterly* 30 (1950): 41–47.

GRAY, JOSEPH (1890–   )

1926   Salaman, M. C. "Etchings of Joseph Gray." *The Studio* 92 (1926): 12.

GREATOREX, ELIZA (1820–1897)

1881   Koehler, S. R. "Mrs. Eliza Greatorex." *American Art Review* 2 (1881): 12.

1970   Library of Congress. *American Prints in the Library of Congress: A Catalog of the Collection.* Compiled by Karen F. Beall. p. 179. Baltimore: The Library of Congress, The Johns Hopkins Press, 1970.

GREAVES, DERICK (1927–   )

1971   Man, Felix H., ed. *Europäische Graphik.* Vol. 7. Munich: Galerie Wolfgang Ketterer. 1971.

GREENWOOD, MARION (1909–1970)

1949   Reese, Albert. *American Prize Prints of the 20th Century.* p. 69. New York: American Artists Group, 1949.

1970   Library of Congress. *American Prints in the Library of Congress: A Catalog of the Collection.* Compiled by Karen F. Beall. p. 180. Baltimore: The Library of Congress, The Johns Hopkins Press, 1970.

1973   Mount Holyoke College Art Museum, and the Weyhe Gallery. *14 American Women Printmakers of the 30's and 40's.* South Hadley, Mass. and New York, 1973.

GRIESHABER, HELMUT A. P. (HAP) (1909–   )

1959   Boeck, Wilhelm. *HAP Grieshaber: Holzschnitte.* Pfüllingen: Neske–Verlag, 1959.

1964   Fürst, Margot. *HAP Grieshaber: der Holzschneider.* Stuttgart: Gerd Hatje, 1964.

1964   Man, Felix H., ed. Europäische Graphik. Vol. 2. Munich: Galerie Wolfgang Ketterer, 1964.

88   1965   *Grieshaber: Der Drucker und Holzschneider.* Stuttgart: Gerd Hatje, 1965.

1969   Städtische Kunstgalerie Bochum. *Grieshaber 60.* Bochum, 1969.

1969   Stanley, Robert G. "H.A.P. Grieshaber, Printmaker 'Malgré Tout'," *Artist's Proof* 9 (1969): 72–74.

1972   Sotriffer, Kristian. *Expressionism and Fauvism.* New York: McGraw-Hill Book Co., 1972.

GRIGGS, FREDERICK LANDSEER (1876–1938)

1924   Dodgson, Campbell. "Etchings of Frederick Landseer Griggs." *Print Collector's Quarterly* 11 (1924): 95–124.

1926   Salaman, M. C. *F. L. M. Griggs.* Modern Masters of Etching Series, no. 12. London, The Studio, Ltd., 1926.

1928   Alexander, Russel. *The Engraved Works of F. L. Griggs, A.R.A., R.E.* Statford-on-Avon, 1928.

1933   Dodgson, Campbell. "The Later Etched Works of F. L. Griggs, R.A." *Print Collector's Quarterly* 20 (1933): 321–345.

1939   Dodgson, Campbell. "The Latest Etchings of F. L. Griggs." *Print Collector's Quarterly* 26 (1939): 265–291.

1941   Wright, Harold J. L. *The Etched Works of F. L. Griggs, R.A., R.E., F.S.A.: With a Catalogue by Campbell Dodgson, C.B.E.* London: The Print Collector's Club, 1941.

1966   Comstock, Francis Adams. *A Gothic Vision: F. L. Griggs and his Work.* Boston Public Library, 1966.

GRIS, JUAN (1887–1927)

1946   Kahnweiler, Daniel-Henry. *Juan Gris. His Life and Work.* Paris: Gallimard, 1946. English translation London, 1947; New York, 1969,

1947   Kahnweiler, Daniel-Henry. *Juan Gris. His Life and Work.* Paris 1946. English translation, London, 1947.

1958   Soby, James Thrall. *Juan Gris.* New York: Museum of Modern Art, 1958.

1969   Kahnweiler, Daniel-Henry. *Juan Gris. His Life and Work.* Paris, 1946. English translation. London, 1947. New York: Abrams, 1969.

1971   Victoria and Albert Museum. *Homage to Senefelder.* Introduction by Felix H. Man. London, 1971.

1956   Galerie Carré. *Oeuvre gravé de Gromaire*. Paris, 1956.

1968   Frapier, Jacques. *Marcel Gromaire: Gravures, Dessins: Catalogue d'Exposition*. Oslo, 1968–69.

1969   Avati, M. *Album des Peintres-Graveurs Français, 80ᵉ anniversaire*. Paris, 1969.

1972   Sotriffer, Kristian. *Expressionism and Fauvism*. New York: McGraw-Hill Book Co., 1972.

GROPPER, WILLIAM (1897–   )

1941   A. C. A. Gallery. *Gropper*. New York, 1941.

1949   Reese, Albert. *American Prize Prints of the 20th Century*. p. 70. New York: American Artists Group, 1949.

1965   Associated American Artists. *William Gropper: Etchings*. New York, 1965.

1970   Library of Congress. *American Prints in the Library of Congress: A Catalog of the Collection*. Compiled by Karen F. Beall. p. 182. Baltimore: The Library of Congress, The Johns Hopkins Press, 1970.

1973   Uptown Gallery. *William Gropper (Retrospective)*. New York, 1973.

GROSS, ANTHONY (1905–   )

1924   Laver, J. "The Etchings of Anthony Gross." *Bookman's Journal* 11 (1924): 28.

1964   Associated American Artists. *Anthony Gross: A Retrospective Covering Thirty Years of Etching*. Foreword by Graham Reynolds. New York, 1964.

1968   Victoria and Albert Museum. *The Etchings of Anthony Gross*. London, 1968.

GROSS, CHAIM (1904–   )

1969   Associated American Artists. *The Jewish Holidays Suite: Eleven Original Color Lithographs by Chaim Gross*. New York, 1969.

GROSS-BETTELHEIM, JOLAN *See* BETTELHEIM, JOLAN GROSS

90   **GROSSMAN, ELIAS M. (1898–1947)**

1949   Reese, Albert. *American Prize Prints of the 20th Century.* p. 72. New York: American Artists Group, 1949.

1970   Library of Congress. *American Prints in the Library of Congress: A Catalog of the Collection.* Compiled by Karen F. Beall. p. 183. Baltimore: The Library of Congress, The Johns Hopkins Press, 1970.

GROSZ, GEORGE (1893–1959)

1955   Grosz, George. *Ein Kleines Ja und Ein Grosses Nein.* Hamburg, 1955.

1957   Peters, H., ed. *Die Bauhaus Mappen: Neue Europäische Graphik 1921–1923.* Cologne: C. Czwiklitzer, 1957.

1961–2 Bittner, H. *George Grosz: Catalogue of an Exhibition.* Cologne, 1961 and Berlin: Akademie der Künste, 1962.

1965   Wingler, H. M. *Graphic Work from the Bauhaus.* Greenwich, Conn.: New York Graphic Society, 1965.

1970   Library of Congress. *American Prints in the Library of Congress: A Catalog of the Collection.* Compiled by Karen F. Beall. p. 183. Baltimore: The Library of Congress, The Johns Hopkins Press, 1970.

1971   Dückers, Alexander. *George Grosz: Frühe Druckgraphik, Sammel-werke Illustrierte Bücher 1914–1923.* Berlin: Berlin-Dahlem Museum, 1971.

1972   Sotriffer, Kristian. *Expressionism and Fauvism.* New York: McGraw-Hill Book Co., 1972.

GROTH, JOHN (1908–   )

1970   Library of Congress. *American Prints in the Library of Congress: A Catalog of the Collection.* Compiled by Karen F. Beall. p. 183. Baltimore: The Library of Congress, The Johns Hopkins Press, 1970.

GROUX, HENRI JULES-CHARLES-CORNEILLE DE (1867–1930)

1970   Stein, Donna and Karshan, Donald. *L'Estampe Originale: A Catalogue Raisonné.* New York: The Museum of Graphic Art, 1970.

1970   Stein, Donna and Karshan, Donald. *L'Estampe Originale: A Catalogue Raisonné*. New York: The Museum of Graphic Art, 1970.

GUIEN, JEAN *See* QUIEN, JEAN

GUILLAUMIN, JEAN-BAPTISTE-ARMAND (1841–1927)

1944   Johnson, Una E. *Ambroise Vollard, Éditeur*. New York: Wittenborn and Co., 1944.

1971   Victoria and Albert Museum. *Homage to Senefelder*. Introduction by Felix H. Man. London, 1971.

GUILLOUX, CHARLES (19th C.)

1970   Stein, Donna and Karshan, Donald. *L'Estampe Originale: A Catalogue Raisonné*. New York: The Museum of Graphic Art, 1970.

GUITET, JAMES (1925–   )

1962   Ragon, M. *James Guitet*. Paris: J. R. Arnaud, 1962.

GUNTHER, MAX (1934–   )

1966   Associated American Artists. *Max Gunther*. New York, 1966.

GUTTUSO, RENATO (1912–   )

1966   Man, Felix H. *Europäische Graphik*. Vol. 4. Munich: Galerie Wolfgang Ketterer, 1966.

GWATHMEY, ROBERT (1903–   )

1949   Reese, Albert. *American Prize Prints of the 20th Century*. p. 73. New York: American Artists Group, 1949.

1970   Library of Congress. *American Prints in the Library of Congress: A Catalog of the Collection*. Compiled by Karen F. Beall. p. 184. Baltimore: The Library of Congress, The Johns Hopkins Press, 1970.

1972   Heckscher Museum. *Artists of Suffolk County: Part 6, Contemporary Prints*. Huntington, N.Y., 1972.

GWYNNE-EVANS, (MRS.) HESTER *See* FROOD, HESTER

1880   Drake, William. *A Descriptive Catalogue of the Etched Work of Sir Francis Seymour Haden.* London: Macmillan & Co., 1880.

1910   Harrington, H. N. *The Engraved Work of Seymour Haden, An Illustrated and Descriptive Catalogue.* Liverpool: H. Young & Sons, 1910.

1911   "Bibliography of Seymour Haden." *Print Collector's Quarterly* 1 (1911): 316–318.

1911   Harrington, H. N. "The Watercolors and Drawings of Sir Francis Seymour Haden, P.R.E." *Print Collector's Quarterly* 1 (1911): 405–420.

1911   Keppel, F. "Personal Characteristics of Sir Seymour Haden, P.R.E." *Print Collector's Quarterly* 1 (1911): 291–316, 421–442.

1911   Keppel, F. "Seymour Haden: The Tracy Dows Collection." *Print Collector's Quarterly* 1 (1911): 9–31.

1923   Salaman, Malcolm. *The Etchings of Sir Francis Seymour Haden, P.R.E.* London: Halton and Truscott Smith, Ltd., 1923.

1926   Salaman, Malcolm. *Sir Francis Seymour Haden, P.R.E.* Modern Masters of Etching Series, no. 11. London: The Studio, 1926.

1967   Kovler Gallery. *Forgotten Printmakers of the 19th Century.* Chicago, 1967.

1970   Ober, William B., M.D. "Sir Francis Seymour Haden, P.R.E. (1818–1910): Etcher and Surgeon." *Artist's Proof* 10 (1970): 39–47.

1973   Associated American Artists. *Sir Francis Seymour Haden: Etchings, Drypoints, and Mezzotints.* Introduction by Richard Schneiderman. New York, 1973.

HAHN, HAROLD MAXWELL (1920–   )

1949   Reese, Albert. *American Prize Prints of the 20th Century.* p. 74. New York: American Artists Group, 1949.

1970   Library of Congress. *American Prints in the Library of Congress: A Catalog of the Collection.* Compiled by Karen F. Beall. p. 185. Baltimore: The Library of Congress, The Johns Hopkins Press, 1970.

HALL, FREDERICK GARRISON (1879–1946)

1920   Rihani, Ameen. "Etchings of Frederick Garrison Hall." *Print Connoisseur* 1 (1920): 219.

1921   "List of Etchings by Frederick Garrison Hall." *Print Connoisseur* 1   **93**
       (1921): 229–236.

1925   Bergengren, R. "The Little People of F. G. Hall." *Print Connoisseur*
       5 (1925): 327.

1970   Library of Congress. *American Prints in the Library of Congress: A
       Catalog of the Collection*. Compiled by Karen F. Beall. p. 186.
       Baltimore: The Library of Congress, The Johns Hopkins Press,
       1970.

n.d.   Hall, Elton Wayland. *Frederick Garrison Hall: Etchings, Book-
       plates, Designs*. Boston: Boston Public Library, n.d.

HALL, OLIVER, R.A. (1869–1957)

1928   Rutter, Frank. "The Etchings of Oliver Hall, R.A." *Print Collector's
       Quarterly* 15 (1928): 35–49.

HAMAGUCHI, YOZO (1909–   )

1961   Krzhshnik, Z. *Catalogue of the Biennale of Graphic Art in Ljublana*.
       Ljublana: Yugoslavia, 1961.

1973   Nantenshi Gallery. *Hamaguchi: Graphic Works*. Tokyo, 1973.
       [American distributor: New York: Wittenborn and Co.].

HAMILTON, RICHARD (1922–   )

1973   Davison Art Center. *The Prints of Richard Hamilton*. Middletown,
       Conn.: Wesleyan University, 1973.

1973   Loring, John. "Not Just so Many Marvelously Right Images."
       Print Collector's Newsletter 4 (1973): 98–100.

1973   *The Prints of Richard Hamilton*. London and New York: Peters-
       burg Press, 1973.

HAMMER, VICTOR KARL (1882–1967)

1940   Rusk, William Sener. "Dry techniques of Victor Hammer." *Print
       Collector's Quarterly* 27 (1940): 239–246.

HANDFORTH, THOMAS (1897–1948)

1926   Whitmore, Elizabeth. "Etchings and Drawings of Thomas Hand-
       forth." *American Magazine of Art* 17 (1926): 185.

1949   Reese, Albert. *American Prize Prints of the 20th Century*. p. 75. New
       York: American Artists Group, 1949.

94 1970 Library of Congress. *American Prints in the Library of Congress: A Catalog of the Collection.* Compiled by Karen F. Beall. pp. 187–188. Baltimore: The Library of Congress, The Johns Hopkins Press, 1970.

HANKEY, WILLIAM LEE-, R.E. *See* LEE-HANKEY, WILLIAM, R.E.

HANSEN, ARMIN CARL (1886–1957)

1934 Kistler, Aline. "Armin Hansen: Etcher of the Sea." *Prints* 5 (1934): 1–9.

HANSEN-BAHIA, KARL HEINZ (1915–   )

1960 Grossman, Rudolf and Frenzel, Christian Otto. *Hansen-Bahia: Stationen und Wegmarken eines Holzschneiders.* Hamburg: H. Christians Verlag, 1960.

HARDIE, MARTIN, R.E. (1875–1952)

1913 Wedmore, Sir F. *Etched Work of Martin Hardie.* London: Hazell, Watson and Viney, Ltd., 1913.

1925 Fiume, N. G. "Martin Hardie, R.E." *L'Art Belle* 2 (1925).

1928 Laver, James. "The Later Drypoints of Martin Hardie, R.I., R.E." *Bookman's Journal* 16 (1928).

1937 Laver, James. "The Etchings and Drypoints of Martin Hardie." *Print Collector's Quarterly* 24 (1937): 121–143.

1938 Laver, James. "Catalogue of the Etchings and Drypoints of Martin Hardie, C.B.E., R.E." *Print Collector's Quarterly* 25 (1938): 81–98.

1938 Laver, James. "Catalogue of the Etchings and Drypoints of Martin Hardie, C.B.E., R.E.; continued." *Print Collector's Quarterly* 25 (1938): 217–234.

HART, GEORGE OVERBURY "POP" (1868–1933)

1928 Cahill, Holger. *George O. "Pop" Hart: 24 Selections from his Work.* New York: The Downtown Gallery, 1928.

1935 The Newark Museum. *George Overbury "Pop" Hart, 1868–1933.* Newark, 1935.

1935 Wickey, Harry. "The Vital Genius of Pop Hart." *Prints* 6 (1935): 20–25.

1949 Reese, Albert. *American Prize Prints of the 20th Century.* p. 228. New York: American Artists Group, 1949.

1970 Library of Congress. *American Prints in the Library of Congress: A*   **95**
   Catalog of the Collection. Compiled by Karen F. Beall. p. 189.
   Baltimore: The Library of Congress, The Johns Hopkins Press,
   1970.

HARTLEY, ALFRED, R.E. (1855–1933)

1915 Stokes, A. G. Folliott. "Alfred Hartley, Painter and Etcher." *Studio*
   64 (1915): 99.

HARTLEY, MARSDEN (1877–1943)

1952 McCausland, Elizabeth. *Marsden Hartley.* Minneapolis: University
   of Minnesota, 1952.

1962 McCausland, Elizabeth. "The Lithographs of Marsden Hartley."
   Artist's Proof 3 (1962): 30–32.

1970 Library of Congress. *American Prints in the Library of Congress: A*
   Catalog of the Collection. Compiled by Karen F. Beall. p. 190.
   Baltimore: The Library of Congress, The Johns Hopkins Press,
   1970.

1972 Eldredge, Charles C. *Marsden Hartley: Lithographs and Related*
   Works. University of Kansas, 1972.

1973 Eldredge, Charles C. "Marsden Hartley: Lithographer." *The Amer-*
   ican Art Journal 5 (1973): 46–53.

HARTUNG, HANS (1904–)

1965 Associated American Artists. *Hans Hartung: Etchings and Lith-*
   ographs. New York, 1965.

1965 Schmücking, R. *Verzeichnis der Graphik 1921–1965.* Brunswick:
   Schmücking, 1965.

1970 Gili, Gustavo, ed. *Hans Hartung.* Barcelona: Coleccióon las
   Estampes de la Cometa, 1970.

HARVEY, HERBERT JOHNSON (1884–1928)

1927 Laver, J. "Etchings of Herbert Johnson Harvey." *Bookman's*
   Journal 15 (1927): 42.

HASKELL, ERNEST (1876–1925)

1936 Mather, Frank Jewett, Jr. "Ernest Haskell's Etchings." *Prints* 6
   (1936): 118–124.

1931 Pousette-Dart, Nathaniel. *Ernest Haskell, His Life and Work.* New
   York: T. S. Hutson, 1931.

96   1949   Reese, Albert. *American Prize Prints of the 20th Century*. p. 229. New York: American Artists Group, 1949.

1950   Arms, John Taylor. "Ernest Haskell: An Appreciation by John Taylor Arms." *Print Collector's Quarterly* 30 (1950): 23–32.

1970   Library of Congress. *American Prints in the Library of Congress: A Catalog of the Collection*. Compiled by Karen F. Beall. pp. 192–197. Baltimore: The Library of Congress, The Johns Hopkins Press, 1970.

HASSAM, CHILDE (1859–1935)

1925   Cortissoz, Royal. *Catalogue of the Etchings and Drypoints of Childe Hassam*. New York and London: Charles Scribner's Sons, 1925.

1929   *Childe Hassam*. American Etchers Series, Vol. 3. New York: The Crafton Collection; London: P. and D. Colnaghi and Co., 1929.

1933   The Leonard Clayton Gallery. *Handbook of the Complete Set of Etchings and Drypoints of Childe Hassam, N.A. from 1883–1933*. Introduction by Paula Eliasoph. New York, 1933.

1935   Cortissoz, Royal, et. al. "Childe Hassam and his Prints: A Compendium of Comment." *Prints* 6 (1935): 2–14.

1949   Reese, Albert. *American Prize Prints of the 20th Century*. p. 230. New York: American Artists Group, 1949.

1962   Griffith, Fuller. *The Lithographs of Childe Hassam: A Catalogue*. Bulletin no. 232. Washington, D.C.: U.S. National Museum, Smithsonian Institution, 1962.

1970   Library of Congress. *American Prints in the Library of Congress: A Catalog of the Collection*. Compiled by Karen F. Beall. pp. 197–202. Baltimore: The Library of Congress, The Johns Hopkins Press, 1970.

1973   Cole, Sylvan, Jr. *Childe Hassam: Etchings, Lithographs*. New York: Associated American Artists, 1973.

HAUPERS, CLEMENT BERNARD (1900–   )

1949   Reese, Albert. *American Prize Prints of the 20th Century*. p. 76. New York: American Artists Group, 1949.

HAVELL, ROBERT, JR. (1793–1878)

1916   Williams, George Alfred. "Robert Havell, Jr.: Engraver of Audubon's 'The Birds of America'." *Print Collector's Quarterly* 6 (1916): 227–257.

1917   Williams, George Alfred. "Portraits of Robert Havell, Jr." *Print*   **97**
            Collector's Quarterly 7 (1917): 298–304.

1966   Toledano, Roulhac. *Audubon in Louisiana.* New Orleans, La.:
            Louisiana State Museum, 1966.

HAY, JAMES HAMILTON (1874–1916)

1927   Marriott, C. "Drypoints of J. Hamilton Hay." *Print Collector's
            Quarterly* 14 (1927): 163–188.

HAYTER, STANLEY WILLIAM (1901–   )

1949   Reese, Albert. *American Prize Prints of the 20th Century.* p. 77. New
            York: American Artists Group, 1949.

1957   De Cordova Museum. *Stanley William Hayter: Prints.* Lincoln,
            Mass., 1957.

1967   Reynolds, Graham. *The Engravings of S. W. Hayter.* London:
            Victoria and Albert Museum, 1967.

1973   Corcoran Gallery of Art. *Stanley William Hayter: Paintings,
            Drawings and Prints 1922–1950.* Washington, D.C.: Corcoran
            Gallery of Art, 1973.

1973   Jane Haslem Gallery. *The Innovators: Renaissance in American
            Printmaking.* Washington, D.C., 1973.

1974   Associated American Artists. *Stanley William Hayter: Nine En-
            gravings 1933–1946.* New York, 1974.

HEASLIP, WILLIAM (1898–1970)

1935   Morrow, B. F. "Highlights of Copper: William Heaslip." *Prints* 5
            (1935): 38–41.

HECKEL, ERICH (1883–1970)

1957   Buchheim, L. G. *Erich Heckel–Holzschnitte 1905–1956.* Feldafing,
            1957.

1964   Dube, A. and W. D. *Erich Heckel, das graphische Werk.* 2 vols.
            New York, 1964.

1965   Wingler, H. M. *Graphic Work from the Bauhaus.* Greenwich,
            Conn.: New York Graphic Society, 1965.

1966–67 Man, Felix H., ed. *Europäische Graphik.* Vols. 4, 5. Munich:
            Galerie Wolfgang Ketterer, 1966, 1967.

98 1969 Gropper Art Gallery. *The Graphic Work of Erich Heckel; Woodcuts, Lithographs and Etchings from 1907–1968.* Cambridge, Mass., 1969.

HECKENBLEIKNER, LOUIS (1893–   )

1949 Reese, Albert. *American Prize Prints of the 20th Century.* p. 78. New York: American Artists Group, 1949.

1970 Library of Congress. *American Prints in the Library of Congress: A Catalog of the Colllection.* Compiled by Karen F. Beall. p. 203. Baltimore: The Library of Congress, The Johns Hopkins Press, 1970.

HECKMAN, ALBERT WILLIAM (1893–   )

1949 Reese, Albert. *American Prize Prints of the 20th Century.* p. 79. New York: American Artists Group, 1949.

1970 Library of Congress. *American Prints in the Library of Congress: A Catalog of the Collection.* Compiled by Karen F. Beall. p. 203. Baltimore: The Library of Congress, The Johns Hopkins Press, 1970.

HEEMSKERCK, JACOBA VAN (1876–1923)

1957 Peters, H., ed. *Die Bauhaus-Mappen: Neue Europäische Graphik 1921–1923.* Cologne: C. Czwiklitzer, 1957.

1965 Wingler, H. M. *Graphic Work from the Bauhaus.* Greenwich, Conn.: New York Graphic Society, 1965.

HEGENBARTH, JOSEPH (1884–1961)

1959 Löffler, Fritz. *Joseph Hegenbarth.* Dresden, 1959.

1972 Sotriffer, Kristian. *Expressionism and Fauvism.* New York: McGraw-Hill Book Co., 1972.

HEIL, CHARLES EMILE (1870–   )

1923 Brown, Warren Wilmer. "The Bird and Animal Etchings of Charles E. Heil." *Print Connoisseur* 3 (1923): 352.

1923 "List of Etchings by Charles E. Heil." *Print Connoisseur* 3 (1923): 364–367.

HEINTZELMAN, ARTHUR WILLIAM (1891–1965)

1920 Holman, Louis Arthur. *Arthur William Heintzelman, Etcher.* Boston: C. E. Goodspeed, 1920.

1922   "Catalogue Raisonné of the Etchings of Arthur William Heintzelman." *Print Connoisseur* 2 (1922): 187–195.

1925   Salaman, M. C. "Etchings of Arthur W. Heintzelman." *The Studio* 89 (1925): 77.

1928   Galerie Marcel Guiot. *Arthur William Heintzelman: estampes, dessins.* Paris, 1928.

1928   Guiot, Marcel. *Arthur William Heintzelman . . . Aquafortiste.* 2 vols. Paris, 1928.

1930   *Arthur Wm. Heintzelman.* American Etchers Series, vol. 6. New York: The Crafton Collection, and London: P. and D. Colnaghi and Co., 1930.

1937   Arms, John Taylor. "Arthur William Heintzelman, Friend and Artist." *Print Collector's Quarterly* 24 (1937): 41–61.

1937   Heintzelman, Arthur W. "Checklist of Prints." *Print Collector's Quarterly* 24 (1937): 423–440.

1949   Reese, Albert. *American Prize Prints of the 20th Century.* p. 80. New York: American Artists Group, 1949.

1970   Library of Congress. *American Prints in the Library of Congress: A Catalog of the Collection.* Compiled by Karen F. Beall. pp. 204–206. Baltimore: The Library of Congress, The Johns Hopkins Press, 1970.

HELLER, HELEN WEST (1885–1955)

1942   Harms, Dr. Ernst. "Helen West Heller: The Woodcutter." *Print Collector's Quarterly* 29 (1942): 251.

1949   Reese, Albert. *American Prize Prints of the 20th Century.* p. 81. New York: American Artists Group, 1949.

1970   Library of Congress. *American Prints in the Library of Congress: A Catalog of the Collection.* Compiled by Karen F. Beall. p. 206–207. Baltimore: The Library of Congress, The Johns Hopkins Press, 1970.

HELLEU, PAUL-CÉSAR (1859–1927)

1897   *Catalogue des Pointes-seches d'Helleu.* Paris: Librairie Lemercier, 1897.

1913   Montesquiou, Robert de. *Paul Helleu Peintre et Graveur.* Paris: Floury, 1913.

1957   Bibliothèque Nationale. *Helleu: exhibition catalogue.* Paris, 1957.

1967   Kovler Gallery. *Forgotten Printmakers of the 19th Century*. Chicago, 1967.

1970   Lumley Cazalet Ltd. *Paul Helleu: Drypoints*. London, 1970.

1970   Stein, Donna and Karshan, Donald. *L'Estampe Originale: A Catalogue Raisonné*. New York: The Museum of Graphic Art, 1970.

1974   Knoedler Gallery. *Paul-César Helleu: Glimpses of the Grace of Women*. New York, 1974.

HENDERSON, ELSIE (MRS. E. M. CONDENHOVE) (1880–)

1928   Nicholson, C. A. "The Prints of Elsie Henderson." *Print Collector's Quarterly* 15 (1928): 315.

HEPWORTH, BARBARA (1903–)

1969   Man, Felix H., ed. *Europäische Graphik*. Vol. 6. Munich: Galerie Wolfgang Ketterer, 1969.

HERKOMER, SIR HUBERT VON (1849–1914)

1901   Baldry, A. L. *Hubert von Herkomer*. London, 1901.

1910   Baldry, A. L. "Hubert von Herkomer." *Studio* 49 (1910): 277.

1911   Herkomer, Hubert von. *The Herkomers*. 2 vols. London, 1911.

HERMAN-PAUL (1874–)

1944   Johnson, Una E. *Ambroise Vollard, Éditeur*. New York: Wittenborn and Co., 1944.

HERMES, GERTRUDE (MRS. HUGHES-STANTON) (1901–)

1929   Fletcher, John Gould. "Gertrude Hermes and Blair Hughes-Stanton." *Print Collector's Quarterly* 16 (1929): 183–198.

HERVIER, ADOLPHE (1821–1879)

1925   Weitenkampf, Frank. "Adolphe Hervier." *Print Collector's Quarterly* 12 (1925): 205–223.

HICKEN PHILIP BURNHAM (1910–)

1949   Reese, Albert. *American Prize Prints of the 20th Century*. p. 82. New York: American Artists Group, 1949.

1952   De Cordova Museum. *Philip Hicken: Serigraphs.* Lincoln, Mass., 1952.

1970   Library of Congress. *American Prints in the Library of Congress: A Catalog of the Collection.* Compiled by Karen F. Beall. p. 208. Baltimore: The Library of Congress, The Johns Hopkins Press, 1970.

HIGGINS, EUGENE (1874–1958)

1931   Arms, John Taylor. "Eugene Higgins: Etcher of Life." *Prints* 1 (1931): 1–13.

1949   Reese, Albert. *American Prize Prints of the 20th Century.* p. 83. New York: American Artists Group, 1949.

1970   Library of Congress. *American Prints in t!e Library of Congress: A Catalog of th8 Collection.* Compiled by Karen F. Beall. pp. 208–214. Baltimore: The Library of Congress, The Johns Hopkins Press, 1970.

HILL, JOHN HENRY (1839–)

1880   Koehler, S. R. *American Art Review* 1 (1880): 429.

HILL, POLLY KNIPP (1900-)

1949   Reese, Albert. *American Prize Prints of the 20th Century.* p. 84. New York: American Artists Group, 1949.

1970   Library of Congress. *American Prints in the Library of Congress: A Catalog of the Collection.* Compiled by Karen F. Beall. p. 214. Baltimore: The Library of Congress, The Johns Hopkins Press, 1970.

HILLS, ROBERT (1769–1844)

1874   Senneville, P. "Hills, Graveur Anglais." *Gazette des Beaux-Arts* 9 (1874): 234.

HIOS, THEO (1910–)

1972   Heckscher Museum. *Artists of Suffolk County: Part 6, Contemporary Prints.* Huntington, N.Y., 1972.

HIRSCH, JOSEPH (1910–)

1949   Reese, Albert. *American Prize Prints of the 20th Century.* p. 85. New York: American Artists Group, 1949.

1970   Cole, Sylvan, Jr., ed. *The Graphic Work of Joseph Hirsch.* New York: Associated American Artists, 1970.

102   1970   Library of Congress. *American Prints in the Library of Congress: A Catalog of the Collection.* Compiled by Karen F. Beall. p. 214. Baltimore: The Library of Congress, The Johns Hopkins Press, 1970.

HIRSCHFELD, ALBERT (1903–   )

1970   Goodrich, Lloyd. *The World of Al Hirschfeld.* New York: Harry Abrams, 1970.

HNIZDOVSKY, JACQUES (1915–   )

1970   Library of Congress. *American Prints in the Library of Congress: A Catalog of the Collection.* Compiled by Karen F. Beall. p. 214. Baltimore: The Library of Congress, The Johns Hopkins Press, 1970.

1971   Associated American Artists. *Hnizdovsky: Ten Years of Woodcut 1960–1970.* New York, 1971.

HOBBS, MORRIS HENRY (1892–   )

1949   Reese, Albert. *American Prize Prints of the 20th Century.* p. 86. New York: American Artists Group, 1949.

1970   Library of Congress. *American Prints in the Library of Congress: A Catalog of the Collection.* Compiled by Karen F. Beall. p. 215. Baltimore: The Library of Congress, The Johns Hopkins Press, 1970.

HOCKNEY, DAVID (1937–   )

1963   *David Hockney: A Rake's Progress and Other Etchings.* London: Editions Alecto, The Print Centre, 1963.

1971   Man, Felix H., ed. *Europäische Graphik.* Vol. 7. Munich: Galerie Wolfgang Ketterer, 1971.

1973   André Emmerich Gallery Downtown. *David Hockney: The Weather and Other Lithographs.* New York, 1973.

1973   M. Knoedler and Co. *David Hockney: Print Retrospective.* New York, 1973.

1973   Plagens, Peter. "David Hockney's New Prints." *Print Review [New York: Pratt Graphics Center and Kennedy Galleries, Inc.]* 2 (1973): 5–14.

HODGKIN, HOWARD (1932–   )

1966   Editions Alecto, Ltd. *Howard Hodgkin.* London, 1966.

1971   Man, Felix H., ed. *Europäische Graphik*. Vol. 7. Munich: Galerie
Wolfgang Ketterer, 1971.

HODLER, FERDINAND (1853–1918)

1913   *Ferdinand Hodler: der Holzfäller*. Frankfurt: Frankfurter Kunstverein, 1913.

1921–24 Loosli, Carl A. *Ferdinand Hodler; Leben, Werk und Nachlass*. 4
Vols. Bern: Sluter, 1921–24.

1971   Victoria and Albert Museum. *Homage to Senefelder*. Introduction
by Felix H. Man. London, 1971.

HOEHN, HARRY (1918–   )

1972   Heckscher Museum. *Artists of Suffolk County: Part 6, Contemporary
Prints*. Huntington, N.Y., 1972.

HOEHRMAN, RALPH W.

1972   Corcoran Museum of Art. *Ralph W. Hoehrman: Prints and
Drawings*. Washington, D.C., 1972.

HOETGER, BERNHARD (1874–1949)

1957   Peters, H., ed. *Die Bauhaus-Mappen: Neue Europäische Graphik
1921–1923*. Cologne: C. Czwiklitzer, 1957.

1965   Wingler, H. M. *Graphic Work from the Bauhaus*. Greenwich,
Conn.: New York Graphic Society, 1965.

HOFER, KARL (1878–1955)

1957   *Catalogue of the Memorial Exhibitions*. Berlin and Karlsruhe,
1956–1957.

1971   Victoria and Albert Museum. *Homage to Senefelder*. Introduction
by Felix H. Man. London, 1971.

1972   Sotriffer, Kristian. *Expressionism and Fauvism*. New York:
McGraw-Hill Book Co., 1972.

n.d.   Rathenau, Ernest, ed. *Karl Hofer: das Graphische Werk*. Berlin:
Euphorion Verlag, n.d.

HOFFMAN, IRWIN D. (1901–   )

1949   Reese, Albert. *American Prize Prints of the 20th Century*. p. 87. New
York: American Artists Group, 1949.

104   1970   Library of Congress. *American Prints in the Library of Congress: A Catalog of the Collection.* Compiled by Karen F. Beall. p. 217. Baltimore: The Library of Congress, The Johns Hopkins Press, 1970.

HOGARTH, WILLIAM (1697–1764)

1907   Dobson, A. *William Hogarth.* London: Heinemann, 1907.

1940   McDonald, Robert. "Hogarth as a Tonic." *Print Collector's Quarterly* 27 (1940): 433–455.

1964   Paulson, Ronald. *Hogarth's Graphic Works.* 2 vols. New Haven: Yale University Press, 1964. rev. ed., 1970.

1968   Burke, Joseph and Caldwell, Colin. *Hogarth: The Complete Engravings.* New York: Abrams, 1968.

1970   Paulson, Ronald. *Hogarth's Graphic Works.* 2 vols. New Haven: Yale University Press, 1964. 2nd ed., rev. New Haven: Yale University Press, 1970.

1971   Paulson, Ronald. *Hogarth: His Life, Art and Times.* 2 vols. New Haven: Yale University Press, 1971

HOGUE, ALEXANDRE (1898–   )

1949   Reese, Albert. *American Prize Prints of the 20th Century.* p. 88. New York: American Artists Group, 1949.

HOLROYD, SIR CHARLES, R.E. (1861–1917)

1923   Dodgson, Campbell. "Sir Charles Holroyd's Etchings." *Print Collector's Quarterly* 10 (1923): 309.

1923   Dodgson, Campbell. "Sir Charles Holroyd's Etchings: List of the Etchings." *Print Collector's Quarterly* 10 (1923): 347–367.

HOMER, WINSLOW (1836–1910)

1937   McCausland, Elizabeth. "Winslow Homer." *Prints* 7 (1937): 214–220.

1961   Gardner, Albert Ten Eyck. *Winslow Homer, American Artist: his World and his Work.* New York: Clarkson N. Potter, 1961.

1968   Goodrich, Lloyd. *The Graphic Art of Winslow Homer.* New York: The Museum of Graphic Art, 1968.

1969   Gelman, Barbara. *The Wood Engravings of Winslow Homer.* New York: Crown Publishers, Inc., 1969.

1970   Library of Congress. *American Prints in the Library of Congress: A*   **105**
Catalog of the Collection. Compiled by Karen F. Beall. pp. 218–220.
Baltimore: The Library of Congress, The Johns Hopkins Press,
1970.

HOOVER, ELLISON (1888–1955)

1949   Reese, Albert. *American Prize Prints of the 20th Century.* P. 89. New
York: American Artists Group, 1949.

1970   Library of Congress. *American Prints in the Library of Congress: A*
Catalog of the Collection. Compiled by Karen F. Beall. p. 220.
Baltimore: The Library of Congress, The Johns Hopkins Press,
1970.

HOPPER, EDWARD (1882–1967)

1949   Reese, Albert. *American Prize Prints of the 20th Century.* p. 90. New
York: American Artists Group, 1949.

1962   Zigrosser, Carl. *The Complete Graphic Work of Edward Hopper:*
Catalogue of the Exhibition. Philadelphia: Philadelphia Museum of
Art, 1962.

1962   Zigrosser, Carl. "The Etchings of Edward Hopper." *Prints.* New
York: Holt, Rinehart and Winston, 1962.

1970   Library of Congress. *American Prints in the Library of Congress: A*
Catalog of the Collection. Compiled by Karen F. Beall. pp. 220–222.
Baltimore: The Library of Congress, The Johns Hopkins Press,
1970.

HORNBY, LESTER GEORGE (1882–   )

1909   "Some Etchings by Lester G. Hornby." *Studio* 46 (1909): 17.

1912   Taylor, E. A. "Etchings by American Artists in Paris: 2, Lester G.
Hornby." *Studio* 56 (1912): 286.

1918   "Six Etchings by Lester G. Hornby." *Studio* 75 (1918): 13.

1921   Holman, Louis Arthur. *Hornby's Etchings of the Great War: With a*
Complete List of all his Plates (1906–1920). Boston: C. E. Goodspeed and Co., 1921.

HORSLEY, JOHN COLCOTT (1817–1903)

1903   Horsley, John C. *Recollections of a Royal Academician.* London: J.
Murray, 1903.

HORTER, EARL (1881–1940)

1970   Library of Congress. *American Prints in the Library of Congress: A Catalog of the Collection*. Compiled by Karen F. Beall. p. 223. Baltimore: The Library of Congress, The Johns Hopkins Press, 1970.

HOSEMANN, THEODOR (1807–1875)

1920   Brieger, L. *Theodor Hosemann*. Munich, 1920.

1971   Victoria and Albert Museum. *Homage to Senefelder*. Introduction by Felix H. Man. London, 1971.

HOUDARD, CHARLES-LOUIS (19th C.)

1970   Stein, Donna and Karshan, Donald. *L'Estampe Originale: A Catalogue Raisonné*. New York: The Museum of Graphic Art, 1970.

HOUGHTON, ARTHUR BOYD (1836–1875)

1923   Sullivan, Edmund J. "Arthur Boyd Houghton: An Artist's Artist." Part 1. *Print Collector's Quarterly* 10 (1923): 95–122.

1923   Sullivan, Edmund J. "Arthur Boyd Houghton." Part 2. *Print Collector's Quarterly* 10 (1923): 125–148.

HOUSMAN, CLEMENCE (20th C.)

1924   Guthrie, James. "The Wood Engravings of Clemence Housman." *Print Collector's Quarterly* 11 (1924): 191–204.

HOWARTH, ALBANY E. (1872–1936)

1909   Dirkes, R. "Etchings of A. E. Howarth." *Art Journal* (1909): 143.

1913   "Some Etchings and Drypoints by Albany E. Howarth, A.R.E." *Studio* 58 (1913): 122.

HRDLICKA, ALFRED (1928–   )

1968   Rucker, Elisabeth. *Alfred Hrdlicka: Das Druckgraphische Werk*. Nuremberg: Kunsthalle, 1968.

1969   Montequercia, F. "Alfred Hrdlicka." *Artist's Proof* 9 (1969): 87–89.

1969   Sotriffer, Kristian. *Alfred Hrdlicka—Randolectil: 1947–1968*. Vienna and Munich: Anton Schroll, 1969.

1972   Sotriffer, Kristian. *Expressionism and Fauvism.* New York: McGraw-Hill Book Co., 1972.

HUBBARD, E. HESKETH (1892–   )

1924   Macfall, C. H. C. *Art of Hesketh Hubbard.* London, 1924.

HUET, CHRISTOPHE (–1759)

1923   Zigrosser, Carl. "A Note on Goya and Christophe Huet." *Print Collector's Quarterly* 10 (1923): 472–474.

HUET, PAUL (1803–1869)

1893–1901   Hédiard, G. *Les Maitres de la Lithographie.* Paris, 1893–1901.

1911   Delteil, Loys. *Le Peintre-Graveur Illustré: Paul Huet.* Vol. 17. Paris: Chez l'auteur, 1911.

1967   Kovler Gallery. *Forgotten Printmakers of the 19th Century.* Chicago, 1967.

1969   Delteil, Loys. *Le-Peintre-Graveur Illustré: Paul Huet.* Vol. 17. 1911. Reprint. New York: Da Capo Press, 1969.

HUGHES-STANTON, BLAIR (1902–   )

1929   Fletcher, John Gould. "Gertrude Hermes and Blair Hughes-Stanton." *Print Collector's Quarterly* 16 (1929): 183–198.

1934   Fletcher, John Gould. "Blair Hughes-Stanton." *Print Collector's Quarterly* 21 (1934): 353–372.

HUGHES-STANTON, GERTRUDE *See* HERMES, GERTRUDE

HUNDERTWASSER, FRIEDRICH *pseudonym:* FRIEDRICH STOWASSER (1928–   )

1969   Felix Landau Gallery. *Graphics, Publications, and Artist's Editions.* Los Angeles, Cal., 1969.

HUNT, WILLIAM HOLMAN (1827–1910)

1971   William Weston Gallery. *An Exhibition of English Etchings of the Victorian Era.* London, 1971.

HUNTLEY, VICTORIA HUTSON (1900–   )

1949   Reese, Albert. *American Prize Prints of the 20th Century.* p. 91. New York: American Artists Group, 1949.

1970   Library of Congress. *American Prints in the Library of Congress: A Catalog of the Collection.* Compiled by Karen F. Beall. p. 225. Baltimore: The Library of Congress, The Johns Hopkins Press, 1970.

HURD, PETER (1904–   )

1939   Gardner, Paul. "Peter Hurd." *The Print Collector's Chronicle* 1 (1939): 37–39, 48–49.

1949   Reese, Albert. *American Prize Prints of the 20th Century.* p. 92. New York: American Artists Group, 1949.

1968   Meigs, John, ed. *Peter Hurd: The Lithographs.* Lubbock, Texas: Baker Gallery Press, 1968.

1970   Library of Congress. *American Prints in the Library of Congress: A Catalog of the Collection.* Compiled by Karen F. Beall. p. 225. Baltimore: The Library of Congress, The Johns Hopkins Press, 1970.

HUTTY, ALFRED HEBER (1877–1954)

1929   *Alfred Hutty.* American Etchers Series, vol. 2. New York: The Crafton Collection, Inc., and London: P. and D. Colnaghi and Co., 1929.

1949   Reese, Albert. *American Prize Prints of the 20th Century.* p. 23. New York: American Artists Group, 1949.

1970   Library of Congress. *American Prints in the Library of Congress: A Catalog of the Collection.* Compiled by Karen F. Beall. p. 226. Baltimore: The Library of Congress, The Johns Hopkins Press, 1970.

IBELS, HENRI GABRIEL (1867–1936)

1970   Kovler Gallery. *The Graphic Art of Valloton and the Nabis.* pp. 56–57, 80. Chicago, 1970.

1970   Stein, Donna and Karshan, Donald. *L'Estampe Originale: A Catalogue Raisonné.* New York: The Museum of Graphic Art, 1970.

ICART, LOUIS (1888–   )

1973   Schnessel, S. M. *A Collector's Guide to Louis Icart.* Princeton, N.J.: The Exhumation, 1973.

IKEDA, MASUO (1934–   )

1965   Lieberman, William S. *Masuo Ikeda: Prints 1961–1965.* New York: Museum of Modern Art, 1965.

1970   Miller, Jo. *Masuo Ikeda: Etchings and Lithographs from 1968 to* **109** *1970.* New York: Associated American Artists, 1970.

1972   Miller, Jo. "Masuo Ikeda." *Newsletter on Comtemporary Japanese Prints.* [Issued by Helen and Felix Juda Collection, Los Angeles, Cal.] Vol. 2, no. 3. September, 1972.

IMLER, EDGAR (1894–   )

1949   Reese, Albert. *American Prize Prints of the 20th Century.* p. 64. New York: American Artists Group, 1949.

1970   Library of Congress. *American Prints in the Library of Congress: A Catalog of the Collection.* Compiled by Karen F. Beall. p. 228. Baltimore: The Library of of Congress, The Johns Hopkins Press, 1970.

INGRES, JEAN-AUGUSTE-DOMINIQUE (1780–1867)

1870   Delaborde, V. H. *Ingres: sa vie, ses travaux, sa doctrine.* Paris: H. Plon, 1870.

1908   Delteil, Loys. *Le Peintre-Graveur Illustré: Ingres and Delacroix.* Vol. 3. Paris: Chez l'auteur, 1908.

1969   Delteil, Loys. *Le Peintre-Graveur Illustré: Ingres and Delacroix.* Vol. 3. 1908. Reprint. New York: Da Capo Press, 1969.

1970   Man, Felix H. *Artist's Lithographs.* pp. 35–36. New York: G. P. Putnam's Sons, 1970.

1971   Victoria and Albert Museum. *Homage to Senefelder.* Introduction by Felix H. Man. London, 1971.

ISABEY, EUGÈNE (1803–1886)

1893–1901 Hédiard, G. *Les Maitres de la Lithographie.* Paris, 1893–1901.

1915   Weitenkampf, Frank. "Eugène Isabey." *Print Collector's Quarterly* 5 (1915): 295–314.

1939   Curtis, Atherton. *Catalogue de l'oeuvre Lithographié d'Eugène Isabey.* Paris: Paul Prouté, 1939.

ISANDER, GUSTAF (1863–1929)

1934   Jungmarker, Gunnar. "Gustaf Isander: A Unique Figure in Swedish Art." *Print Collector's Quarterly* 21 (1934): 273.

ISRÄELS, JOSEF (1824–1911)

1879   Duranty. "Eaux-fortes de M. Josef Isräels." *Gazette des Beaux-Arts.* [Paris] 19 (1879): 395–397.

110   1890   Zilcken, Phillip. *Essai de Catalogue descriptif des eaux-fortes de Josef Isräels.* La Haye, 1890.

1910   Hubert, H. J. *The Etched Works of Josef Isräels.* Amsterdam, 1910.

ITTEN, JOHANNES (1888–1967)

1965   Wingler, H. M. *Graphic Work from the Bauhaus.* Greenwich, Conn.: New York Graphic Society, 1965.

1971   Victoria and Albert Museum. *Homage to Senefelder.* Introduction by Felix H. Man. London, 1971.

JACKSON, JOHN-BAPTISTE (1701–1754)

1962   Kainen, J. *18th Century Master of the Color Woodcut.* Washington, 1962.

JACQUE, CHARLES ÉMILE (1813–1894)

1866   Guiffrey, J. *L'oeuvre de Charles Jacque: Catalogue de ses eaux-fortes et pointes sèches.* Paris, 1866.

1884   Guiffrey, J. *Nouvelles Eaux-fortes de Charles Jacque: Supplement au catalogue par J. Guiffrey.* Paris, 1884.

1912   Wickenden, R. J. "Charles Jacque." *Print Collector's Quarterly* 2 (1912): 74–101.

1922   Delteil, Loys. "Charles Émile Jacque." *Print Connoisseur* 2 (1922): 305.

1967   Kovler Gallery. *Forgotten Printmakers of the 19th Century.* Chicago, 1967.

JACQUEMART, JULES (1837–1880)

1921   Metcalfe, Louis R. "The Etchings of Jules Jacquemart." *Print Collector's Quarterly* 8 (1921): 407–432.

JAMES, WALTER (1869–   )

1911   Salaman, M. C. "Pictures and Etchings of the Hon. Walter James." *Studio* 54 (1911): 103.

JANINET, JEAN FRANÇOIS (1752–1814)

1880–82 Béraldi, H. and Portalis, R. *Les graveurs du XVIIIᵉ Siècle.* Vol. 2. Paris: D. Morgand and C. Fatout, 1880–1882.

1921   Delteil, Loys. "Jean François Janinet." *Print Connoisseur* 2 (1921): 155.

1969   Man, Felix H., ed. *Europäische Graphik*. Vol. 6. Munich: Galerie Wolfgang Ketterer, 1969.

1969   Schmied, Wieland, ed. *Horst Janssen: Ballhaus Jahnke, Radierungen*. (from the C. Vogel collection) Frankfort: Insel, 1969.

1971   Victoria and Albert Museum. *Homage to Senefelder*. Introduction by Felix H. Man. London, 1971.

1973   *Horst Janssen: Drawings and Graphics (1969–1973)*. Hanover: Kestner-Gesellschaft, 1973.

JASINSKI, FÉLIX-STANISLAS (1862–1901)

1934   Wellisz, Léopold. "Félix-Stanislas Jasinski, Graveur. Paris: Van Oest, 1934.

JAWLENSKY, ALEXEI VON (1864–1941)

1957   Peters, H., ed. *Die Bauhaus Mappen: Neue Europäische Graphik 1921–1923*. Cologne: C. Czwiklitzer, 1957.

1959   Weiler, C. *Alexei Jawlensky: With a Catalogue of Works*. Cologne, 1959.

1965   Wingler, H. M. *Graphic Work from the Bauhaus*. Greenwich, Conn.: New York Graphic Society, 1965.

1972   Sotriffer, Kristian. *Expressionism and Fauvism*. New York: McGraw-Hill Book Co., 1972.

JEFFRIES, KATHLEEN

1924   Laver, James. "The Etchings of Kathleen Jeffries." *Bookman's Journal* 10 (1924): 124.

JELINEK, HANS (1910–   )

1949   Reese, Albert. *American Prize Prints of the 20th Century*. p. 95. New York: American Artists Group, 1949.

1970   Library of Congress. *American Prints in the Library of Congress: A Catalog of the Collection*. Compiled by Karen F. Beall. p. 231. Baltimore: The Library of Congress, The Johns Hopkins Press, 1970.

JENKINS, PAUL (1923–   )

1964   Hann, O. *Jenkins*. Paris: P. Tisnes and Stuttgart: Hatje, 1964.

1971 Victoria and Albert Museum. *Homage to Senefelder.* Introduction by Felix H. Man. London, 1971.

JOHN, AUGUSTUS (1878–1961)

1909 Dodgson, Campbell. "Augustus John: als Zeichner und Radirer." *Graphischen Kunst* 32 (1909): 43.

1917 Allhusen, E. L. "Etched Work of Augustus John." *Print Collector's Quarterly.* 7 (1917): 91–102.

1920 Dodgson, Campbell. *A Catalogue of Etchings by Augustus John: 1901–1914.* London: C. Chenil and Co., Ltd., 1920

1931 Dodgson, Campbell. "Additions to the Catalogue of the Etchings by Augustus John, R.A." *Print Collector's Quarterly* 18 (1931): 271–287.

JOHNS, JASPER (1930–   )

1969 Marion Koogler McNay Art Institute. *Jasper Johns: The Graphic Work—Catalogue of an Exhibition.* San Antonio, Tex., 1969.

1970 Field, Richard S. *Jasper Johns: Prints 1960–1970.* New York: Praeger, and Philadelphia: Philadelphia Museum of Art, 1970.

1970 Field, Richard S. "The Making of 'Souvenir'." *Print Collector's Newsletter* 1 (1970): 29–31.

1970 John Berggruen Gallery. *Jasper Johns: Retrospective Exhibition.* San Francisco, 1970.

1970 Kozloff, Max. *Jasper Johns.* New York: Harry N. Abrams, 1970.

1970 Young, Joseph E. "Jasper Johns' Lead-Relief Prints." *Artist's Proof* 10 (1970): 36–38.

1972 Coplans, John. "Fragments According to Johns: An Interview with Jasper Johns." *Print Collector's Newsletter* 3 (1972): 29–32.

1972 Hopps, Walter. "Jasper Johns: Fragments—According to What." *Print Review.* New York: Pratt Graphics Center and Kennedy Galleries, Inc. 1 (1972): 41–50.

1972 Littman, Robert. *Jasper Johns: 'Decoy'—The Print and the Painting.* Hempstead, N.Y.: Hofstra University, Emily Lowe Gallery, 1972.

JOHNSON, LESTER (1919–   )

1972 Heckscher Museum. *Artists of Suffolk County: Part 6, Contemporary Prints.* Huntington, N.Y., 1972.

1970   Johnson, Malcolm. *David Claypool Johnston: American Graphic Humorist.* Worcester, Mass.: Worcester Art Museum; Boston: Boston Public Library, 1970.

JONES, ALLEN (1937–   )

1966   Editions Alecto Ltd. *Catalogue (Allen Jones).* London, 1966.

1968   "Two Artists Discuss their Work." *Studio, International Supplement,* June 1968: pp. 335–336.

1971   Man, Felix H., ed. *Europäische Graphik.* Vol. 7. Munich: Galerie Wolfgang Ketterer, 1971.

JONES, JOHN PAUL (1924–   )

1963   Johnson, Una and Miller, Jo. *John Paul Jones: Prints and Drawings 1948–1963.* American Graphic Artists of the 20th Century Series, monograph no. 1. New York: Brooklyn Institute of Arts and Sciences, Shorewood Publishers, 1963.

1970   Library of Congress. *American Prints in the Library of Congress: A Catalog of the Collection.* Compiled by Karen F. Beall. p. 232. Baltimore: The Library of Congress, The Johns Hopkins Press, 1970.

JONES, STANLEY (20th C.)

1971   Man, Felix H., ed. *Europäische Graphik.* Vol. 7. Munich: Galerie Wolfgang Ketterer, 1971.

JONES, SYDNEY R. (1881–   )

1922   "Four Etchings by Sydney R. Jones." *Studio* 84 (1922): 99.

1925   Salaman, M. C. "Mr. Sydney R. Jones's Cambridge Etchings." *Studio* 90 (1925): 159.

JONGKIND, JOHAN BARTHOLD (1819–1891)

1906   Delteil, Loys. *Le Peintre-Graveur Illustré: Jongkind.* Vol. 1. Paris: Chez l'auteur, 1906.

1928   Roger-Marx, Claude. "The Engraved Work of Jongkind." *Print Collector's Quarterly* 15 (1928): 111–130.

1969   Delteil, Loys. *Le Peintre-Graveur Illustré: Jongkind.* Vol. 1. 1906. Reprint. New York: Da Capo Press, 1969.

114   **JORN, ASGER (1914–1973)**

1950   Dotremont, C. *Asger Jorn.* Copenhagen, 1950.

1972   Sotriffer, Kristian. *Expressionism and Fauvism.* New York: McGraw-Hill Book Co., 1972.

JOSSOT, HENRI-GUSTAVE (1866–   )

1970   Stein, Donna and Karshan, Donald. *L'Estampe Originale: A Catalogue Raisonné.* New York: The Museum of Graphic Art, 1970.

JOUVET-MAGRON, DOMINIQUE (20th C.)

1923   "Catalogue of the Etchings of Dominique Jouvet-Magron." *Print Connoisseur* 3 (1923): 95.

1923   Clément-Janin. "Dominique Jouvet-Magron." *Print Connoisseur* 3 (1923): 93.

1923   Dezert, G. Desdevises Du. "Dominique Jouvet-Magron." *Print Connoisseur* 3 (1923): 91.

JOYAU, AMÉDÉE

1938   Curtis, Atherton. *L'oeuvre gravé d'Amédée Joyau.* Paris: Paul Prouté, 1938.

JULES, MERVIN (1912–   )

1949   Reese, Albert. *American Prize Prints of the 20th Century.* p. 96. New York: American Artists Group, 1949.

1970   Library of Congress. *American Prints in the Library of Congress: A Catalog of the Collection.* Compiled by Karen F. Beall. p. 233. Baltimore: The Library of Congress, The Johns Hopkins Press, 1970.

KAHN, MAX (1904–   )

1949   Reese, Albert. *American Prize Prints of the 20th Century.* p. 97. New York: American Artists Group, 1949.

1970   Library of Congress. *American Prints in the Library of Congress: A Catalog of the Collection.* Compiled by Karen F. Beall. p. 234. Baltimore: The Library of Congress, The Johns Hopkins Press, 1970.

1962   Andrew D. White Museum of Art. *Paintings, Drawings and
       Graphics by Peter Kahn.* Ithaca, N. Y.: Cornell University, 1962.

KANDINSKY, WASSILY (1866–1944)

1954   Grohmann, Will. *Kandinsky: Oeuvre Gravé.* Paris: Galerie Berg-
       gruen, 1954.

1958   Grohmann, Will. *Wassily Kandinsky: Life and Work.* New York:
       Harry N. Abrams, 1958.

1962   Lindsay, K. "Graphic Art in Kandinsky's Oeuvre." *Prints.* Edited
       by Carl Zigrosser. New York: Holt, Rinehart and Winston, 1962.

1964   Grohmann, Will. "Wassily Kandinsky." Paris, 1954. Translation.
       Artist's Proof 7 (1964): 34–37.

1965   Wingler, H. M. *Graphic Work from the Bauhaus.* Greenwich,
       Conn.: New York Graphic Society, 1965.

1970   Roethel, Hans Konrad. *Kandinsky: Das Graphische Werk.* Cologne:
       Verlag Du Mont Schauberg, 1970.

1972   Sotriffer, Kristian. *Expressionism and Fauvism.* New York:
       McGraw-Hill Book Co., 1972.

1974   Roethel, Hans Konrad. *The Graphic Work of Kandinsky: A Loan
       Exhibition.* New York: Solomon R. Guggenheim Museum, 1974.

1974   The William Benton Museum of Art. *Vasily Kandinsky: An
       Introduction to his Work.* Introduction by Stephanie Terenzio.
       Storrs, Conn.: The University of Connecticut, 1974.

KAPLAN, JEROME (1920–)

1970   Library of Congress. *American Prints in the Library of Congress: A
       Catalog of the Collection.* Compiled by Karen F. Beall. p. 135.
       Baltimore: The Library of Congress, The Johns Hopkins Press,
       1970.

1973   *Jerome Kaplan: Prints 1948–1973.* Philadelphia: The Print Club of
       Philadelphia, 1973.

KAPPEL, PHILIP (1901–)

1929   *Philip Kappel.* American Etchers Series. Vol. 4. New York: The
       Crafton Collection, and London: P. and D. Colnaghi and Co.,
       1929.

1949   Reese, Albert. *American Prize Prints of the 20th Century*. p. 98. New York: American Artists Group, 1949.

1970   Library of Congress. *American Prints in the Library of Congress: A Catalog of the Collection*. Compiled by Karen F. Beall. p. 235. Baltimore: The Library of Congress, The Johns Hopkins Press, 1970.

KARP, LEON (1903–   )

1949   Reese, Albert. *American Prize Prints of the 20th Century*. p. 99. New York: American Artists Group, 1949.

1970   Library of Congress. *American Prints in the Library of Congress: A Catalog of the Collection*. Compiled by Karen F. Beall. p. 235. Baltimore: The Library of Congress, The Johns Hopkins Press, 1970.

KATZ, HILDA (1909–   )

1970   Library of Congress. *American Prints in the Library of Congress: A Catalog of the Collection*. Compiled by Karen F. Beall. pp. 235–237. Baltimore: The Library of Congress, The Johns Hopkins Press, 1970.

KATZ, LEO (1887–   )

1949   Reese, Albert. *American Prize Prints of the 20th Century*. p. 100. New York: American Artists Group, 1949.

1970   Library of Congress. *American Prints in the Library of Congress: A Catalog of the Collection*. Compiled by Karen F. Beall. p. 237. Baltimore: The Library of Congress, The Johns Hopkins Press, 1970.

KAY, (MRS.) KATHERINE *See* CAMERON, KATHERINE

KEENE, CHARLES S. (1823–1891)

1897   Pennell, Joseph. *Work of Charles Keene*. London, 1897.

1902–03 Spielman, M. H. "Charles Keene and his Newly Found Plates." *Magazine of Art* (1902–03): 490.

1903   Spielman, M. H. *Twenty-one Etchings by Charles S. Keene*. London, 1903.

1908   Veth, Jan. "Charles Keene." *Kunst und Kunstler* 6 (1908): 284.

1930   Reid, Forrest. "Charles Keene, Illustrator." *Print Collector's Quarterly* 17 (1930): 23–47.

1972   Waldman, Diane. *Ellsworth Kelly: Drawings, Collages, Prints.*
Greenwich, Conn.: New York Graphic Society, 1972.

KELLY, FRANCIS (1927–   )

1971   William Weston Gallery. *Francis Kelly: English Landscape Etching.*
London, 1971.

KENT, CORITA (SISTER MARY CORITA) (1918–   )

1970   Library of Congress. *American Prints in the Library of Congress: A
Catalog of the Collection.* Compiled by Karen F. Beall. pp. 238–239.
Baltimore: The Library of Congress, The Johns Hopkins Press,
1970.

KENT, NORMAN (1903–1972)

1949   Reese, Albert. *American Prize Prints of the 20th Century.* p. 101.
New York: American Artists Group, 1949.

1970   Library of Congress. *American Prints in the Library of Congress: A
Catalog of the Collection.* Compiled by Karen F. Beall. p. 239.
Baltimore: The Library of Congress, The Johns Hopkins Press,
1970.

KENT, ROCKWELL (1882–1971)

1933   Kent, Rockwell, and Zigrosser, Carl. *Rockwellkentiana.* New York:
Harcourt, Brace and Co., 1933.

1938   Zigrosser, Carl. "Rockwell Kent." *Print Collector's Quarterly* 25
(1938): 137–155.

1942   Zigrosser, Carl. *The Artist in America: 24 Close-ups of Contemporary
Printmakers.* New York: Alfred Knopf, 1942.

1949   Reese, Albert. *American Prize Prints of the 20th Century.* p. 102.
New York: American Artists Group, 1949.

1970   Library of Congress. *American Prints in the Library of Congress: A
Catalog of the Collection.* Compiled by Karen F. Beall. pp. 239–240.

Baltimore: The Library of Congress, The Johns Hopkins Press,
1970.

1971   Denison University. *Rockwell Kent: In Memoriam.* Granville, Ohio,
1971.

1972   The American Academy of Arts and Letters. *Memorial Exhibition.*
New York, 1972.

118 [1975] Jones, Dan Burne. *The Prints of Rockwell Kent: A Catalogue Raisonné.* Work in Progress. University of Chicago Press, [Projected date: 1975]

KERKOVIUS, RUTH (1921–   )

1969 Associated American Artists. *Ruth Kerkovius: Recent Etchings.* New York, 1969.

1970 Library of Congress. *American Prints in the Library of Congress: A Catalog of the Collection.* Compiled by Karen F. Beall. p. 240. Baltimore: The Library of Congress, The Johns Hopkins Press, 1970.

KIMBALL, CHARLES FREDERICK (1831–1903)

1881 Koehler, S. R. *American Art Review* 2 (1881): 244.

KIMBALL, WAYNE (1943–   )

1973 Roswell Museum. *Wayne Kimball: Lithographs.* Roswell, N. Mex., 1973.

1973 Wilfer, Joseph. *Wayne Kimball: An Exhibition of Prints.* Madison, Wis.: Madison Art Center, 1973.

KINGSLEY, ELBRIDGE (1842–1918)

1901 Dwight, Clara Leigh. *Catalogue of the Works of Elbridge Kingsley.* [Compiled for Mt. Holyoke College, Mass.] New York, 1901.

1970 Library of Congress. *American Prints in the Library of Congress: A Catalog of the Collection.* Compiled by Karen F. Beall. p. 241. Baltimore: The Library of Congress, The Johns Hopkins Press, 1970.

KINNEY, TROY (1871–1938)

1920 *Catalogue of the Etchings of Troy Kinney.* Introduction by Robert Cole. New York: W. E. Rudge, 1920.

1920 "Catalogue Raisonné of the Etchings and Dry-points of Troy Kinney." *The Print Connoisseur* 1 (1920): 142–157.

1929 *The Etchings of Troy Kinney.* Garden City, N.Y.: Doubleday, Doran and Co., 1929.

1930 *Troy Kinney.* American Etchers Series. Vol. 9. New York: The Crafton Collection, Inc., London: P. and D. Colnaghi and Co., 1930.

1938   Kinney, Troy. "Troy Kinney: An Autobiography." *Print Collector's Quarterly* 25 (1938): 265–283.

1970   Library of Congress. *American Prints in the Library of Congress: A Catalog of the Collection.* Compiled by Karen F. Beall. p. 242. Baltimore: The Library of Congress, The Johns Hopkins Press, 1970.

KIRCHNER, ERNST LUDWIG (1880–1938)

1916–27 Schiefler, Gustav. *Die Graphik: Ernst Ludwig Kirchner.* 2 vols. Berlin: Euphorion, 1916, 1917–27.

1965   Dube-Heynig, Annemarie and Wolf-Dieter. *Kirchner: His Graphic Art.* Greenwich, Conn.: New York Graphic Society, 1965.

1967   Dube-Heynig, Annemarie and Wolf-Dieter. *Ernst Ludwig Kirchner: Das Graphische Werk.* 2 vols. Munich: Prestel-Verlag, 1967.

1972   Allan Frumkin Gallery. *Ernst Ludwig Kirchner: Woodcuts, Lithographs, Etchings: 1906–1924.* Chicago, 1972.

1972   Sotriffer, Kristian. *Expressionism and Fauvism.* New York: McGraw-Hill Book Co., 1972.

KITAJ, R. B. (1932–   )

1971   Marlborough Fine Art, Ltd. *R. B. Kitaj: The Complete Graphic Works 1963–1970.* London, 1971.

KLEE, PAUL (1879–1940)

1920   Klee, Paul. "Schopferische Konfession." *Tribune der Kunst und Zeit* [Berlin] 1 (1920).

1945   Soby, James T. *The Prints of Paul Klee.* New York: Valentin, 1945.

1954   Grohmann, Will. *Paul Klee.* Stuttgart, 1954.

1955   Grohmann, Will. *Paul Klee.* New York: Harry N. Abrams, 1955.

1963   Kornfeld, E. W. *Verzeichnis Des Graphischen Werkes von Paul Klee.* Berne: Verlag Kornfeld and Klipstein, 1963.

1972   Sotriffer, Kristian. *Expressionism and Fauvism.* New York: McGraw-Hill Book Co., 1972.

1973   Klee, Paul. "Graphic Art." Translation by Flavia Somasca and Clive Foster. Reprint of "Schopferische Konfession," Berlin, 1920. *Print Collector* [Milan: Grafica Sipiel, s.r.] 2 (1973): 20–25.

120   1973   Sanna, Jole de. "Early Etchings by Klee." *Print Collector* [Milan: Grafica Sipiel, s.r.] 5 (1973): 20–39.

KLEIBER, HANS (1887–   )

1937   *Hans Kleiber: Catalog.* Appreciation by Bertha E. Jacques. 1937.

1970   Library of Congress. *American Prints in the Library of Congress: A Catalog of the Collection.* Compiled by Karen F. Beall. p. 243. Baltimore: The Library of Congress, The Johns Hopkins Press, 1970.

KLEIN, CÉSAR (1879–1954)

1962   Pfefferkorn, Rudolf. *César Klein.* Die Kunst unserer Zeit Series. Vol. 14. Berlin: Rembrandt-Verlag, 1962.

1972   Sotriffer, Kristian. *Expressionism and Fauvism.* New York: McGraw-Hill Book Co., 1972.

KLEIN, JOHANN ADAM (1792–1875)

1863   Jahn, C. *Das Werk von J. A. Klein.* Munich, 1863.

1925   Dussler, L. *Die Incunabeln der Deutschen Lithographie.* Berlin: H. Tiedemann, 1925.

1971   Victoria and Albert Muse)m. *Homage to Senefelder.* Introduction by Felix H. Man. London, 1971.

KLINGER, MAX (1857–1920)

1909   Singer, H. W. *Max Klingers Radierungen, Stiche und Steindrucke.* Berlin: Amsler and Ruthart, 1909.

1930   Beyer, Carl. *Max Klingers graphisches Werk, von 1909–1919.* Leipzig: P. H. Beyer and Son, 1930.

1957   Pommeranz-Liedtke, G. *Der Graphische Zylers von Max Klinger biz zur Gegen wart All.* Deutsche Akademie der Kunst, 1957.

1972   Margonari, Renzo. *Max Klinger: Engravings.* Milan: galleria dell'incisione, 1972.

1974   Carus Gallery. *Klinger: Exhibition List.* New York, 1974.

KLOSS, GENE (1903–   )

1949   Reese, Albert. *American Prize Prints of the 20th Century.* p. 103. New York: American Artists Group, 1949.

1970   Library of Congress. *American Prints in the Library of Congress: A Catalog of the Collection.* Compiled by Karen F. Beall. p. 243. Baltimore: The Library of Congress, The Johns Hopkins Press, 1970.

KNAPTON, CHARLES (1700–1760)

1922   Hake, H. M. "Pond's and Knapton's Imitations of Drawings." *Print Collector's Quarterly* 9 (1922): 325–349.

KNATHS, KARL (1891–1971)

1972   The American Academy of Arts and Letters. *Memorial Exhibition.* New York, 1972.

KNIGHT, LAURA, A.R.A., A.R.E. (1877–1971)

1924   Grimsditch, H. B. "Some Recent Etchings and Aquatints by Laura Knight." *Studio* 87 (1924): 260.

1932   Salaman, Malcolm C. *Laura Johnson Knight.* Modern Masters of Etching Series, no. 29. London: The Studio, Ltd., 1932.

KOBELL, WILHELM VON (1766–1855)

1923   Lessing, Waldemar. *Wilhelm von Kobell.* Munich: F. Bruckmann A.G., 1923.

KOHN, BERNARD (20th C.)

1973   Selig, J. Daniel. *The Lyrical Vision: Graphic Art of Bernard Kohn.* Reading, Pa.: The Reading Public Museum, 1973.

KOHN, MISCH (1916–   )

1961   Zigrosser, Carl. *Misch Kohn.* New York: American Federation of Arts, 1961.

1970   Library of Congress. *American Prints in the Library of Congress: A Catalog of the Collection.* Compiled by Karen F. Beall. pp. 244–246. Baltimore: The Library of Congress, The Johns Hopkins Press, 1970.

1973   Jane Haslem Gallery. *The Innovators: Renaissance in American Printmaking.* Washington, D.C., 1973.

KOKOSCHKA, OSKAR (1886–   )

1947   Hoffman, Edith. *Kokoschka: Life and Work, With Catalogue 1908–1945.* London: Faber and Faber, 1947.

122 1950   Arntz, Wilhelm. *Das Graphische Werk Oskar Kokoschkas: [Catalogue of exhibition] 'Oskar Kokoschka auf seinem scheffen 1907–1950.'* Munich: Haus der Kunst, 1950.

1962   Hodin, J. P. "Notes on Oskar Kokoschka's Graphic Style." *Prints.* Edited by Carl Zigrosser. New York: Holt, Rinehart and Winston, 1962.

1962   Tate Gallery. *Kokoschka: A Retrospective Exhibition of Paintings, Drawings, Lithographs, Stage Designs and Books.* London, 1962.

1965   Wingler, H. M. *Graphic Work from the Bauhaus.* Greenwich, Conn.: New York Graphic Society, 1965.

1966   Man, Felix H., ed. *Europäische Graphik.* Vol. 5. Munich: Galerie Wolfgang Ketterer, 1966.

1967   The British Museum. *Kokoschka: Word and Vision 1906–1966.* London, 1967.

1971   Victoria and Albert Museum. *Homage to Senefelder.* Introduction by Felix H. Man. London, 1971.

1971   Victoria and Albert Museum. *Kokoschka: Prints and Drawings—an Exhibition.* London, 1971.

1971   Wingler, H. M. *Kokoschka: Das Graphische Werk.* Munich, 1971.

1972   Sotriffer, Kristian. *Expressionism and Fauvism.* New York: McGraw-Hill Book Co., 1972.

KOLLWITZ, KÄTHE SCHMIDT (1867–1945)

1946   Zigrosser, Carl. *Käthe Kollwitz.* New York: Bittner, 1946.

1955   Klipstein, August. *Käthe Kollwitz: Verzeichnis des graphischen Werkes.* Berne: Kornfeld and Klipstein, 1955.

1968   University of Connecticut. *The Landauer Collection of Käthe Kollwitz Prints.* Storrs, Conn.: University of Connecticut Museum of Art, 1968.

1969   Zigrosser, Carl. *Prints and Drawings of Käthe Kollwitz.* New York: Dover, 1969.

1970   Peter Deitsch Gallery. *Käthe Kollwitz.* New York, 1970.

KOPMAN, BENJAMIN (1887–1965)

1949   Reese, Albert. *American Prize Prints of the 20th Century.* p. 104. New York: American Artists Group, 1949.

1970 Library of Congress. *American Prints in the Library of Congress: A Catalog of the Collection.* Compiled by Karen F. Beall. p. 246. Baltimore: The Library of Congress, The Johns Hopkins Press, 1970.

1973 Associated American Artists. *Chaim Koppelman: Twenty Years of Printmaking: Checklist of the Graphic Work.* New York, 1973.

KRASNER, LEE (1911–)

1972 Heckscher Museum. *Artists of Suffolk County: Part 6, Contemporary Prints.* Huntington, N.Y., 1972.

KRIEHUBER, JOSEF (1800–1876)

1902 Wurzbach, W. von. *Josef Kriehuber: Katalog der von ihm Lithografirten portraits.* Munich: H. Helbing, 1902.

1971 Victoria and Albert Museum. *Homage to Senefelder.* Introduction by Felix H. Man. London, 1971.

KRIWET, FERDINAND (1942–)

1962 *Catalogue of the Exhibition "Strukturale Malerei."* Berlin, 1962.

KRUCK, CHRISTIAN (1925–)

1966-67 Man, Felix H., ed. *Europäische Graphik.* Vols. 4, 5. Munich: Galerie Wolfgang Ketterer, 1966–67.

1971 Victoria and Albert Museum. *Homage to Senefelder.* Introduction by Felix H. Man. London, 1971.

KRUSE, ALEXANDER ZERDIN (1890–)

1949 Reese, Albert. *American Prize Prints of the 20th Century.* p. 105. New York: American Artists Group, 1949.

1970 Library of Congress. *American Prints in the Library of Congress: A Catalog of the Collection.* Compiled by Karen F. Beall. p. 247. Baltimore: The Library of Congress, The Johns Hopkins Press, 1970.

KUBIN, ALFRED (1877–1959)

1957 Raabe, P. *Alfred Kubin: Leben, Werk, Wirkung: With a Catalogue of Works.* Hamburg: Rowohlt, 1957.

1965 Wingler, H. M. *Graphic Work from the Bauhaus.* Greenwich, Conn.: New York Graphic Society, 1965.

124 1972   Sotriffer, Kristian. *Expressionism and Fauvism*. New York:
McGraw-Hill Book Co., 1972.

KUEHNE, MAX (1880–1968)

1949   Reese, Albert. *American Prize Prints of the 20th Century*. p. 106.
New York: American Artists Group, 1949.

1970   Library of Congress. *American Prints in the Library of Congress: A
Catalog of the Collection*. Compiled by Karen F. Beall. p. 248.
Baltimore: The Library of Congress, The Johns Hopkins Press,
1970.

KUHN, WALT (1877–1949)

1967   Kennedy Galleries. *Walt Kuhn as Printmaker*. New York, 1967.

1974   Harlan, Gallery. *Walt Kuhn as Printmaker*. Tucson, Ariz., 1974.

KUMJÁTI, JULIUM (1894–   )

1933   Salaman, Malcolm C. "The Etchings of Julium Kumjáti." *Print
Collector's Quarterly* 20 (1933): 247–268.

KUMM, MARGUERITE ELIZABETH (1902–   )

1949   Reese, Albert. *American Prize Prints of the 20th Century*. p. 107.
New York: American Artists Group, 1949.

1970   Library of Congress. *American Prints in the Library of Congress: A
Catalog of the Collection*. Compiled by Karen F. Beall. p. 248.
Baltimore: The Library of Congress, The Johns Hopkins Press,
1970.

KUNIYOSHI, YASUO (1893–1953)

1942   Zigrosser, Carl. *The Artist in America: 24 Close-ups of Contemporary
Printmakers*. New York: Alfred A. Knopf, 1942.

1948   Whitney Museum of American Art. *Yasuo Kuniyoshi: Retrospective*.
New York, 1948.

1949   Reese, Albert. *American Prize Prints of the 20th Century*. p. 108.
New York: American Artists Group, 1949.

1965   "A Checklist of the Etchings of Yasuo Kuniyoshi." *Journal of the
Archives of American Art* 5 (1965).

1969   University of Florida. *Yasuo Kuniyoshi*. Gainesville, Fla., 1969.

1970   Library of Congress. *American Prints in the Library of Congress: A*
        Catalog of the Collection. Compiled by Karen F. Beall. p. 248.
        Baltimore: The Library of Congress, The Johns Hopkins Press,
        1970.

KUPPERMAN, LAWRENCE (1909–   )

1949   Reese, Albert. *American Prize Prints of the 20th Century.* p. 109.
        New York: American Artists Group, 1949.

1970   Library of Congress. *American Prints in the Library of Congress: A*
        Catalog of the Collection. Compiled by Karen F. Beall. p. 248.
        Baltimore: The Library of Congress, The Johns Hopkins Press,
        1970.

LABOUREUR, EMILE (1877–1943)

1909   Lotz-Brissoneau, A. *Eaux-fortes, Bois et Lithographies d'Emile*
        Laboureur. Paris: Chez Sagot, 1909.

1928   Laurencin, M. *Cahier de l'oeuvre gravé par Laboureur.* Paris:
        Bibliothèque Nationale, Cabinet des Estampes, 1928.

1929   Godefroy, L. *L'oeuvre gravé de Laboureur.* Paris, 1929.

1945   Prinet, J. "Les Illustrations de Laboureur." *Portique* 1 (1945).

1954   Bibliothèque Nationale. *Laboureur: Estampes, dessins, livres il-*
        lustrés. Paris, 1954.

1962   Loyer, Jacqueline. *L'oeuvre gravé de Laboureur: Suite et fin du*
        Catalogue Godefroy. Paris: Tournon, M. Lecomte, 1962.

LACOSTE, CHARLES (1870–   )

1970   Stein, Donna and Karshan, Donald. *L'Estampe Originale: A*
        Catalogue Raisonné. New York: The Museum of Graphic Art,
        1970.

LACOURIÈRE, ROGER

1949   McNulty, K. *Roger Lacourière, Engraver and Master Printer:*
        Catalogue of an Exhibition. New York: New York Public Library,
        1949.

LA FARGE, JOHN (1835–1910)

1915   Weitenkampf, Frank. "John La Farge, Illustrator." *Print Collector's*
        Quarterly 5 (1915): 473–494.

1967   Toledo Museum of Art. *John La Farge.* Toledo, Ohio, 1967.

LAFRENSEN, NICOLAS *See* LAVREINCE, NICOLAS

LAHEY, RICHARD FRANCIS (1893–   )

1949 Reese, Albert. *American Prize Prints of the 20th Century*. p. 110. New York: American Artists Group, 1949.

LALANNE, MAXIME (1827–1886)

1889 Béraldi, Henri. *Les Graveurs du XIXᵉ Siècle*. Vol. 9. Paris: L. Conquet, 1889.

1913 Bradley, W. A. "Maxime Lalanne." *Print Collector's Quarterly* 3 (1913): 70–85.

1923 Delteil, Loys. "Maxime Lalanne." *Print Connoisseur* 3 (1923): 390.

LAM, WILFREDO (1902–   )

1960 Cherpin, J. *Wilfredo Lam*. Paris: Musée de poche, 1960.

1970 Gimpel and Weitzenhoffer Ltd. *Original Prints of the Surrealists*. New York, 1970.

LAMI, EUGÈNE (1800–1890)

1914 Lemoisne, P. A. *L'Oeuvre d'Eugène Lami (1800–1890): Lithographies, Dessins, Aquarelles, Peintures. Essai d'un catalogue*. Paris, 1914.

1930 Reitlinger, Henry. "Lami and Monnier." *Print Collector's Quarterly* 17 (1930): 73–91.

LANDACRE, PAUL (1893–1963)

1942 Zigrosser, Carl. *The Artist in America: 24 Close-Ups of Contemporary Printmakers*. New York: Alfred Knopf, 1942.

1949 Reese, Albert. *American Prize Prints of the 20th Century*. p. 111. New York: American Artists Group, 1949.

1970 Library of Congress. *American Prints in the Library of Congress: A Catalog of the Collection*. Compiled by Karen F. Beall. pp. 250–251. Baltimore: The Library of Congress, The Johns Hopkins Press, 1970.

LANDAU, JACOB (1917–   )

1969 Associated American Artists. *Jacob Landau: Exhibition Catalogue*. New York, 1969.

1970   Library of Congress. *American Prints in the Library of Congress: A Catalog of the Collection.* Compiled by Karen F. Beall. p. 251. Baltimore: The Library of Congress, The Johns Hopkins Press, 1970.

LANDECK, ARMIN (1905–   )

1940   Reece, Childe. "Armin Landeck." *Print Collector's Quarterly* 27 (1940): 457–499.

1949   Reese, Albert. *American Prize Prints of the 20th Century.* p. 112. New York: American Artists Group, 1949.

1970   Library of Congress. *American Prints in the Library of Congress: A Catalog of the Collection.* Compiled by Karen F. Beall. pp. 252–253. Baltimore: The Library of Congress, The Johns Hopkins Press, 1970.

LANDERS, BERTHA (1911–   )

1949   Reese, Albert. *American Prize Prints of the 20th Century.* p. 113. New York: American Artists Group, 1949.

1970   Library of Congress. *American Prints in the Library of Congress: A Catalog of the Collection.* p. 253. Baltimore: The Library of Congress, The Johns Hopkins Press, 1970.

LANDON, EDWARD AUGUST (1911–   )

1949   Reese, Albert. *American Prize Prints of the 20th Century.* p. 114. New York: American Artists Group, 1949.

1970   Library of Congress. *American Prints in the Library of Congress: A Catalog of the Collection.* Compiled by Karen F. Beall. p. 253. Baltimore: The Library of Congress, The Johns Hopkins Press, 1970.

LANDSEER, SIR EDWIN (1802–1873)

1876   Graves, A. *Catalogue of the Works of Sir Edwin Landseer.* London, 1876.

LANDSEER, THOMAS (1795–1880)

1903   Graves, A. "Thomas Landseer." *The Printseller* 1 (1903): 101.

LANG, LÉON (1899–   )

1937   Dodgson, Campbell. "The Lithographs of Léon Lang." *Print Collector's Quarterly* 24 (1937): 265–281.

128   **LANGE, OTTO (1879–1944)**

1972   Sotriffer, Kristian. *Expressionism and Fauvism*. New York: McGraw-Hill Book Co., 1972.

LANKES, JULIUS J. (1884–1960)

1921   Brown, B. *J. J. Lankes: Painter-graver on Wood*. Kansas City, Mo., 1921.

1924   "List of Woodcuts by J. J. Lankes." *The Print Connoisseur* 4 (1924): 314–321.

1924   Whitaker, Charles Harris. "The Work of J. J. Lankes." *Print Connoisseur* 4 (1924): 303.

1937   Whitaker, C. H. *A Descriptive Checklist of the Woodcut Bookplates of J. J. Lankes*. Millersville, Penn., 1937.

1942   Zigrosser, Carl. *The Artist in America: 24 Close-Ups of Contemporary Printmakers*. New York: Alfred Knopf, 1942.

1949   Reese, Albert. *American Prize Prints of the 20th Century*. p. 115. New York: American Artists Group, 1949.

1970   Library of Congress. *American Prints in the Library of Congress: A Catalog of the Collection*. Compiled by Karen F. Beall. pp. 254–255. Baltimore: The Library of Congress, The Johns Hopkins Press, 1970.

Lankes, J. J. *The Woodcut Record*. Unpublished manuscript catalog in collection of the Virginia State Library, Richmond, Va.

LANYON, ELLEN (1926–   )

1970   Library of Congress. *American Prints in the Library of Congress: A Catalog of the Collection*. Compiled by Karen F. Beall. p. 256. Baltimore: The Library of Congress, The Johns Hopkins Press, 1970.

1972   Wilfer, Joseph Edward. *Wonder Production: Volume 1: Catalogue of Exhibition*. Madison, Wis.: Madison Art Center, 1972.

LAPINSKI, TADEUSZ (1928–   )

1971   Davis, Bernard. *Tadeusz Lapinski: Color Lithographs*. Miami, Fla.: Miami Museum of Modern Art, 1971.

1973   Jane Haslem Gallery. *The Innovators: Renaissance in American Printmaking*. Washington, D.C., 1973.

1973   Kainen, Jacob. *Tadeusz Lapinski: Recent Lithographs.* New York:
Kennedy Graphics, 1973.

LAPRADE, PIERRE (1875–1931)

1944   Johnson, Una E. *Ambroise Vollard, Éditeur.* New York: Wittenborn and Co., 1944.

LARIONOV, MICHAEL (1881–1964)

1965   Wingler, H. M. *Graphic Work from the Bauhaus.* Greenwich,
Conn.: New York Graphic Society, 1965.

1972   Sotriffer, Kristian. *Expressionism and Fauvism.* New York:
McGraw-Hill Book Co., 1972.

LARKINS, WILLIAM M., A.R.E.

1926   Laver, James. "The Etched Work of William M. Larkins."
Bookman's Journal 14 (1926): 157.

LARSENS, JOHANNES

1938   Rasmussen, H. M. *Johannes Larsens, Grafiske Arbejoer: en illust-
reret fortegnelse.* Copenhagen: Fischer, 1938.

LARSSON, CARL (1853–1919)

1923   Allhusen, E. L. "The Etched Work of Carl Larsson." *Print
Collector's Quarterly* 10 (1923): 197–218.

1923   Dodgson, Campbell. "Carl Larsson Lithographs: A Postscript by
the Editor." *Print Collector's Quarterly* 10 (1923): 220.

LASANSKY, MAURICIO (1914–   )

1949   Reese, Albert. *American Prize Prints of the 20th Century.* p. 116.
New York: American Artists Group, 1949.

1960   Zigrosser, Carl. *Mauricio Lasansky.* New York: American Federation of Arts, 1960.

1970   Library of Congress. *American Prints in the Library of Congress: A
Catalog of the Collection.* Compiled by Karen F. Beall. pp. 257–258.
Baltimore: The Library of Congress, The Johns Hopkins Press,
1970.

1973   Rhodes, Stephen. *Mauricio Lasansky: 43 Prints: The Thematic
Context of Mauricio Lasansky's Prints.* Fort Dodge, Iowa: Blanden
Art Gallery, 1973.

130 1973   Jane Haslem Gallery. *The Innovators: Renaissance in American Printmaking.* Washington, D. C.,1973.

LASINIO, CARLO (1759–1838)

1918   Singer, H. W. *Monatshefte für Kunstwissenschaft* 11 (1918): 58–73.

LASSAW, IBRAM (1913–   )

1972   Heckscher Museum. *Artists of Suffolk County: Part 6, Contemporary Prints.* Huntington, N.Y., 1972.

LATENAY, GERARD DE (20th C.)

1924   "Checklist of the Etchings of Gerard de Latenay." *Print Connoisseur* 4 (1924): 131.

LATHROP, DOROTHY PULIS (1891–   )

1949   Reese, Albert. *American Prize Prints of the 20th Century.* p. 117. New York: American Artists Group, 1949.

1970   Library of Congress. *American Prints in the Library of Congress: A Catalog of the Collection.* Compiled by Karen F. Beall. p. 259. Baltimore: The Library of Congress, The Johns Hopkins Press, 1970.

LAVREINCE, NICOLAS (1737–1807)

1928   Francis, Eric C. "N. Lavreince." *Print Collector's Quarterly* 15 (1928): 11–33.

LAWSON, ROBERT (1892–1957)

1949   Reese, Albert. *American Prize Prints of the 20th Century.* p. 118. New York: American Artists Group, 1949.

1970   Library of Congress. *American Prints in the Library of Congress: A Catalog of the Collection.* Compiled by Karen F. Beall. p. 259. Baltimore: The Library of Congress, The Johns Hopkins Press, 1970.

LEAF, RUTH (1923–   )

1949   Reese, Albert. *American Prize Prints of the 20th Century.* p. 120. New York: American Artists Group, 1949.

1970   Library of Congress. *American Prints in the Library of Congress: A Catalog of the Collection.* Compiled by Karen F. Beall. p. 260. Baltimore: The Library of Congress, The Johns Hopkins Press, 1970.

1924   Thomas, Thomas H. "The Lithographs of Edward Lear." *Print Connoisseur* 4 (1924): 283.

LEBRUN, RICO (1900-   )

1970   Library of Congress. *American Prints in the Library of Congress: A Catalog of the Collection.* Compiled by Karen F. Beall. p. 260. Baltimore: The Library of Congress, The Johns Hopkins Press, 1970.

LE CLERC, SÉBASTIEN (1637–1714)

1877   Hissink, G. W. *Sébastien Le Clerc et son oeuvre gravé: étude biographique et catalogue raisonné.* Paris, 1877.

1969   Hissink, G. W. *Sébastien Le Clerc et son oeuvre gravé: étude biographique et catalogue raisonné.* 1877. Reprint. Amsterdam: G. W. Hissink, 1969.

LE CORBUSIER (EDOUARD JEANNERET) (1887–1965)

n.d.   *Le Corbusier: Oeuvre Lithographique 1954–1961.* Zurich: Centre Le Corbusier, n.d.

LEE, DORIS EMRICK (1905–   )

1946   American Artists Group. *Doris Lee.* New York, 1946.

1949.   Reese, Albert. *American Prize Prints of the 20th Century.* p. 119. New York: American Artists Group, 1949.

1970   Library of Congress. *American Prints in the Library of Congress: A Catalog of the Collection.* Compiled by Karen F. Beall. p. 260. Baltimore: The Library of Congress, The Johns Hopkins Press, 1970.

1973   Mount Holyoke College Art Museum and the Weyhe Gallery. *14 American Women Printmakers of the 30s and 40's.* South Hadley, Mass. and New York, 1973.

LEECH, JOHN (1817–1864)

1892   Chambers, C. E. S. *A List of Works Containing Illustrations by John Leech.* Edinburgh, 1892.

1914   *Catalogue of an Exhibition of Works by John Leech.* New York: Grolier Club, 1914.

132   **LEE-HANKEY, WILLIAM, R.E. (1869–1952)**

1918   Salaman, M. C. "Some Recent Prints by W. Lee-Hankey, R.E."
         Studio 74 (1918): 81.

1921   Hardie, Martin. *The Etched Work of W. Lee-Hankey from 1904–
         1920*. London: Lefevre and Son, 1921.

1924   Laver, James. "The Art of William Lee-Hankey." *Bookman's
         Journal* (1924): 14.

LÉGER, FERNAND (1881–1955)

1920   *Die Schaffenden*.Vol. 2. Berlin, 1920.

1928   Tériade, E. *Fernand Léger*. Paris: Cahiers d'Art, 1928.

1949   Cooper, Douglas. *Fernand Léger*. London and Paris, 1949.

1953   Kuh, K. *Léger*. Chicago: The Art Institute of Chicago, 1953.

1965   Wingler,H. M. *Graphic Work from the Bauhaus*. Greenwich, Conn.:
         New York Graphic Society, 1965.

1971   Victoria and Albert Museum. *Homage to Senefelder*. Introduction
         by Felix H. Man. London, 1971.

LEGRAND, EDY (1892–   )

1932   Bliss, Douglas Percy. "The Engraved Work of Edy Legrand." *Print
         Collector's Quarterly* 19 (1932): 117–134.

LEGRAND, LOUIS (1863–1951)

1896   Ramiro, E. *Louis Legrand, peintre-graveur*. Paris: H. Floury, 1896.

1967   Kovler Gallery. *Forgotten Printmakers of the 19th Century*. Chicago,
         1967.

LEGROS, ALPHONSE (1837–1911)

1877   Malassis, A. P. and Thibaudeau, A. W. *Catalogue raisonné de
         l'oeuvre gravé ... Alphonse Legros*. Paris, 1877.

1889   Béraldi, Henri. *Les Graveurs du XIXᵉ Siècle*. Vol. 9. Paris: L.
         Conquet, 1889.

1912   Cary, Elisabeth L. "Alphonse Legros." *Print Collector's Quarterly* 2
         (1912): 439–458.

1912   Haviland, Paul Burty. "Alphonse Legros." *Print Collector's Quar-
         terly* 2 (1912): 435–438.

1923   *A Catalogue of the Etchings, Drypoints, and Lithographs by Alphonse Legros in the Collection of Frank E. Bliss.* London, 1923.   **133**

1925   Lane, J. W., Jr. "Alphonse Legros." *Print Connoisseur* 5 (1925): 167.

1926   Salaman, M. C. *Alphonse Legros.* Modern Masters of Etching Series, no. 9. London: The Studio, Ltd., 1926.

1929   Wright, H. J. L. *Catalogue Raisonné of the Works of Alphonse Legros.* 1929.

1967   Kovler Gallery. *Forgotten Printmakers of the 19th Century.* Chicago, 1967.

LEHEUTRE, GUSTAVE (1861–1932)

1921   Delteil, Loys. *Le Peintre-Graveur Illustré: Leheutre.* Vol. 12. Paris: Chez l'auteur, 1921.

1944   Johnson, Una E. *Ambroise Vollard, Éditeur.* New York: Wittenborn and Co., 1944.

1969   Delteil, Loys. *Le Peintre-Graveur Illustré: Leheutre.* Vol. 12. 1921. Reprint. New York: Da Capo Press, 1969.

LEHMBRUCK, WILHELM (1881–1919)

1964   Petermann, Erwin. *Die Druckgraphik von Wilhelm Lehmbruck.* Stuttgart: G. Hatje, 1964.

1964   Petermann, Erwin. *Wilhelm Lehmbruck: Catalogue of All Known Lithographs and Etchings.* New York: Wittenborn, Inc., 1964.

LEIGHTON, CLARE VERONICA HOPE (1899–   )

1935   Hardie, Martin. "The Wood Engravings of Clare Leighton." *Print Collector's Quarterly* 22 (1935): 139–165.

1949   Reese, Albert. *American Prize Prints of the 20th Century.* p. 121. New York: American Artists Group, 1949.

1970   Library of Congress. *American Prints in the Library of Congress: A Catalog of the Collection.* Compiled by Karen F. Beall. pp. 263–265. Baltimore: The Library of Congress, The Johns Hopkins Press, 1970.

1973   Mount Holyoke College Art Museum and the Weyhe Gallery. *14 American Women Printmakers of the 30's and 40's.* South Hadley, Mass. and New York, 1973.

134   **LE MOAL, JEAN (1909–   )**

1960   Bourniquel, C. *Le Moal*. Paris: Musée de poche, 1960.

LEMUD, AIMÉ DE (1816–1886)

1881   Bouvenne, A. *Catalogue de l'oeuvre lithographie et gravé d'Aimé de Lemud*. Paris, 1881.

LENTZ, ELIZABETH (20th C.)

1949   Reese, Albert. *American Prize Prints of the 20th Century*. p. 122. New York: American Artists Group, 1949.

1970   Library of Congress. *American Prints in the Library of Congress: A Catalog of the Collection*. Compiled by Karen F. Beall. p. 265. Baltimore: The Library of Congress, The Johns Hopkins Press, 1970.

LEPÈRE, AUGUSTE-LOUIS (1849–1918)

1905   Lotz-Brissoneau, A. *L'Oeuvre Gravé d'Auguste Lepère*. Paris: Chez Edmond Sagot, 1905.

1912   Cary, Elisabeth Luther. "Auguste Lepère." *Print Collector's Quarterly* 2 (1912): 31–49.

1914   Cary, E. L. *Auguste Lepère*. New York: F. Keppel and Co., 1914.

1931   Saunier, C. *Auguste Lepère: with Texier-Bernier's Continuation of the Catalogue by Lotz-Brissoneau*. Paris: M. Le Garrec, 1931.

1967   Kovler Gallery. *Forgotten Printmakers of the 19th Century*. Chicago, 1967.

1970   Stein, Donna and Karshan, Donald. *L'Estampe Originale: A Catalogue Raisonné*. New York: The Museum of Graphic Art, 1970.

LE PRINCE, JEAN BAPTISTE (1734–1781)

1879   Hédou, Jules. *Jean Le Prince*. Paris: P. Baur, 1879.

LE VEAU, J. J. A. (1729–1785)

1903   Hédou, Jules. *J. J. A. Le Veau*. Paris: N. Charavay, 1903.

LEVINE, JACK (1915–   )

1966   Getlein, F. *Jack Levine*. New York: Abrams, 1966.

1970   Library of Congress. *American Prints in the Library of Congress: A Catalog of the Collection.* Compiled by Karen F. Beall. p. 265. Baltimore: The Library of Congress, The Johns Hopkins Press, 1970.

LEWIS, ALLEN (1873–1957)

1949   Reese, Albert. *American Prize Prints of the 20th Century.* p. 123. New York: American Artists Group, 1949.

1970   Library of Congress. *American Prints in the Library of Congress: A Catalog of the Collection.* Compiled by Karen F. Beall. p. 266. Baltimore: The Library of Congress, The Johns Hopkins Press, 1970.

LEWIS, MARTIN (1881–1962)

1931   *Martin Lewis.* American Etchers Series, vol. 11. New York: The Crafton Collection, Inc., and London: P. and D. Colnaghi and Co., 1931.

1931   Salaman, M. C. *Martin Lewis.* Modern Masters of Etching Series, no. 26. London: The Studio, Ltd., 1931.

1934   Reece, Childe. "Martin Lewis." *Prints* 4 (1934): 1–12.

1949   Reese, Albert. *American Prize Prints of the 20th Century.* p. 124. New York: American Artists Group, 1949.

1970   Library of Congress: *American Prints in the Library of Congress: A Catalog of the Collection.* Compiled by Karen F. Beall. pp. 266-267. Baltimore: The Library of Congress, The Johns Hopkins Press, 1970.

1973   McCarron, Paul. *Martin Lewis: The Graphic Work.* New York: Kennedy Galleries, 1973.

LEYS, HENRI (1815–1869)

1925   Delteil, Loys. *Le Peintre-Graveur Illustré: Leys, Braekeleer, Ensor. Vol. 19. Paris: Chez l'auteur, 1925.*

1969   Delteil, Loys. *Le Peintre-Graveur Illustré: Leys, Braekeleer, Ensor.* Vol. 19. 1925. Reprint. New York: Da Capo Press, 1969.

LHERMITE, LÉON AUGUSTIN (1844–1925)

1889   Béraldi, Henri. *Les graveurs du XIXe Siècle.* Vol. 9. Paris: L. Conquet, 1889.

1905   Henriet, Frédéric. *Léon Lhermite.* Paris, 1905.

136　　　　　**LICHTENSTEIN, ROY (1923–　　)**

1969　Waldman, D. *Roy Lichtenstein: Drawings and Prints.* New York: Chelsea House, 1969.

1970　Bianchini, Paul. *Roy Lichtenstein: Drawings and Prints.* New York: Chelsea House, 1970.

1970　Chafetz, Sidney. "Four Early Lichtenstein Prints." *Artist's Proof* 10 (1970): 48–52.

1970　Library of Congress: *American Prints in the Library of Congress: A Catalog of the Collection.* Compiled by Karen F. Beall. p. 267. Baltimore: The Library of Congress, The Johns Hopkins Press, 1970.

1971　Victoria and Albert Museum. *Homage to Senefelder.* Introduction by Felix H. Man. London, 1971.

1972　Heckscher Museum. *Artists of Suffolk County: Part 6, Contemporary Prints.* Huntington, N.Y., 1972.

LIEBERMANN, MAX (1847–1935)

1902　Schiefler, G. *Das Graphische Werk von Max Liebermann.* Vol. 1. Berlin, 1902.

1914　Schiefler, G. *Das Graphische Werk von Max Liebermann.* Vol. 2. Berlin, 1914.

1922　Friedländer, M. J. *Max Liebermann's Graphische Kunst.* Dresden: Arnold, 1922.

1923　Schiefler, G. *Das Graphische Werk von Max Liebermann.* 2nd ed. Berlin, 1923.

1971　Victoria and Albert Museum. *Homage to Senefelder.* Introduction by Felix H. Man. London, 1971.

LILIEN, EPHRAIM MOSES (1874–1925)

1922　*List of the Original Etchings of Ephraim Moses Lilien.* Berlin: B. Harz, 1922.

LIMBACH, RUSSEL T. (1904–　　)

1949　Reese, Albert. *American Prize Prints of the 20th Century.* p. 125. New York: American Artists Group, 1949.

1970   Library of Congress. *American Prints in the Library of Congress: A*
        Catalog of the Collection. Compiled by Karen F. Beall. p. 268.
        Baltimore: The Library of Congress, The Johns Hopkins Press,
        1970.

LINDNER, RICHARD (1901–   )

1970   Ashton, Dore. *Richard Lindner.* New York: Harry N. Abrams,
        1970.

LINDQUIST, EVAN (1936–   )

1973   Missouri State Council on the Arts. *Engravings by Evan Lindquist.*
        St. Louis, Mo., 1973.

LINDSAY, SIR LIONEL (1874–1961)

1916–17 "Lionel Lindsay." *Art in Australia* (1916–17): 50.

1928   MacDonald, James S. and Wright, H. J. M., "Art of Lionel
        Lindsay." *Art in Australia* (1928).

1934   MacDonald, James S. "The Woodcuts of Lionel Lindsay." *Print
        Collector's Quarterly* 21 (1934): 165.

1949   *Etchings and Drypoints: Lionel Lindsay.* Sydney: Ure Smith, 1949.

LINDSAY, NORMAN ALFRED W. (1879–   )

1927   *The Etchings of Norman Lindsay.* London, 1927.

LINNELL, JOHN (1792–1882)

1872   Stephens, F. G. "John Linnell." *Portfolio* 3 (1872): 45.

LIPINSKY, LINO S. (1908–   )

1949   Reese, Albert. *American Prize Prints of the 20th Century.* p. 126.
        New York: American Artists Group, 1949.

LIPMAN-WULF, PETER (1905–   )

1970   Library of Congress. *American Prints in the Library of Congress: A*
        Catalog of the Collection. Compiled by Karen F. Beall. p. 268.
        Baltimore: The Library of Congress, The Johns Hopkins Press,
        1970.

1972   Heckscher Museum. *Artists of Suffolk County: Part 6, Contemporary*
        Prints. Huntington, N.Y., 1972.

LISSITSKY, (EL) ELIEZER MARKOVITCH (1890–1941)

1958   Richter, Horst. *El Lissitsky: Verzeichnis der lithographien*. Cologne: Verlag galerie Christophe Czwiklitzer, 1958.

1967   Lissitsky-Küppers, Sophie. *El Lissitsky: Maler, Architekt, Typograf, Fotograf*. Dresden, 1967.

1968   Lissitsky-Küppers, Sophie. *El Lissitsky: Life, Letters*. Translated by H. Aldwinkle and M. Whittail. Greenwich, Conn.: New York Graphic Society, 1968.

LIVINGSTONE, BIGANESS (MRS. MELVIN LIVINGSTONE) (1926–   )

1952   DeCordova Museum. *Biganess Livingstone: Prints*. Lincoln, Mass., 1952.

LOCKE, CHARLES WHEELER (1899–   )

1949   Reese, Albert. *American Prize Prints of the 20th Century*. p. 127. New York: American Artists Group, 1949.

1970   Library of Congress. *American Prints in the Library of Congress: A Catalog of the Collection*. Compiled by Karen F. Beall. p. 269. Baltimore: The Library of Congress, The Johns Hopkins Press, 1970.

LOGGIE, HELEN A. (1935-   )

1949   Reese, Albert. *American Prize Prints of the 20th Century*. p. 128. New York: American Artists Group, 1949.

LONGO, VINCENT JOHN (1923–   )

1970   Baro, Gene. *Vincent Longo: A Print Retrospective, 1954–1970*. Washington, D.C.: Corcoran Gallery of Art, 1970.

1970   Library of Congress. *American Prints in the Library of Congress: A Catalog of the Collection*. Compiled by Karen F. Beall. p. 270. Baltimore: The Library of Congress, The Johns Hopkins Press, 1970.

LORJOU, BERNARD (1908–   )

1965   Galerie A. Gattlen. *Bernard Lorjou: Catalogue d'exposition*. Lausanne, 1965.

LOUND, THOMAS (1802–1861)

1974   *Thomas Lound: Etchings*. London: Christopher Drake, Ltd., 1974.

1971   Roswell Museum. *Bruce Stark Lowney: Lithographer*. Roswell, New
       Mexico, 1971.

LOZOWICK, LOUIS (1893–1973)

1949   Reese, Albert. *American Prize Prints of the 20th Century*. p. 129.
       New York: American Artists Group, 1949.

1969   Newark Public Library. *Louis Lozowick Graphic Retrospective*.
       Newark, N.J., 1969.

1970   Library of Congress. *American Prints in the Library of Congress: A
       Catalog of the Collection*. Compiled by Karen F. Beall. p. 271.
       Baltimore: The Library of Congress, The Johns Hopkins Press,
       1970.

1971   Robert Hull Fleming Museum. *Paintings, Drawings and Lithographs
       of Louis Lozowick*. Burlington, Vt.: University of Vermont, 1971.

1973   Singer, E. F. "The Lithography of Louis Lozowick." *American
       Artist* (1973): 37–41.

1973   Whitney Museum of American Art. *Louis Lozowick: Lithographs*.
       Introduction by Elke M. Solomon. New York, 1973.

LUCE, MAXIMILIEN (1858–1941)

1970   Stein, Donna and Karshan, Donald. *L'Estampe Originale: A
       Catalogue Raisonné*. New York: The Museum of Graphic Art,
       1970.

LUCIONI, LUIGI (1900–   )

1949   Reese, Albert. *American Prize Prints of the 20th Century*. p. 130.
       New York: American Artists Group, 1949.

1970   Library of Congress. *American Prints in the Library of Congress: A
       Catalog of the Collection*. Compiled by Karen F. Beall. p. 271.
       Baltimore: The Library of Congress, The Johns Hopkins Press,
       1970.

LUM, BERTHA BOYNTON (1934–   )

1970   Library of Congress. *American Prints in the Library of Congress: A
       Catalog of the Collection*. Compiled by Karen F. Beall. pp. 271–273.
       Baltimore: The Library of Congress, The Johns Hopkins Press,
       1970.

LUMSDEN, ERNEST S., R. E. (1883–   )

1921   Salaman, M. C. "The Etchings of E. S. Lumsden, R. E." *Print Collector's Quarterly* 8 (1921): 91–119.

1924   Allhusen, E. L. "Some Etched Portraits by E. S. Lumsden, R. E." *Print Connoisseur* 4 (1924): 3.

1924   "List of Portrait Etchings by E. S. Lumsden, R. E." *Print Connoisseur* 4 (1924): 19.

1925   Salaman, M. C. "Masterly Etchings by E. S. Lumsden." *Apollo* 2 (1925): 296.

1928   Salaman, M. C. *E. S. Lumsden.* Modern Masters of Etching Series, no. 17. London: The Studio, Ltd., 1928.

1936   Copley, John. "The Later Etchings of E. S. Lumsden." *Print Collector's Quarterly* 23 (1936): 211–238.

LUNOIS, ALEXANDRE (1863–1916)

1914   André, Edouard. *Alexandre Lunois: peintre, graveur, et lithographe.* Paris: H. Floury, 1914.

1944   Johnson, Una E. *Ambroise Vollard, Éditeur.* New York: Wittenborn and Co., 1944.

1967   Kovler Gallery. *Forgotten Printmakers of the 19th Century.* Chicago, 1967.

1970   Stein, Donna and Karshan, Donald. *L'Estampe Originale: A Catalogue Raisonné.* New York: The Museum of Graphic Art, 1970.

1971   Victoria and Albert Museum. *Homage to Senefelder.* Introduction by Felix H. Man. London, 1971.

McARDELL, JAMES (1729–1765)

1903   Goodwin, Gordon. *James McArdell.* British Mezzotinters Series. London: A. H. Bullen, 1903.

McBEY, JAMES (1883–1959)

1924   Salaman, Malcolm. *James McBey.* Modern Masters of Etching Series, no. 2. London: The Studio, Ltd., 1924.

1925   Hardie, Martin. *James McBey: Catalogue Raisonné 1902–1924.* London, 1925.

1929   Salaman, Malcolm C. *The Etchings of James McBey*. London and   **141**
New York, 1929.

1935   Seachrest, Effie. "James McBey: Master of Light and Space."
Prints 5 (1935): 28–35.

1938   Hardie, Martin. "The Etched Work of James McBey: 1925–1937."
Print Collector's Quarterly 25 (1938): 421–445.

MacCOY, GUY (1904–   )

1949   Reese, Albert. *American Prize Prints of the 20th Century*. p. 131.
New York: American Artists Group, 1949.

1970   Library of Congress. *American Prints in the Library of Congress: A
Catalog of the Collection*. Compiled by Karen F. Beall. p. 174.
Baltimore: The Library of Congress, The Johns Hopkins Press,
1970.

McCRADY, JOHN (1911–   )

1949   Reese, Albert. *American Prize Prints of the 20th Century*. p. 139.
New York: American Artists Group, 1949.

MacDONALD, ARTHUR NELSON (1865–1940)

1922   French, Thomas Ewing. "MacDonald: Master Graver." *Print
Connoisseur* 2 (1922): 321.

MACDONALD, CATHERINE (1936–   )

1972   Heckscher Museum. *Artists of Suffolk County: Part 6, Contemporary
Prints*. Huntington, N.Y., 1972.

MACDONALD-WRIGHT, STANTON (1890–1973)

1967   National Collection of Fine Arts. *Stanton Macdonald-Wright*.
Washington, D.C.: The Smithsonian Press, 1967.

1970   The Grunwald Graphic Arts Foundation. *Stanton Macdonald-
Wright: A Retrospective Exhibition 1911–1970*. Los Angeles: The
U.C.L.A. Art Galleries, 1970.

MACKE, AUGUST (1887–1914)

1953   Vriesan, Gustav. *August Macke*. Stuttgart: W. Kohlhammer, 1953.

1965   Wingler, H. M. *Graphic Work from the Bauhaus*. Greenwich,
Conn.: New York Graphic Society, 1965.

142   1972   Sotriffer, Kristian. *Expressionism and Fauvism.* New York: McGraw-Hill Book Co., 1972.

MACKENZIE, J. HAMILTON (–1926)

1920   Taylor, E. A. "J. Hamilton Mackenzie: Painter and Etcher." *Studio* 78 (1920): 148.

McLACHLAN, THOMAS HOPE (1845–1897)

1903   "Thomas Hope McLachlan." *Magazine of Art* 1 (1903): 117.

1904   Dodgson, Campbell. "Die Radierungen von T. H. McLachlan." *Graphischen Kunst* 27 (1904): 18.

MAC LAUGHLAN, DONALD SHAW (1876–1938)

1916   Palmer, Cleveland. "The Recent Etchings of Donald Shaw MacLaughlan." *Print Collector's Quarterly* 6 (1916): 111–126.

1924   Bruette, Marie. *A Descriptive Catalogue of the Etched Work of Donald Shaw McLaughlan.* Chicago: A. Rouillier Art Galleries, 1924.

1926   Laver, James. "Etchings of Donald Shaw MacLaughlan." *Print Collector's Quarterly* 13 (1926): 323–344.

1934   Jaffe, Nell L. "A Notable Gift of Prints." *Prints* 4 (1934): 26–37.

1970   Library of Congress. *American Prints in the Library of Congress: A Catalog of the Collection.* Compiled by Karen F. Beall. pp. 276–285. Baltimore: The Library of Congress, The Johns Hopkins Press, 1970.

McNAB, ALLAN (1901–   )

1926   "Three Etchings by Allan McNab." *Studio* 112 (1926): 320.

MACRET, CHARLES-FRANÇOIS-ADRIEN (1751–1783)

1914   Delignières, Émile. *Les Macrets: Graveurs Abbévillois: Catalogue Raisonné de leur Gravé.* Abbéville, 1914.

MACRET, JEAN-CÉSAR (1768–   )

1914   Delignières, Émile. *Les Macrets: Graveurs Abbévillois: Catalogue Raisonné de leur Gravé.* Abbéville, 1914.

Mc VEIGH, BLANCHE (1895–   )

1949   Reese, Albert. *American Prize Prints of the 20th Century.* p. 140. New York: American Artists Group, 1949.

1970   Library of Congress. *American Prints in the Library of Congress: A* **143**
        Catalog of the Collection. Compiled by Karen F. Beall. p. 289.
        Baltimore: The Library of Congress, The Johns Hopkins Press,
        1970.

Mc VICKER, JAY J. (1911–   )

1949   Reese, Albert. *American Prize Prints of the 20th Century.* p. 141.
        New York: American Artists Group, 1949.

1970   Library of Congress. *American Prints in the Library of Congress: A*
        Catalog of the Collection. Compiled by Karen F. Beall. p. 286.
        Baltimore: The Library of Congress, The Johns Hopkins Press,
        1970.

MAGRITTE, RENÉ (1898–1967)

1970   Gimpel and Weitzenhoffer Ltd. *Original Prints of the Surrealists.*
        New York, 1970.

1972   William Weston Gallery. *Catalogue of an Exhibition.* London, July
        1972.

MAILLOL, ARISTIDE JOSEPH BONAVENTURE (1861–1944)

1925   Lafargue, M. *Maillol Sculpture et Lithographe.* Paris, 1925.

1944   Johnson, Una E. *Ambroise Vollard, Éditeur.* New York: Witten-
        born and Co., 1944.

1945   Rewald, J. "Maillol Illustrateur." *Portique* [Paris] 1 (1945).

1951   Rewald, John, ed. *The Woodcuts of Aristide Maillol.* New York:
        Pantheon Books Inc., 1951.

1965   Guérin, M. *Catalogue Raisonné de l'oeuvre gravé et lithographié*
        d'Aristide Maillol. Geneva: Cailler, 1965.

MAIRS, CLARA GARDNER (1879–   )

1949   Reese, Albert. *American Prize Prints of the 20th Century.* p. 132.
        New York: American Artists Group, 1949.

1970   Library of Congress. *American Prints in the Library of Congress: A*
        Catalog of the Collection. Compiled by Karen F. Beall. p. 287.
        Baltimore: The Library of Congress, The Johns Hopkins Press,
        1970.

MALARDOT, ANDRÉ CHARLES (1817–1879)

1935   Godefroy, Louis. "André Charles Malardot: An Unknown Rival of
        Rodolphe Bresdin." *Print Collector's Quarterly* 22 (1935): 79–84.

144   **MALEVICH, KASIMIR (1878–1935)**

1970   Andersen, T. *Malevich: Catalogue Raisonné of the Berlin Exhibition of 1927.* Amsterdam, 1970.

MANESSIER, ALFRED (1911–)

1955   Cayrol, J. *Manessier.* Paris: Musée de poche, 1955.

1955   Dorival, B. "A. Manessier: Artisan réligieux." *L'Oeil* [Paris] 10: (1955).

1966   Cayrol, J. *Manessier.* Paris: Musée de poche, 1966.

MANET, ÉDOUARD (1832–1883)

1906   Moreau-Nelaton, E. *Manet: graveur et lithographe.* Paris, 1906.

1921   Zigrosser, Carl. "Manet's Etchings and Lithographs." *Print Connoisseur* 1 (1921): 381.

1925   Rosenthal, L. *Manet: Aquafortiste et Lithographe.* Paris, 1925.

1936   Roger-Marx, Claude. "Manet: Etcher, Lithographer and Illustrator." *Print Collector's Quarterly* 23 (1936): 303–322.

1944   Guérin, M. *L'Oeuvre Gravé de Manet.* Paris, 1944.

1967   Hanson, A. C. *Édouard Manet: 1832–1883.* Philadelphia: Philadelphia Museum of Art, 1966 and Chicago: Art Institute of Chicago, 1967.

1969   Guérin, Marcel. *L'Oeuvre Gravé de Manet.* 1944. Reprint. New York: Da Capo Press, 1969.

1969   Isaacson, Joel. *Manet and Spain.* Ann Arbor, Mich.: University of Michigan Museum of Art, 1969.

1970   Harris, Jean. *Édouard Manet: Graphic Works: A Definitive Catalogue Raisonné.* New York: Collector's Editions, 1970.

1972   Leymarie, Jean and Melot, Michel. *The Graphic Works of the Impressionists: The Complete Prints of Manet, Pissarro, Renoir, Cézanne, and Sisley.* New York: Abrams, 1972.

MANGRAVITE, PEPPINO (1896–)

1949   Reese, Albert. *American Prize Prints of the 20th Century.* p. 133. New York: American Artists Group, 1949.

1972   Heckscher Museum. *Artists of Suffolk County: Part 6, Contemporary Prints.* Huntington, N. Y., 1972.

MANNING, W. WESTLEY (1868–)

1929   *The Aquatints of W. Westley Manning.* London: P. & D. Colnaghi & Co., 1929.

MANZÙ, GIACOMO (1908–)

1967   Rewald, John. *Giacomo Manzù.* Greenwich, Conn.: New York Graphic Society, 1967.

1968   Ciranna, Alfonso. *Giacomo Manzù: Catalogo delle Opere Grafiche (Incisioni e Litografie) 1929–1968.* Milan, 1968.

MARC, FRANZ (1880–1916)

1916   Walden, Herwath. *Franz Marc: Gemälde und Aquarelle/ Holzschnitte.* Berlin: Der Sturm, 1916.

1936   Schardt, A. J. *Franz Marc.* Berlin: Rembrandt, 1936.

1950   Lankheit, Klaus. *Franz Marc.* Berlin, 1950.

1965   Wingler, H. M. *Graphic Work from the Bauhaus.* Greenwich, Conn.: New York Graphic Society, 1965.

1967   *Franz Marc: das Graphische Werk: Exhibition Catalogue.* Berne, 1967.

1970   Lankheit, Klaus. *Franz Marc: Katalog der Werke.* Cologne: Dumont Schauberg, 1970.

1972   Sotriffer, Kristian. *Expressionism and Fauvism.* New York: McGraw-Hill Book Co., 1972.

MARCENAY DE GHUY, ANTOINE DE (1728–1811)

1764   *Idée de la gravure: Lettre sur l'encyclopédie au mot graveur, et catalogue raisonné des planches de l'oeuvre de M. de Marcenay de Ghuy.* Paris, 1764.

1901   Morand, L. *Antoine de Marcenay de Ghuy: peintre et graveur: catalogue de son oeuvre.* Paris, 1901.

MARCKS, GERHARD (1889–)

1965   Wingler, H. M. *Graphic Work from the Bauhaus.* Greenwich, Conn.: New York Graphic Society, 1965.

146 1966 Man, Felix H., ed. *Europäische Graphik*. Vol. 4. Munich: Galerie Wolfgang Ketterer, 1966.

1969 University of California Art Galleries. *Gerhard Marcks: Catalogue of a Retrospective Exhibition*. Los Angeles, 1969.

Hoffman, R. *Catalogue of Marcks' Prints*. Hamburg. Work in progress.

MARCOLA, GIOVANNI BATTISTA (1711–1780)

1940 Middeldorf, Ulrich. "A Drawing by Giovanni Battista Marcola." *Print Collector's Quarterly* 27 (1940): 89–97.

MARCOUSSIS, LOUIS (1883–1941)

1961 Lanfranchis, J. *Marcoussis: sa vie, son oeuvre*. Paris, 1961.

1965 Wingler, H. M. *Graphic Work from the Bauhaus*. Greenwich, Conn.: New York Graphic Society, 1965.

1974 Scott Elliot Gallery. *Louis Marcoussis: Checklist*. January, 1974.

MARCUS, PETER (1889–1934)

1924–25 "Etchings by Peter Marcus." *International Studio*. 80 (1924–25): 324.

MARGO, BORIS (1902–   )

1949 Reese, Albert. *American Prize Prints of the 20th Century*. p. 134. New York: American Artists Group, 1949.

1968 Schmeckebier, L. and Gelb, J. *Boris Margo: Graphic Work 1932–1968*. Syracuse, N.Y.: Syracuse University School of Art, 1968.

1970 Library of Congress. *American Prints in the Library of Congress: A Catalog of the Collection*. Compiled by Karen F. Beall. p. 287. Baltimore: The Library of Congress, The Johns Hopkins Press, 1970.

1973 Jane Haslem Gallery. *The Innovators: Renaissance in American Printmaking*. Washington, D.C., 1973.

MARGULIES, JOSEPH (1896–   )

1935 Morrow, B. F. "Highlights of Copper: Joseph Margulies." *Prints* 5 (1935): 30–35.

1948   Mauroner, Fabio. "Michiel Marieschi." *Print Collector's Quarterly* 27 (1948): 179–215.

MARIN, JOHN (1872–1953)

1908   Saunier, C. "John Marin: Peintre-Graveur." *L'Art Decoratif* 18 (1908): 17.

1924–25 Cary, E. L. "Modern American Prints." *International Studio* 80 (1924–25): 214.

1935   Benson, Emanuel Mervin. *John Marin: the Man and his Work.* Washington, D.C.: The American Federation of Arts, 1935.

1936   Museum of Modern Art. *John Marin: Watercolors, Oil Paintings, Etchings.* New York, 1936.

1942   Zigrosser, Carl. *The Artist in America: 24 Close-ups of Contemporary Printmakers.* New York: Alfred A. Knopf, 1942.

1969   Gray, Cleve. "John Marin: The Etched Line." *Artist's Proof* 9 (1969): 78–89.

1969   Zigrosser, Carl. *The Complete Etchings of John Marin: Catalogue Raisonné.* Philadelphia: Philadelphia Museum of Art, 1969.

1970   Library of Congress. *American Prints in the Library of Congress: A Catalog of the Collection.* Compiled by Karen F. Beall. p. 289–290. Baltimore: The Library of Congress, The Johns Hopkins Press, 1970.

1970   Zigrosser, Carl. "Errata in the Catalogue of the Etchings of John Marin." *Print Collector's Newsletter* 1 (1970): 82–83.

1972   Sotriffer, Kristian. *Expressionism and Fauvism.* New York: McGraw-Hill Book Co., 1972.

MARINI, MARINO (1901-   )

1960   Hoffman, W. *Malerei und Graphik.* Stuttgart: Hatje, 1960.

1960   *Marino Marini: Graphic Work and Paintings.* Introduction by P. M. Bardi. New York: Abrams, 1960.

1965   Philadelphia Museum of Art. *Marino Marini: Graphics and Related Works.* Philadelphia, 1965.

148   1967   Carandente, Giovanni. *Marino Marini: Lithographs 1942–1965.*
New York: Harry N. Abrams, 1967.

1969   Man, Felix H., ed. *Europäische Graphik.* Vol. 6. Munich: Galerie
Wolfgang Ketterer, 1969.

1970   San Lazzaro, Gualtieri Di. *Marino Marini: Complete Works.* New
York: Tudor, 1970.

MARKOW, JACK (1905–   )

1949   Reese, Albert. *American Prize Prints of the 20th Century.* p. 135.
New York: American Artists Group, 1949.

1970   Library of Congress. *American Prints in the Library of Congress: A
Catalog of the Collection.* Compiled by Karen F. Beall. p. 292.
Baltimore: The Library of Congress, The Johns Hopkins Press,
1970.

MARQUET, ALBERT (1875–1947)

1922   Fosca, F. *Marquet.* Paris, 1922.

1933   Jourdain, F. *Marquet.* Paris, 1933.

1967   Besson, G. *Introduction à l'Exposition Marquet.* Paris: Galerie
Schmit, 1967.

MARSH, REGINALD (1898–1954)

1956   Sasowsky, Norman. *Reginald Marsh: Etchings, Engravings, Lithographs.* New York: Prager, 1956.

1970   Library of Congress. *American Prints in the Library of Congress: A
Catalog of the Collection.* Compiled by Karen F. Beall. p. 292–296.
Baltimore: The Library of Congress, The John Hopkins Press,
1970.

MARTELLY, JOHN S. DE *see* DE MARTELLY, JOHN S.

MARTIN, CAMILLE (1861–1898)

1970   Stein, Donna and Karshan, Donald. *L'Estampe Originale: A
Catalogue Raisonné.* New York: The Museum of Graphic Art,
1970.

MARTIN, HENRI (1860–1936)

1944   Johnson, Una E. *Ambroise Vollard, Èditeur.* New York: Wittenborn and Co., 1944.

1942 Wickenden, Robert J. "Louis Marvy." *Print Collector's Quarterly* 29 (1942): 209–235.

SISTER MARY CORITA *see* KENT, CORITA

MASEREEL, FRANS-LAURET (1889–1971)

1949 Ziller, G. *Frans Masereel: With a Chronological Catalogue of his Works.* Dresden, 1949.

1954 Schneider, Walter Otto. *Frans Masereel: his Work.* 1954. Unpublished manuscript at the Print Room of the New York Public Library.

1972 Sotriffer, Kristian. *Expressionism and Fauvism.* New York: McGraw-Hill Book Co., 1972.

MASON, ALICE TRUMBULL (1904–1971)

1949 Reese, Albert. *American Prize Prints of the 20th Century.* p. 137. New York: American Artists Group, 1949.

1970 Library of Congress. *American Prints in the Library of Congress: A Catalog of the Collection.* Compiled by Karen F. Beall. p. 297. Baltimore: The Library of Congress, The Johns Hopkins Press, 1970.

MASSON, ANDRÉ (1896–   )

1947 Leiris, M. and Limbour, G. *André Masson et Son Univers.* Geneva and Paris, 1947.

1954 *Catalogue de l'Exposition: Masson.* Brème, 1954.

1970 Gimpel and Weitzenhoffer Ltd. *Original Prints of the Surrealists.* New York, 1970.

1973 Passeron, Roger. *André Masson: The Engravings 1924–1972.* Fribourg, Switzerland: Office du Livre, s.a., 1973.

MATARÉ, EWALD (1887–1965)

1957–58 Peters, Heinz. *Ewald Mataré: das graphische Werk.* Cologne: C. Czwiklitzer, 1957–58.

MATHEY, PAUL (1844–1929)

1923 Clément-Janin. "Paul Mathey: Painter, Etcher." *Print Connoisseur* 3 (1923): 23.

150 1923   "List of Etchings of Paul Mathey." *Print Connoisseur* 3 (1923): 35.

MATISSE, HENRI (1869–1954)

1933   Roger-Marx, Claude. "The Engraved Work of Henri Matisse." *Print Collector's Quarterly* 20 (1933): 139–157.

1933   Roger-Marx, Claude. *Matisse*. Paris, 1933.

1935   Parker, John. "The Prints of Matisse." *Prints* 6 (1935): 90–93.

1954   Catalogue Berggrüen. *Henri Matisse: Lithographies rares*. Introduction by Marguerite Duthuit. Paris, 1954.

1955   Liebermann, William S. *Etchings by Matisse*. New York: Museum of Modern Art, 1955. 2nd printing 1965.

1956   Liebermann, William S. *Matisse: Fifty Years of his Graphic Work*. New York: George Braziller, 1956.

1961   Klipstein and Kornfeld. *Catalogue de l'exposition Matisse*. Berne, 1961.

1965   Liebermann, William S. *Etchings by Matisse*. 1955. 2nd printing. New York: Museum of Modern Art, 1965.

1970   Guichard-Meili, J. and Woimant, F. *Matisse: l'oeuvre gravé*. Paris: Bibliothèque Nationale, 1970.

1970   Hahnloser-Ingold, Morgrit. *Henri Matisse: Gravures et Lithographies de 1900 à 1929*. Introduction by Hans R. Hahnloser. Pully, Switzerland, and Berne: Kornfeld and Klipstein, 1970.

1971   Goldman, Judith. "Fake Matisse Lithographs on the Market." *Print Collector's Newsletter* 2 (1971): 11.

1972   International Gallery. *Master of Graphic Art: Henri Matisse-Woodcuts and Lithographs, 1904–1929*. Chicago, 1972.

1972   Lambert, Susan. *Matisse Lithographs*. London: Victoria and Albert Museum, 1972.

1972   Reiss-Cohen Gallery. *Henri Matisse: The Graphic Works*. New York, 1972.

1974   Lumley Cazalet, Ltd. *Matisse: Fifty-two Lithographs, Woodcuts, and Aquatints*. London, 1974.

Schniewind, Carl O. Catalogue of Matisse's graphic works established by his family. Museum of Modern Art, unpublished manuscript.

1970   Stein, Donna and Karshan, Donald. *L'Estampe Originale: A Catalogue Raisonné.* New York: The Museum of Graphic Art, 1970.

MAURIN, CHARLES (1856–1914)

1944   Johnson, Una E. *Ambroise Vollard, Éditeur.* New York: Wittenborn and Co., 1944.

1970   Stein, Donna and Karshan, Donald. *L'Estampe Originale: A Catalogue Raisonné.* New York: The Museum of Graphic Art, 1970.

MAUZEY, MERRITT (1898–   )

1942   Zigrosser, Carl. *The Artist in America: 24 Close-ups of Contemporary Printmakers.* New York: Alfred Knopf, 1942.

1949   Reese, Albert. *American Prize Prints of the 20th Century.* p. 138. New York: American Artists Group, 1949.

1970   Library of Congress. *American Prints in the Library of Congress: A Catalog of the Collection.* Compiled by Karen F. Beall. p. 297. Baltimore: The Library of Congress, The Johns Hopkins Press, 1970.

MAZUR, MICHAEL (1935–   )

1970   Mazur, Michael. "Michael Mazur." *Artist's Proof* 10 (1970): 19–29.

MEAD, RODERICK (1900–1971)

1949   Reese, Albert. *American Prize Prints of the 20th Century.* p. 142. New York: American Artists Group, 1949.

1970   Library of Congress. *American Prints in the Library of Congress: A Catalog of the Collection.* Compiled by Karen F. Beall. p. 299. Baltimore: The Library of Congress, The John Hopkins Press, 1970.

1972   Museum of the Southwest. *Roderick Mead 1900–1972: A Retrospective Exhibition.* Midland, Tex., 1972.

MECKSEPER, FRIEDRICH (1936–   )

1973   Galérie Gérald Cramer. *Meckseper: Gravures Originales en noir et en couleur 1956–1973.* Geneva, 1973.

MEEKER, DEAN (1920–   )

1967   De Cordova Museum. *Dean Meeker: Prints*. Lincoln, Mass., 1967.

1970   Library of Congress. *American Prints in the Library of Congress: A Catalog of the Collection*. Compiled by Karen F. Beall. p. 299. Baltimore: The Library of Congress, The Johns Hopkins Press, 1970.

MEIDNER, LUDWIG (1884–1966)

1966   Man, Felix H., ed. *Europäische Graphik*. Vol. 4. Munich: Galerie Wolfgang Ketterer, 1966.

1970   *Ludwig Meidner: Catalogue of an Exhibition*. Frankfort and Darmstadt Kunstverein, 1970.

1971   Victoria and Albert Museum. *Homage to Senefelder*. Introduction by Felix H. Man. London, 1971.

1972   Sotriffer, Kristian. *Expressionism and Fauvism*. New York: McGraw-Hill Book Co., 1972.

1973   University of Southern California Art Galleries. *Ludwig Meidner: Prints, Drawings, Watercolors*. Ernest and Lilly Jacobson Collection. Los Angeles, Cal., 1973.

MEISSNER, LEO JOHN (1895–   )

1949   Reese, Albert. *American Prize Prints of the 20th Century*. p. 143. New York: American Artists Group, 1949.

1970   Library of Congress. *American Prints in the Library of Congress: A Catalog of the Collection*. Compiled by Karen F. Beall. p. 300. Baltimore: The Library of Congress, The Johns Hopkins Press, 1970.

MEISSONIER, JEAN LOUIS ERNEST (1815–1891)

1890   Béraldi, Henri. *Les Graveurs du XIXᵉ Siècle*. Vol. 10. Paris: L. Conquet, 1890.

1967   Kovler Gallery. *Forgotten Printmakers of the 19th Century*. Chicago, 1967.

MENSE, CARL (1886–1965)

1965   Wingler, H. M. *Graphic Work from the Bauhaus*. Greenwich, Conn.: New York Graphic Society, 1965.

1894 Museum of Fine Arts. *Exhibition of the Work of Adolf Menzel.* Boston, 1894.

1896 Dorgerloh, A. *Verzeichnis der Durch Kunstdruck vervielfältigten arbeiten Adolf von Menzel.* Leipzig, 1896.

1916 Cary, Elisabeth Luther. "Adolf von Menzel." *Print Collector's Quarterly* 6 (1916): 299–320.

1920 Kurth, W. *Adolf Menzel's Graphische Kunst.* Dresden, 1920.

1923 Bock, Elfried. *Adolf von Menzel: Verzeichnis seines graphischen Werkes.* Berlin, 1923.

1971 Victoria and Albert Museum. *Homage to Senefelder.* Introduction by Felix H. Man. London, 1971.

MERRITT, ANNA LEA (1844–1930)

1880 Koehler, S. R. *American Art Review.* 1 (1880): 229.

MERYON, CHARLES (1821–1868)

1907 Delteil, Loys. *Le Peintre-graveur Illustré: Meryon.* Vol. 2. Paris: Chez l'auteur, 1907.

1911 Bradley, William Aspenwall. "Meryon and Baudelaire." *Print Collector's Quarterly* 1 (1911):587–609.

1913 Bradley, William Aspenwall. "Charles Meryon-Poet." *Print Collector's Quarterly* 3 (1913): 337–364.

1917 Bradley, William Aspenwall. "Some Meryon Drawings in the MacGeorge Collection." *Print Collector's Quarterly* 7 (1917): 223–255.

1921 Dodgson, Campbell. *The Etchings of Charles Meryon.* London: The Studio, Ltd., 1921.

1921 Wright, Harold J. L. "Undescribed States of Meryon etchings." *Print Collector's Quarterly* 8 (1921): 171–201.

1924 Wright, Harold J. L., ed. *Catalogue Raisonné of the Etchings of Charles Meryon, by Loys Delteil.* London and New York, 1924.

1927 Salaman, Malcolm. *Charles Meryon.*Modern Masters of Etching Series. Vol. 14. London: The Studio, 1927.

154   1969   Delteil, Loys. *Le Peintre-graveur Illustré: Meryon*. Vol. 2. 1907.
Reprint. New York: Da Capo Press, 1969.

1970   Hitchings, Sinclair H. "Meryon's Voyage and Vision of the
Pacific." *Print Collector's Newsletter* 1 (1970): 102–104.

METOUR, EUGENE PAUL (1879–   )

1923   Brown, Warren Wilmer. "Eugene Paul Metour and his Etchings of
Annapolis." *Print Connoisseur* 3 (1923): 179.

1923   "Catalogue Raisonné of the Etchings of Eugene Paul Metour."
Print Connoisseur 3 (1923): 189.

MEUNIER, CONSTANTIN-EMILE (1831–1905)

1970   Stein, Donna and Karshan, Donald. *L'Estampe Originale: A
Catalogue Raisonné*. New York: The Museum of Graphic Art,
1970.

MEYEROWITZ, WILLIAM (1898–   )

1949   Reese, Albert. *American Prize Prints of the 20th Century*. p. 144.
New York: American Artists Group, 1949.

1970   Library of Congress. *American Prints in the Library of Congress: A
Catalog of the Collection*. Compiled by Karen F. Beall. p. 302.
Baltimore: The Library of Congress, The Johns Hopkins Press,
1970.

MIELATZ, CHARLES F. W. (1864–1919)

1922   Harris, G. W. "Mielatz, American Etcher." *International Studio* 75
(1922): 293.

1937   Weitenkampf, Frank. "An Etcher of New York: C. F. W. Mielatz."
Print Collector's Quarterly 24 (1937): 237.

1970   Library of Congress. *American Prints in the Library of Congress: A
Catalog of the Collection*. Compiled by Karen F. Beall. p. 303.
Baltimore: The Library of Congress, The Johns Hopkins Press,
1970.

MILHAU, ZELLA de (1870–1954)

1923   "Zella de Milhau, Etcher." *American Magazine of Art* 14 (1923):
249.

MILLAIS, JOHN EVERETT, SIR (1829–1896)

1908   Victoria and Albert Museum. *Catalogue of Prints and Wood
Engravings after Sir John E. Millais*. London, 1908.

1881 Koehler, S. R. *American Art Review* 2 (1881): 102.

MILLER, HELEN PENDLETON (MRS. KENNETH HAYES MILLER) (1888–1959)

1949 Reese, Albert. *American Prize Prints of the 20th Century*. p. 145. New York: American Artists Group, 1949.

1970 Library of Congress. *American Prints in the Library of Congress: A Catalog of the Collection*. Compiled by Karen F. Beall. p. 304. Baltimore: The Library of Congress, The Johns Hopkins Press, 1970.

MILLER, KENNETH HAYES (1876–1952)

1930 Goodrich, Lloyd. *Kenneth Hayes Miller*. New York: The Arts, 1930.

1931 Burroughs, Alan. *Kenneth Hayes Miller*. New York: Macmillan, 1931.

1949 Reese, Albert. *American Prize Prints of the 20th Century*. p. 146. New York: American Artists Group, 1949.

1970 Library of Congress. *American Prints in the Library of Congress: A Catalog of the Collection*. Compiled by Karen F. Beall. p. 304. Baltimore: The Library of Congress, The Johns Hopkins Press, 1970.

MILLET, JEAN-FRANÇOIS (1814–1875)

1890 Béraldi, Henri. *Les Graveurs du XIXᵉ Siècle*. Vol. 10. pp. 63–71. Paris: L. Conquet, 1890.

1906 Delteil, Loys. *Le Peintre-graveur Illustré: Millet, Rousseau, Dupré, Jongkind*. Vol. 1. Paris: Chez l'auteur, 1906.

1912 "Bibliography of J.-F. Millet." *Print Collector's Quarterly* 2 (1912): 249.

1912 Wickenden, Robert F. "The Art and Etchings of Jean-François Millet." *Print Collector's Quarterly* 2 (1912): 225–250.

1914 Wickenden, Robert F. "Millet's Drawings at the Museum of Fine Arts, Boston." *Print Collector's Quarterly* 4 (1914): 3–30.

1935 "Millets Presented to the Toledo Museum." *Prints* 5 (1935): 38–43.

1948 Arms, John Taylor. "Peasant With a Wheelbarrow." *Print Collector's Quarterly* 29 (1948): 38–41.

156 1969   Delteil, Loys. *Le Peintre-graveur Illustré: Millet, Rousseau, Dupré, Jongkind.* Vol. 1. 1906. Reprint. New York: Da Capo Press, 1969.

MILLIER, ARTHUR (1893–   )

1970   Library of Congress. *American Prints in the Library of Congress: A Catalog of the Collection.* Compiled by Karen F. Beall. p. 305. Baltimore: The Library of Congress, The Johns Hopkins Press, 1970.

1972   Ross, Kenneth and Opliger, Curt. *Arthur Millier.* Los Angeles, Cal.: Municipal Art Gallery, 1972.

MILTON, PETER (1930–   )

1970   Library of Congress. *American Prints in the Library of Congress: A Catalog of the Collection.* Compiled by Karen F. Beall. p. 306. Baltimore: The Library of Congress, The Johns Hopkins Press, 1970.

1971   De Cordova Museum. *Etchings by Peter Milton.* Lincoln, Mass., 1971.

1971   Finkelstein Irving. "Julia Passing: The World of Peter Milton." *Artist's Proof* 11 (1971): 71–77.

1972   Corcoran Gallery of Art. *Peter Milton: Etchings.* Washington, D.C., 1972.

1973   Jane Haslem Gallery. *The Innovators: Renaissance in American Printmaking.* Washington, D.C., 1973.

M'INTOSH, J. PATRICK (1907–   )

1930   Judge, Max. "The Etchings of J. Patrick M'Intosh." *Print Collector's Quarterly* 17 (1930): 197–206.

MIRÓ, JOAN (1893–   )

1947   Leiris, Michel. *The Prints of Joan Miró.* New York: Tudor Publishing Co., 1947.

1957   Wember, Paul. Joan Miró: das Graphische Werk. Krefeld: Kaiser Wilhelm Museum, 1957.

1958   Hunter, Sam. *Joan Miró: his Graphic Work.* New York: Abrams, 1958.

1958   Hunter, Sam. *Joan Miró: l'Oeuvre gravé.* Paris: Calmann-Lévy, 1958.

1967   McNulty, Kneeland. *Joan Miró: Prints and Books*. Philadelphia: **157**
        Philadelphia Museum of Art, 1967.

1972   Leiris, Michel and Mourlot, Fernand. *Joan Miró Lithographs
        1930–1952*. Vol. 1. New York: Tudor Publishing Co., 1972.

MODERSOHN-BECKER, PAULA (1876–1907)

1968   Werner, Wolfgang. *Paula Modersohn-Becker: Gemälde Zeichnun-
        gen, Oeuvre-verzeichnis der Graphik*. Bremen: Graphisches Kabinett
        und Kunsthandlung Ursula Voigt, 1968.

MOHOLY-NAGY, LASZLO (1895–1946)

1970   Library of Congress. *American Prints in the Library of Congress: A
        Catalog of the Collection*. Compiled by Karen F. Beall. p. 308.
        Baltimore: The Library of Congress, The Johns Hopkins Press,
        1970.

MOLZHAHN, JOHANNES (1892–1965)

1957   Peters, H., ed. *Die Bauhaus Mappen: Neue Europäische Graphik
        1921–1923*. Cologne: C. Czwiklitzer, 1957.

1965   Wingler, H. M. *Graphic Work from the Bauhaus*. Greenwich,
        Conn.: New York Graphic Society, 1965.

MONK, WILLIAM, R. E. (1863–1937)

1915   Monk, William. "An English Artist's Impressions of New York."
        Studio 64 (1915): 247.

1937   Yockney, Alfred. "The Etchings of William Monk, R. E." *Print
        Collector's Qarterly* 24 (1937): 308–317.

MONNIER, HENRI (1805–1877)

1879   Fleury, J. *Henri Monnier: sa vie, son oeuvre: avec un catalogue
        complet de l'oeuvre*. Paris, 1879.

1889   Champfleury. M. *Henri Monnier: Sa vie et son oeuvre*. Paris, 1889.

1930   Reitlinger, Henry. "Lami and Monnier." *Print Collector's Quarterly*
        17 (1930): 73–91.

MONTGOMERIE, W. C. (20th C.)

1921   Brinton, Selwyn. "A Modern Etcher." *Art in America* 9 (1921): 128.

1971   Fels, Catherine. *Graphic Work of Louis Monza.* Los Angeles, Cal.: Plantin Press, 1971.

MOORE, HENRY (1898–   )

1968   Gallery Cramer. *Henry Moore: Oeuvre Gravé et Lithographié 1939–1967.* Geneva, 1968.

1969   Man, Felix H., ed. *Europäische Graphik.* Vol. 6. Munich: Galerie Wolfgang Ketterer, 1969.

1973   Gallery Cramer. *Henry Moore: Catalogue of Graphic Work 1931– 1972.* Geneva, 1973.

1974   Russell, John; Gere, John and Moore, Henry. *Auden Poems/Moore Lithographs.* London: The British Museum, 1974.

MOORE, THOMAS STURGE (1870–1944)

1931   French, Cecil. "The Wood-engravings of T. Sturge Moore." *Print Collector's Quarterly* 18 (1931): 203–219.

MORA, FRANCIS LUIS (1874–1940)

1970   Library of Congress. *American Prints in the Library of Congress: A Catalog of the Collection.* Compiled by Karen F. Beall. p. 309. Baltimore: The Library of Congress, The Johns Hopkins Press, 1970.

MORAN, EDWARD (1829–1901)

1965   Heckscher Museum. *The Moran Family: Exhibition Catalogue.* Huntington, N.Y., 1965.

1970   Library of Congress. *American Prints in the Library of Congress: A Catalog of the Collection.* Compiled by Karen F. Beall. p. 310. Baltimore: The Library of Congress, The Johns Hopkins Press, 1970.

MORAN, EDWARD PERCY (1862–1935)

1965   Heckscher Museum. *The Moran Family: Exhibition Catalogue.* Huntington, N.Y., 1965.

1970   Library of Congress. *American Prints in the Library of Congress: A Catalog of the Collection.* Compiled by Karen F. Beall. p. 310. Baltimore: The Library of Congress, The Johns Hopkins Press, 1970.

MORAN, JOHN LEON (1864–1941)

1965   Heckscher Museum. *The Moran Family: Exhibition Catalogue.* Huntington, N.Y., 1965.

1970   Library of Congress. *American Prints in the Library of Congress. A Catalog of the Collection.* Compiled by Karen F. Beall. p. 310. Baltimore: The Library of Congress, The Johns Hopkins Press, 1970.

MORAN, MARY NIMMO (1842–1899)

1881   Koehler, S. R. *American Art Review* 2 (1881): 183.

1965   Heckscher Museum. *The Moran Family: Exhibition Catalogue.* Huntington, N.Y., 1965.

1970   Library of Congress. *American Prints in the Library of Congress: A Catalog of the Collection.* Compiled by Karen F. Beall. p. 310.

        Baltimore: The Library of Congress, The Johns Hopkins Press, 1970.

MORAN, PETER (1842–1915)

1880   Koehler, S. R. *American Art Review* 1 (1880): 149.

1888   Morton, F. W., *Catalogue of the Etched Work of Peter Moran.* New York, 1888.

1965   Heckscher Museum. *The Moran Family: Exhibition Catalogue.* Huntington, N.Y., 1965.

1970   Library of Congress. *American Prints in the Library of Congress: A Catalog of the Collection.* Compiled by Karen F. Beall. p. 310. Baltimore: The Library of Congress, The Johns Hopkins Press, 1970.

MORAN, THOMAS (1837–1925)

1880   Koehler, S. R. "Thomas Moran." *American Art Review* 1 (1880): 151.

1881   Koehler, S. R. "New Etchings by Thomas Moran." *American Art Review* 2 (1881): 104.

1955   Wilson, J. B. *The Significance of Thomas Moran as an American Landscape Painter.* 2 vols. Publication no. 15, 897. Ann Arbor, Mich.: Ohio State University, University Microfilms, 1955.

1965   Heckscher Museum. *The Moran Family: Exhibition Catalogue.* Huntington, N.Y., 1965.

160   1966   Wilkins, T. *Thomas Moran: Artist of the Mountains*. University of Oklahoma Press, 1966. 2nd printing. 1969.

    1970   Library of Congress. *American Prints in the Library of Congress: A Catalog of the Collection*. Compiled by Karen F. Beall. pp. 311–312. Baltimore: The Library of Congress, The Johns Hopkins Press, 1970.

MORANDI, GIORGIO (1890–1964)

    1957   Vitali, Lamberto. *L'Opera grafica di Giorgio Morandi*. Turin: Einaudi, 1957.

    1964   Vitali, Lamberto. *L'Opera grafica di Giorgio Morandi*. rev. ed. Turin: Einaudi, 1964.

    1973   Valsecchi, M. *Le acqueforti di Giorgio Morandi 1912–1945*. Urbino: Instituto Statale d'Arte, 1973.

MOREAU, JEAN MICHEL (1741–1814)

    1880   Mahérault, M. J. F. *L'Oeuvre de Moreau le jeune: Catalogue raisonné*. Paris, 1880.

    1926   Francis, Eric C. "Jean Michel Moreau." *Print Collector's Quarterly* 13 (1926): 211–236.

MOREAU, LOUIS GABRIEL (1740–1806)

    1956   *Les Eaux-fortes de Louis Moreau*. Paris: Paul Prouté, 1956.

MOREAU, LUC-ALBERT (1882-   )

    1930   Roger-Marx, Claude. "The Lithographs of Luc-Albert Moreau." *Print Collector's Quarterly* 17 (1930): 261–278.

MORENA, ALBERICO (1926–   )

    1963   Fendrick, Daniel. "Alberico Morena." *Artist's Proof* 6 (1963): 50–51.

MORGNER, WILHELM (1891–1917)

    1967   Landesmuseum für Kunst und Kunstgeschichte. *Katalog des Westfälischen Kunstvereins*. Münster, 1967.

    1972   Sotriffer, Kristian. *Expressionism and Fauvism*. New York: McGraw-Hill Book Co., 1972.

MORIN, GUSTAVE (1809–1886)

1877   Hédou, J. *Gustave Morin et son oeuvre*. Rouen: E. Augé, 1877.

MORISOT, BERTHE (1841–1895)

1925   Fourreau, Armand. *Berthe Morisot*. Paris: Rieder, 1925.

1950   Morisot, Berthe. *Correspondance de Berthe Morisot avec sa famille et ses amis: Manet, Puvis de Chavannes, Degas, Monet, Renoir et Mallarmé*. Edited by Denis Rouart. Paris: Quatre Chemins, 1950.

MORLAND, GEORGE (1763–1804)

1893–94 *Exhibition of Upward of 300 Mezzotints and other Engravings after George Morland*. London, 1893–94.

1907   Williamson, George Charles. *George Morland: his Life and Works*. London: Bell, 1907.

1933   Buckley, Francis. "George Morland's Sketch Books and their Publisher." *Print Collector's Quarterly* 20 (1933): 211–220.

MORTENSEN, RICHARD (1910–   )

1966   *Künst-unserer Zeit*. Cologne: Du Mont Schauberg, 1966.

MOSER, CARL (1873–1939)

1930   Holzschneider. *Carl Moser*. Bolzano, 1930.

MOSKOWITZ, IRA (1912–   )

1949   Reese, Albert. *American Prize Prints of the 20th Century*. p. 147. New York: American Artists Group, 1949.

1970   Library of Congress. *American Prints in the Library of Congress: A Catalog of the Collection*. Compiled by Karen F. Beall. p. 314. Baltimore: The Library of Congress, The Johns Hopkins Press, 1970.

MOTHERWELL, ROBERT (1915–   )

1974   Colsman-Freyberger, Heidi. "Robert Motherwell: Words and Images." *Print Collector's Newsletter* 4 (1974): 125–129.

MOY, SEONG (1921–   )

1970   Library of Congress. *American Prints in the Library of Congress: A Catalog of the Collection*. Compiled by Karen F. Beall. p. 314. Baltimore: The Library of Congress, The Johns Hopkins Press, 1970.

MUCHA, ALPHONSE MARIA (1860–1939)

1963   Reade, Brian. *Art Nouveau and Alphonse Mucha*. London: Victoria and Albert Museum, 1963.

1965   Mucha, Jiri. *Alphonse Mucha: Meister des Jugendstils*. Prague: Artia, 1965.

1974   Mucha, Jiri, ed. *The Graphic Work of Alphonse Mucha*. New York: St. Martin's Press, 1974.

MUCHE, GEORG (1895–   )

1965   Wingler, H. M. *Graphic Work from the Bauhaus*. Greenwich, Conn.: New York Graphic Society, 1965.

MUELLER, OTTO *See* MÜLLER, OTTO

MÜLLER, OTTO (1874–1930)

1963   Karsch, Florian and Buchheim, L. G. *Otto Müller: Leben und Werk: With a List of Graphic Work*. Feldafing, 1963.

1972   Sotriffer, Kristian. *Expressionism and Fauvism*. New York: McGraw-Hill Book Co., 1972.

MULLICAN, LEE (1919–   )

1950   Swetzoff, Hyman. "The Drawings of Lee Mullican." *Print Collector's Quarterly* 30 (1950): 19–22.

MUNCH, EDVARD (1863–1944)

1907   Schiefler, Gustave. *Verzeichnis des Graphischen Werks Edvard Munch bis 1906*. Berlin: Cassirer, 1907.

1928   Schiefler, Gustave. *Edvard Munch das Graphische Werk 1906–1926*. Berlin: Euphorion, 1928.

1944   Johnson, Una E. *Ambroise Vollard, Éditeur*. New York: Wittenborn and Co., 1944.

1950   Willoch, Sigurd. *Edvard Munch: Etchings*. Oslo: G. Tanum, 1950.

1963   Greve, Eli. *Edvard Munch liv og verk I Lys Av Tresnittene*. Oslo: J. W. Cappelens Forlag, 1963.

1963   Langaard, J. H. and Revold, R. *Edvard Munch: Meisterwerke aus der Sammlung des Künstlers im Munch-Museum in Oslo*. Stuttgart, 1963.

1964   Sarvig, Ole. *Edvard Munch Grafik*. Copenhagen: Bernhard Middel-   **163**
boe, 1964.

1966   Timm, Werner. *Edvard Munch: Graphik*. Inselbücherei no. 536.
Leipzig, 1966.

1969   Feinblatt, Ebria. *Edvard Munch: Lithographs, Etchings, Woodcuts*.
Los Angeles: Los Angeles County Museum of Art, 1969.

1969   Hougen, P. *Edvard Munch: Oeuvre Graphique*. Paris: Musée des
Arts Décoratifs, 1969.

1969   Timm, Werner. *The Graphic Art of Edvard Munch*. Greenwich,
Conn.: New York Graphic Society, 1969 and London: Studio
Vista, 1969.

1972   Sotriffer, Kristian. *Expressionism and Fauvism*. New York:
McGraw-Hill Book Co., 1972.

MÜNTER, GABRIELE (1877–1962)

1967   Städtische Galerie im Lenbachhaus. *Gabriele Münter: Das Druckgraphische Werk*. Munich, 1967.

MURPHY, ALICE HAROLD (1890–   )

1949   Reese, Albert. *American Prize Prints of the 20th Century*. p. 148.
New York: American Artists Group, 1949.

MURPHY, MRS. C. T. *See* BULLER, CECIL

MURPHY, JOHN J. A. (1888–1967)

1924   Fletcher, John Gould. "The Woodcuts of John J. A. Murphy."
Print Collector's Quarterly 11 (1924): 227–252.

1970   Library of Congress. *American Prints in the Library of Congress: A
Catalog of the Collection*. Compiled by Karen F. Beall. p. 316.
Baltimore: The Library of Congress, The Johns Hopkins Press,
1970.

MURPHY, MINNIE LOIS (1901–   )

1949   Reese, Albert. *American Prize Prints of the 20th Century*. p. 149.
New York: American Artists Group, 1949.

1970   Library of Congress. *American Prints in the Library of Congress: A
Catalog of the Collection*. Compiled by Karen F. Beall. p. 316.
Baltimore: The Library of Congress, The Johns Hopkins Press,
1970.

164	MUSIĆ, ZORAN (ANTONIO) (1909–)

1962	Schmücking, R. *Zoran Musić: Das graphische Werk 1947–62.*
Brunswick, Germany: Schmücking, 1962.

MUYDEN, EVERT VAN (1853–1922)

1894	Curtis, A. *Catalogue of the Etched Work of Evert van Muyden.* New
York: F. Keppel, 1894.

MYERS, ETHEL (MRS. JEROME MYERS) (1881–1960)

1973	Mount Holyoke College Art Museum and the Weyhe Gallery. *14
American Women Printmakers of the 30's and 40's.* South Hadley,
Mass. and New York, 1973.

MYERS, JEROME (1867–1940)

1940	Myers, Jerome. *Artist in Manhattan.* New York: American Artists
Group, 1940.

1949	Reese, Albert. *American Prize Prints of the 20th Century.* p. 231.
New York: American Artists Group, 1949.

1967	Wilmington Society of Fine Arts. *Jerome Myers: An Artist in
Manhattan.* Wilmington, Del., 1967.

1970	Library of Congress. *American Prints in the Library of Congress: A
Catalog of the Collection.* Compiled by Karen F. Beall. p. 317.
Baltimore: The Library of Congress, The Johns Hopkins Press,
1970.

NAGLER, FRED (1891–   )

1949	Reese, Albert. *American Prize Prints of the 20th Century.* p. 151.
New York: American Artists Group, 1949.

1970	Library of Congress. *American Prints in the Library of Congress: A
Catalog of the Collection.* Compiled by Karen F. Beall. p. 318.
Baltimore: The Library of Congress, The Johns Hopkins Press,
1970.

NANEO, KENJILO

1972	Kastner, Fenton. *Kenjilo Nanao.* Santa Barbara, Cal.: The Santa
Barbara Museum of Art, 1972.

NANKIVELL, FRANK ARTHUR (1869–1959)

1970	Library of Congress. *American Prints in the Library of Congress: A
Catalog of the Collection.* Compiled by Karen F. Beall. p. 318.
Baltimore: The Library of Congress, The Johns Hopkins Press,
1970.

1890   Béraldi, Henri. *Les Graveurs du XIXᵉ Siècle*. Vol. 10. Paris: L. Conquet, 1890.

1925   Marie, Aristide. *Célestin Nanteuil: Peintre, Aquafortiste et Lithographe*. Paris: Byblis, 1925.

NASH, PAUL (1889–1946)

1928   Fletcher, John Gould. "The Wood-engravings of Paul Nash." *Print Collector's Quarterly* 15 (1928): 209–233.

1944   Read, Herbert. *Paul Nash*. 2nd ed. London: Penguin, 1944.

1949   Nash, Paul. *Outline, an Autobiography and Other Writings*. London: Faber, 1949.

1973   Postan, A. *The Complete Graphics of Paul Nash*. London: Secker and Warburg, 1973.

NASON, THOMAS WILLOUGHBY (1889–1971)

1937   Arms, John Taylor. "The Engravings of Thomas W. Nason." *Print Collector's Quarterly* 24 (1937): 185–207.

1942   Zigrosser, Carl. *The Artist in America: 24 Close-ups of Contemporary Printmakers*. New York: Alfred Knopf, 1942.

1949   Reese, Albert. *American Prize Prints of the 20th Century*. p. 152. New York: American Artists Group, 1949.

1970   Library of Congress. *American Prints in the Library of Congress: A Catalog of the Collection*. Compiled by Karen F. Beall. pp. 318–319. Baltimore: The Library of Congress, The Johns Hopkins Press, 1970.

1972   The American Academy of Arts and Letters. *Memorial Exhibition*. New York, 1972.

NAST, THOMAS (1840–1902)

1970   Library of Congress. *American Prints in the Library of Congress: A Catalog of the Collection*. Compiled by Karen F. Beall. p. 320. Baltimore: The Library of Congress, The Johns Hopkins Press, 1970.

1972   Boime, Albert. "Thomas Nast and French Art." *The American Art Journal* 4 (1972): 43–65.

NAUDIN, BERNARD (1876–1940)

1918   Poncetton, F. *Essai d'un catalogue des eaux-fortes de Bernard Naudin.* Paris, 1918.

NAY, ERNST (1902–1968)

1960   Haftmann, W. *E. W. Nay.* Cologne: DuMont Schauberg, 1960.

1964   Man, Felix H., ed. *Europäische Graphik.* vol. 2. Munich: Galerie Wolfgang Ketterer, 1964.

NEAL, REGINALD M. (1909–   )

1949   Reese, Albert. *American Prize Prints of the 20th Century.* p. 152. New York: American Artists Group, 1949.

1970   Library of Congress. *American Prints in the Library of Congress: A Catalog of the Collection.* Compiled by Karen F. Beall. p. 320. Baltimore: The Library of Congress, The Johns Hopkins Press, 1970.

NESBITT, JACKSON LEE (1913–   )

1949   Reese, Albert. *American Prize Prints of the 20th Century.* p. 153. New York: American Artists Group, 1949

1970   Library of Congress. *American Prints in the Library of Congress: A Catalog of the Collection.* Compiled by Karen F. Beall. p. 320. Baltimore: The Library of Congress, The Johns Hopkins Press, 1970.

NESCH, ROLF (1893–   )

1958   Kunsthalle, Bremen. *Rolf Nesch: Retrospective Exhibition.* Introduction by Alfred Hentzen. Bremen, 1958.

1961   Simmons, Robert H. "With Eye and Heart: The Art of Rolf Nesch." *Artist's Proof* 1 (1961): 2–11.

1962   Hentzen, Alfred. "Rolf Nesch." in *Prints.* Edited by Carl Zigrosser. New York: Holt, Rinehart and Winston, 1962.

1969   Detroit Institute of Arts. *Prints by Rolf Nesch.* Detroit, 1969.

NEUMANN, ROBERT VON (1888–   )

1949   Reese, Albert. *American Prize Prints of the 20th Century.* p. 205. New York: American Artists Group, 1949.

1970   Library of Congress. *American Prints in the Library of Congress: A Catalog of the Collection.* Compiled by Karen F. Beall. p. 485. Baltimore: The Library of Congress, The Johns Hopkins Press, 1970.

NEVELSON, LOUISE (1900–   )

1967   Johnson, Una and Miller, Jo. *Louise Nevelson, Prints and Drawings 1953–1966.* American Graphic Artists of the 20th Century Series, monograph no. 5. New York: Brooklyn Institute of Arts and Sciences, Shorewood Publishers, 1967.

1970   Library of Congress. *American Prints in the Library of Congress: A Catalog of the Collection.* Compiled by Karen F. Beall. p. 321. Baltimore: The Library of Congress, The Johns Hopkins Press, 1970.

NEVINSON, CHRISTOPHER R. (1889–   )

1932   Salaman, Malcolm C. *Christopher R. Nevinson.* Modern Masters of Etching Series, no. 31. London: The Studio, Ltd., 1932.

NEVITT, STEPHEN R. (1949–   )

1973   Columbia Museum of Art. *Stephen Nevitt: A Survey Exhibition.* Columbia, S. C., 1973.

NEWTON, EDITH WHITTLESEY (1878–   )

1949   Reese, Albert. *American Prize Prints of the 20th Century.* p. 154. New York: American Artists Group, 1949.

1970   Library of Congress. *American Prints in the Library of Congress: A Catalog of the Collection.* Compiled by Karen F. Beall. p. 321. Baltimore: The Library of Congress, The Johns Hopkins Press, 1970.

NICHOLSON, SIR WILLIAM (1872–1949)

1970   Stein, Donna and Karshan, Donald. *L'Estampe Originale: A Catalogue Raisonné.* New York: The Museum of Graphic Art, 1970.

NIEUWENKAMP, WIJNAND OTTO JAN (1874–   )

1930   Furst, Herbert. "Wijnand Otto Jan Nieuwenkamp: Etcher, Woodcutter, Lithographer and Ethnographer." *Print Collector's Quarterly* 17 (1930): 333.

NISBET, ROBERT HOGG (1879–1961)

1949   Reese, Albert. *American Prize Prints of the 20th Century.* p. 155.
        New York: American Artists Group, 1949.

1970   Library of Congress. *American Prints in the Library of Congress: A
        Catalog of the Collection.* Compiled by Karen F. Beall. p. 321.
        Baltimore: The Library of Congress, The Johns Hopkins Press,
        1970.

NIXON, JOB, A.R.E. (1891–1938)

1924   Dodgson, Campbell. "Mr. Job Nixon's Etchings." *Studio* 88 (1924):
        188.

1925   Laver, J. "The Etched Work of Job Nixon." *Bookman's Journal* 12
        (1925): 181.

1927   Stokes, Hugh. "Etchings of Job Nixon." *Print Collector's Quarterly*
        14 (1927): 271–293.

NOBLE, JOHN ALEXANDER (1913–   )

1948   Watson, Lyn A. "Sea Going Lithographer." *American Artist.*
        October 1948, pp. 32–35.

NOLDE, EMIL (1867–1956)

1911–27 Schiefler, Gustav. *Das Graphische Werke von Emil Nolde.* Berlin:
        Verlag von Julius Bard, 1911–27.

1966–67 Schiefler, Gustave. *Emil Nolde: Das Graphische Werke.* 2nd ed.,
        revised by Christel Mosel. 2 vols. Cologne: Dumont Schauberg,
        1966–67.

1972   Sotriffer, Kristian. *Expressionism and Fauvism.* New York:
        McGraw-Hill Book Co., 1972.

**NORBLIN, JEAN-PIERRE (NORBLIN de la GOURDAINE)
(1745–1830)**

1848   Hillemacher, Frédéric. *Catalogues des Estampes qui composent
        l'oeuvre de Jean-Pierre Norblin.* Paris: H. Menu, 1848.

1877   Hillemacher, Frédéric. *Catalogues des Estampes qui composent
        l'oeuvre de Jean-Pierre Norblin.* 2nd ed. Paris: H. Menu, 1877.

1895   Franke, Willibold. *Das radierte Werk des Jean-Pierre Norblin de la
        Gourdaine.* Leipzig: K. W. Hiersemann, 1895.

1939   Simon, Karl. "Unbekannte Radierungen von Jean-Pierre Norblin."
        Graphischen Künste [Vienna] 4 (1939): 115–119.

1970   Library of Congress. *American Prints in the Library of Congress: A Catalog of the Collection.* Compiled by Karen F. Beall. p. 322. Baltimore: The Library of Congress, The Johns Hopkins Press, 1970.

1970   University Gallery, University of Minnesota. *The Etchings of Bror Julius Olsson Nordfeldt.* Minneapolis, Minn., 1970.

1974   Urdang, Beth. *B. J. O. Nordfeldt: The Early and Late Years—the Sea.* New York: Zabriskie Gallery, 1974.

NORTON, ELIZABETH (1887–   )

1970   Library of Congress. *American Prints in the Library of Congress: A Catalog of the Collection.* Compiled by Karen F. Beall. pp. 323–324. Baltimore: The Library of Congress, The Johns Hopkins Press, 1970.

NURA, (ULREICH, NURA WOODSON) (–1950)

1949   Reese, Albert. *American Prize Prints of the 20th Century.* p. 156. New York: American Artists Group, 1949.

O'CALLAHAN, KEVIN B. (1902–   )

1949   Reese, Albert. *American Prize Prints of the 20th Century.* p. 157. New York: American Artists Group, 1949.

1970   Library of Congress. *American Prints in the Library of Congress: A Catalog of the Collection.* Compiled by Karen F. Beall. p. 325. Baltimore: The Library of Congress, The Johns Hopkins Press, 1970.

O'CONNOR, THOM (1937–   )

1970   State University of New York at Albany, University Gallery. *Thom O'Connor: A Selection of Prints and Drawings.* Albany, N.Y., 1970.

OGER, FERDINAND HENRI (20th C.)

1924   "Catalogue Raisonné of the Etchings by Ferdinand Henri Oger." *Print Connoisseur* 4 (1924): 58.

1924   Clément-Janin. "Ferdinand Henri Oger." *Print Connoisseur* 4 (1924): 57.

OLDENBURG, CLAES (1929–   )

1969   Baro, Gene. *Claes Oldenburg Drawings and Prints.* London and New York: Chelsea House Publishers, 1969.

170 1969 Young, Joseph E. "Claes Oldenburg at Gemini." *Artist's Proof* 9 (1969): 44–52.

1970 Library of Congress. *American Prints in the Library of Congress: A Catalog of the Collection.* Compiled by Karen F. Beall. p. 326. Baltimore: The Library of Congress, The Johns Hopkins Press, 1970.

1971 Goldman, Judith. "Sort of a Commercial for Objects." *Print Collector's Newsletter* 2 (1972): 117–121.

1971 Margo Leavin Gallery. *Claes Oldenburg: Works in Edition 1971–1972.* Los Angeles, Cal., 1972.

ORLOWSKI, ALEXANDER (1777–1832)

1971 Victoria and Albert Museum. *Homage to Senefelder.* Introduction by Felix H. Man. London, 1971.

OROVIDA (PISSARRO, OROVIDA) (1893–   )

1925 Rutter, Frank. "The Art of Orovida Pissarro." *Artwork* [London] 1 (1925): 152–155.

1926 Nicholson, C. A. "The Etchings of Orovida." *Print Collector's Quarterly* 13 (1926): 177–202.

1940 "Orovida: Supplementary List of Etchings and Aquatints, Continued from Checklist in 'The Print Collector's Quarterly' April, 1926." *Print Collector's Quarterly* 27 (1940): 99–105.

OROZCO, JOSÉ CLEMENTE (1883–1949)

1934 Schmeckebier, Dr. Laurence. "Orozco's Graphic Art." *Print Collector's Quarterly* 21 (1934): 185–194.

1967 Hopkins, Jon H. *Orozco: A Catalogue of his Graphic Work.* Flagstaff, Arizona: Northern Arizona University Publications, 1967.

1970 Marrozzini, Luigi. *Catálogo completo de la obra gráfico de Orozco.* Puerto Rico, 1970.

1972 Sotriffer, Kristian. *Expressionism and Fauvism.* New York: McGraw-Hill Book Co., 1972.

ORR, LOUIS (1879–   )

1913 "Etchings by Louis Orr." *Studio* 60 (1913): 20.

1921 "List of Etchings by Louis Orr." *Print Connoisseur* 2 (1921): 81.

1921–22 Eglington, G. C. "Etchings of Louis Orr." *Print Connoisseur* 2 (1921–22): 69.

1923   Clément-Janin. "Louis Orr." *Print Connoisseur* 3 (1923): 370.

1923   Orr, Louis. "Catalogue Raisonné of the Etchings of Louis Orr." *Print Connoisseur* 3 (1923): 384.

1970   Library of Congress. *American Prints in the Library of Congress: A Catalog of the Collection.* Compiled by Karen F. Beall. p. 327. Baltimore: The Library of Congress, The Johns Hopkins Press, 1970.

OSBORNE, MALCOLM, A.R.A., R.E. (1880–   )

1919   Salaman, M. C. "Etchings and Engravings by Malcolm Osborne A.R.A., R.E." *Studio* 75 (1919): 110.

1924   Laver, J. "The Etched Work of Malcolm Osborne." *Bookman's Journal* 11 (1924): 63.

1925   Salaman, M. C. "Etchings of Malcolm Osborne, A.R.E., R.E." *Print Collector's Quarterly* 12 (1925): 285–313.

1929   Salaman, Malcolm C. *Malcolm Osborne.* Modern Masters of Etching Series, no. 21. London: The Studio, Ltd., 1929.

OSK, ROSELLE HILLENBERG (1884–1954)

1949   Reese, Albert. *American Prize Prints of the 20th Century.* p. 158. New York: American Artists Group, 1949.

1970   Library of Congress. *American Prints in the Library of Congress: A Catalog of the Collection.* Compiled by Karen F. Beall. p. 327. Baltimore: The Library of Congress, The Johns Hopkins Press, 1970.

OSSORIO, ALFONSO (1916–   )

1972   Heckscher Museum. *Artists of Suffolk County: Part 6, Contemporary Prints.* Huntington, N.Y., 1972.

OSTROWSKY, ABBO (1889–   )

1949   Reese, Albert. *American Prize Prints of the 20th Century.* p. 159. New York: American Artists Group, 1949.

1970   Library of Congress. *American Prints in the Library of Congress: A Catalog of the Collection.* Compiled by Karen F. Beall. p. 327. Baltimore: The Library of Congress, The Johns Hopkins Press, 1970.

PAI, LAXMAN (1926–   )

1959   St. George's Gallery Prints. *Laxman Pai: The Life of the Buddha*.
        London, 1959.

1962   Kup, Karl. "Laxman Pai of Bombay and Paris." *Artist's Proof* 4
        (1962): 34–35.

PALENSKE, R. H. (1884–1954)

1938   Smithsonian Institution. *R. H. Palenske: Exhibition of Drypoints
        and Drawings*. Washington, D.C., 1938.

1970   Library of Congress. *American Prints in the Library of Congress: A
        Catalog of the Collection*. Compiled by Karen F. Beall. p. 328.
        Baltimore: The Library of Congress, The Johns Hopkins Press,
        1970.

PALMER, FANNY (1812–1876)

1962   Cowdrey, Mary Bartlett. "Fanny Palmer: an American Lithog-
        rapher." *Prints*. Edited by Carl Zigrosser. New York: Holt,
        Rinehart and Winston, 1962.

PALMER, SAMUEL (1805–1881)

1913   "Bibliography of Samuel Palmer." *Print Collector's Quarterly* 3
        (1913): 223.

1913   Hardie, Martin. "Catalogue of Samuel Palmer's Etchings." *Print
        Collector's Quarterly* 3 (1913): 225–239.

1913   Hardie, Martin. "The Etched Work of Samuel Palmer." *Print
        Collector's Quarterly* 3 (1913): 207–223.

1926   Victoria and Albert Museum. *Catalogue of an Exhibition of
        Etchings by Samuel Palmer*. London, 1926.

1927   Laver, J. "The Place of Samuel Palmer in the History of British
        Etching." *Artwork* 3 (1927): 40.

1937   Alexander, R. G. *A Catalogue of the Etchings of Samuel Palmer*.
        London: Print Collector's Club, 1937

1937   Mather, Frank Jewett, Jr. "Samuel Palmer's Virgil etchings." *Print
        Collector's Quarterly* 24(1937): 253–264.

1968   Lister, Raymond. *Samuel Palmer and his Etchings*. New York:
        Watson-Guptill, 1968.

1968   Selz, Peter. *Eduardo Paolozzi, A Print Retrospective: Exhibition Catalogue.* Berkeley: University of California and London: Editions Alecto, 1968.

1969   Paolozzi, Eduardo. *Eduardo Paolozzi Complete Graphics.*Berlin: Galerie Mikro and London: Petersburg Press, 1969.

1973   Whitford, Frank. *Eduardo Paolozzi.* London: Tate Gallery, 1973.

PAONE, PETER (1936–)

1970   Library of Congress. *American Prints in the Library of Congress: A Catalog of the Collection.* Compiled by Karen F. Beall. p. 328. Baltimore: The Library of Congress, The Johns Hopkins Press, 1970.

PARIS, HAROLD PERSICO (1925–)

1961   McKnulty, Kneeland. "Hosannah: The Work of Harold Paris." *Artist's Proof* 1 (1961): 12–17.

1970   Library of Congress. *American Prints in the Library of Congress: A Catalog of the Collection.* Compiled by Karen F. Beall. p. 329. Baltimore: The Library of Congress, The Johns Hopkins Press, 1970.

1972   University Art Museum. *Harold Paris: The California Years.* Berkeley, Cal., 1972.

PARRISH, STEPHEN (1846–1938)

1881   Koehler, S. R. *American Art Review* 2 (1881): 5.

1886   Hitchcock. R. "Stephen Parrish." *Art Review* (1886).

n.d.   *A Catalogue of Etchings by Stephen Parrish: 1879–1883.* Privately published, n.d.

PARTRIDGE, ROI (1888–)

1924   Brown, Howell C. "Roi Partridge: Etcher." *American Magazine of Art* 15 (1924): 352.

1970   Library of Congress. *American Prints in the Library of Congress: A Catalog of the Collection.* Compiled by Karen F. Beall. p. 330. Baltimore: The Library of Congress, The Johns Hopkins Press, 1970.

174   1973   "Roi Partridge." *American Artist Magazine* November, 1973.

PASCIN, JULES (PINCAS) (1885–1930)

1945   Georges, Waldemar. *Pascin Retrospective: 1885–1930: Peintures, Aquarelles, Dessins, Gravures.* Paris: Galeries Jean-Marc Vidal, 1945.

1966   Freudenheim, T. L. *Pascin: Exhibition Catalogue.* Berkeley: University of California, 1966.

1970   Library of Congress. *American Prints in the Library of Congress: A Catalog of the Collection.* Compiled by Karen F. Beall. p. 331. Baltimore: The Library of Congress, The Johns Hopkins Press, 1970.

PAUL, HERMANN RENÉ GEORGES (1864–1940)

1970   Stein, Donna and Karshan, Donald. *L'Estampe Originale: A Catalogue Raisonné.* New York: The Museum of Graphic Art, 1970.

PAULI, FRITZ (1891–1968)

1926   Schaffner, Paul. *Fritz Eduard Pauli: Radierungen.* With a catalog of graphic works by August Klipstein. Erlenbach-Zurich: F. Rentsch, 1926.

PEALE, CHARLES WILLSON (1741–1827)

1939   Sellers, Charles Coleman. *The Artist of the Revolution; the Early Life of Charles Willson Peale.* Hebron, Conn.: Feather and Good, 1939.

1970   Library of Congress. *American Prints in the Library of Congress: A Catalog of the Collection.* Compiled by Karen F. Beall. p. 332. Baltimore: The Library of Congress, The Johns Hopkins Press, 1970.

PEARLSTEIN, PHILIP (1924–   )

1973   Adrian, Dennis. "The Prints of Philip Pearlstein." *Print Collector's Newsletter* 4 (1973): 49–52.

1973   Dückers, Alexander. *Philip Pearlstein: Drawings and Prints 1946–1972.* Berlin: Staatliche Museum, 1973.

PEARSON, RALPH M. (1883–1958)

1925   Osburn, Luna C. "Ralph M. Pearson: Painter, Etcher and Modernist." *American Magazine of Art* 16 (1925): 467.

1921   Fechter, Paul. *Das Graphische Werk: Max Pechstein.* Berlin, 1921.

1965   Wingler, H. M. *Graphic Work from the Bauhaus.* Greenwich, Conn.: New York Graphic Society, 1965.

1972   Sotriffer, Kristian. *Expressionism and Fauvism.* New York: McGraw-Hill Book Co., 1972.

PENNELL, JOSEPH (1857–1926)

1912   Pennell, Joseph. "Joseph Pennell's Lithographs of the Panama Canal." *Print Collector's Quarterly* 2 (1912): 291–316.

1927   Cary, Elisabeth Luther. "Joseph Pennell: A Note." *Print Collector's Quarterly* 14 (1927): 47–68.

1928   Wuerth, Louis A. *Catalogue of the Etchings of Joseph Pennell.* Boston: Little, Brown and Co., 1928.

1931   Salaman, Malcolm C. *Joseph Pennell. Modern Masters of Etching Series, no. 28.* London: The Studio Ltd., 1931.

1931   Wuerth, Louis A. *Catalogue of the Lithographs of Joseph Pennell.* Boston: Little, Brown and Co., 1931.

1949   Reese, Albert. *American Prize Prints of the 20th Century.* p. 232. New York: American Artists Group, 1949.

1970   Library of Congress. *American Prints in the Library of Congress: A Catalog of the Collection.* Compiled by Karen F. Beall. pp. 333–395. Baltimore: The Library of Congress, The Johns Hopkins Press, 1970.

1970   Stein, Donna and Karshan, Donald. *L'Estampe Originale: A Catalogue Raisonné.* New York: The Museum of Graphic Art, 1970.

1970   Young, Mahonri Sharp. "The Remarkable Joseph Pennell." *The American Art Journal* 2 (1970): 81–92.

PETERDI, GABOR (1915–   )

1959   De Cordova Museum. *Gabor Peterdi: Prints.* Lincoln, Mass., 1959.

1959   Johnson, Una E. *Gabor Peterdi: 25 years of his prints, 1934–1959.* Brooklyn, N. Y.: Brooklyn Museum, 1959.

1962   The Cleveland Museum of Art. *Catalog of an Exhibition of Prints and Drawings by Gabor Peterdi.* Cleveland, Ohio: The Print Club, 1962.

176   1964   Yale University Art Gallery. *Gabor Peterdi: Paintings, Drawings and Prints*. New Haven, 1964, and Washington, D.C.: Corcoran Gallery of Art, 1964.

1970   Library of Congress. *American Prints in the Library of Congress: A Catalog of the Collection*. Compiled by Karen F. Beall. p. 396. Baltimore: The Library of Congress, The Johns Hopkins Press, 1970.

1970   Peterdi, Gabor. *Gabor Peterdi: Graphics 1934–1969*. New York: Touchstone Publishers, 1970.

1973   Jane Haslem Gallery. *The Innovators: Renaissance in American Printmaking*. Washington, D.C., 1973.

PETERSEN, MARTIN (1870–   )

1949   Reese, Albert. *American Prize Prints of the 20th Century*.p. 160. New York: American Artists Group, 1949.

PETERSEN, ROLAND CONRAD (1926–   )

1973   Hayter, S. W. *Color Etchings by Roland Petersen*. Santa Barbara, Cal.: The Santa Barbara Museum of Art, 1973.

PETTIT, GENO (20th C.)

1949   Reese, Albert. *American Prize Prints of the 20th Century*. p. 161. New York: American Artists Group, 1949.

PICASSO, PABLO (1881–1973)

1933   Geiser, Bernard. *Picasso, Peintre-graveur: Catalogue illustré de l'oeuvre gravé et lithographie 1899–1931*. Vol. 1. Berne, 1933—. 2nd ed. Berne, 1955.

1944   Johnson, Una E. *Ambroise Vollard, Éditeur*. New York: Wittenborn and Co., 1944.

1948   Geiser, Bernard. *Pablo Picasso: Lithographs: 1945–1948*. New York: Valentin, 1948.

1949   Mourlot, Fernand. *Picasso Lithographie*. Vol. 1. Monte Carlo: A. Sauret, 1949.

1950   Mourlot, Fernand. *Picasso Lithographie*. Vol. 2. Monte Carlo: A. Sauret, 1950.

1955   Geiser, Bernard. *Picasso, Peintre-Graveur: Catalogue illustré de l'oeuvre gravé et lithographie 1899–1931*. Vol. 1. 2d. ed. Berne, 1955.

1956   Mourlot, Fernand. *Picasso Lithographie*. Vol. 3. Monte Carlo: A.   **177**
Sauret, 1956.

1964   Mourlot, Fernand. *Picasso Lithographie*. Vol. 4. Monte Carlo: A.
Sauret, 1964.

1968   Bloch, Georges. *Picasso: Catalogue de l'oeuvre gravé et lithographié
1904–1967*. Vol. 1. Berne: Kornfeld and Klipstein, 1968.

1968   Geiser, Bernard. *Picasso, Peintre-Graveur: Catalogue illustré de
l'oeuvre gravé et lithographié 1932–1934*. Vol. 2. Berne: Kornfeld
and Klipstein, 1968.

1968   Karshan, Donald H. *Picasso Linocuts: 1958–1963*. New York:
Tudor Publishing Co., 1968.

1970   Mourlot, Fernand. *Picasso Lithographs 1919–1969*. Boston: Boston
Book and Art Publisher, 1970.

1971   Bloch, Goerges. *Picasso: Catalogue de l'oeuvre gravé et lithographié
1966–1969*. Vol. 2. Berne: Kornfeld and Klipstein, 1971.

PICKHARDT, CARL E., JR. (1908–   )

1949   Reese, Albert. *American Prize Prints of the 20th Century*. p. 162.
New York: American Artists Group, 1949.

1970   Library of Congress. *American Prints in the Library of Congress: A
Catalog of the Collection*. Compiled by Karen F. Beall. p. 400.
Baltimore: The Library of Congress, The Johns Hopkins Press,
1970.

PINWELL, GEORGE JOHN (1842–1875)

1924   Hartley, Harold. "George John Pinwell." *Print Collector's Quarterly*
11 (1924): 163–189.

PIRANESI, GIOVANNI BATTISTA (1720–1778)

1912   Moore, Benjamin Burges. "Giovanni Battista Piranesi." Part 1.
Print Collector's Quarterly 2 (1912): 105–148.

1912   Moore, Benjamin Burges. "Giovanni Battista Piranesi." Part 2.
Print Collector's Quarterly 2 (1912): 341–364.

1915   Ivins, William M., Jr. "Piranesi and 'Le Carceri d'Invenzione'."
Print Collector's Quarterly 5 (1915): 191–218.

1922   Hind, Arthur Mayger. *Giovanni Battista Piranesi: A Critical Study,
with list of all his published works of the Prisons and the Views of
Rome*. London: The Cotswold Gallery, 1922.

178 1937 Chamberlain, Samuel. "The Triumphal Arches of Piranesi." *Print Collector's Quarterly* 24 (1937): 63–79.

1967 Hind, Arthur Mayger. *Giovanni Battista Piranesi: A Critical Study, With List of all his Published Works of the Prisons and the Views of Rome.* 1922. Reprint. New York: Da Capo Press, 1967.

1974 *Etchings by Giovanni Battista Piranesi: 1720–1778.* London: P. and D. Colnaghi and Co., Ltd., 1974.

PISSARRO, CAMILLE (1830–1903)

1922 Rodo, Ludovic. "The Etched and Lithographed Work of Camille Pissarro." *Print Collector's Quarterly* 9 (1922): 275–301.

1923 Delteil, Loys. *Le Peintre-Graveur Illustré: Pissarro, Sisley, Renoir.* Vol. 17. Paris: Chez l'auteur, 1923.

1932 Cailac, Jean. "The Prints of Camille Pissarro: A Supplement to the Catalogue by Loys Delteil." *Print Collector's Quarterly* 19 (1932): 75–86.

1969 Delteil, Loys. *Le Peintre-Graveur Illustré: Pissarro, Sisley, Renoir.* Vol. 17. 1923. Reprint. New York: Da Capo Press, 1969.

1970 Stein, Donna and Karshan, Donald. *L'Estampe Originale: A Catalogue Raissonné.* New York: The Museum of Graphic Art, 1970.

1972 Leymarie, Jean and Melot, Michel. *The Graphic Works of the Impressionists: The Complete Prints of Manet, Pissarro, Renoir, Cezanne and Sisley.* New York: Abrams, 1972.

1973 Shapiro, Barbara S. *Camille Pissarro: The Impressionist Printmaker.* Boston, Mass.: Boston Museum of Fine Arts, Meriden Gravure, 1973.

PISSARRO, GEORGE HENRI (1871–1961)

1970 Stein, Donna and Karshan, Donald. *L'Estampe Originale: A Catalogue Raisonné.* New York: The Museum of Graphic Art, 1970.

PISSARRO, LUCIEN (1863–1944)

1944 Johnson, Una E. *Ambroise Vollard, Éditeur.* New York: Wittenborn and Co., 1944.

1948 Robb, Brian. *The Wood-engravings of Lucien Pissarro.* London, 1948.

1970   Stein, Donna and Karshan, Donald. *L'Estampe Originale: A Catalogue Raisonné*. New York: The Museum of Graphic Art, 1970.

PISSARRO, OROVIDA *See* OROVIDA

PITCAIRN-KNOWLES, JAMES (1864–   )

1944   Johnson, Una E. *Ambroise Vollard, Éditeur*. New York: Wittenborn and Co., 1944.

PITTERI, MARCO (1703–1786)

1950   Mauroner, Fabio. "A Catalogue of the Portrait Engravings of Marco Pitteri." *Print Collector's Quarterly* 30 (1950): 15–18.

1950   McComp, A. K. "The Engravings of Marco Pitteri." *Print Collector's Quarterly* 30 (1950): 5–14.

PITTMAN, ROSS A. (1883–   )

1949   Reese, Albert. *American Prize Prints of the 20th Century*. p. 163. New York: American Artists Group, 1949.

PITZ, HENRY C. (1895–   )

1949   Reese, Albert. *American Prize Prints of the 20th Century*. p. 164. New York: American Artists Group, 1949.

PLATT, CHARLES ADAMS (1861–1933)

1889   Rice, Richard Austin. *A Descriptive Catalogue of the Etched Work of Charles A. Platt*. New York: The DeVinne Press, 1889.

1925   Anderson, Joan. "Charles A. Platt." *International Studio* 82 (1925): 180.

1970   Library of Congress. *American Prints in the Library of Congress: A Catalog of the Collection*. Compiled by Karen F. Beall. pp. 401–403. Baltimore: The Library of Congress, The Johns Hopkins Press, 1970.

PLOWMAN, GEORGE TAYLOR (1869–1932)

1914   Plowman, George T. *Etching and Other Graphic Arts*. New York: John Lane Company, 1914.

1921   "Catalogue Raisonné of the Etchings and Drypoints of George Taylor Plowman." *The Print Connoisseur* 2 (1921): 43–49.

PLUM, JASPER (1893–   )

1942   Zigrosser, Carl. *The Artist in America: 24 Close-Ups of Contemporary Printmakers.* New York: Alfred Knopf, 1942.

POLIAKOFF, SERGE (1906–1969)

1956   Ragon, M. *Poliakoff.* Paris: Musée de poche, 1956.

POLLAK, MAX (1886–   )

1932   Binder, Bruno. "The Etcher Max Pollak." *Print Collector's Quarterly* 19 (1932): 341–358.

POLLARD, JAMES (1797–1859)

1930   Daniell, Frederick C. "Coaching Prints after James Pollard." *Print Collector's Quarterly* 17 (1930): 169–195.

POLLEY, FREDERICK (1875–1958)

1924   "Etchings of Old Germantown by Frederick Polley." *American Magazine of Art* 15 (1924): 134.

POLLOCK, JACKSON (1912–1956)

1971   Kainen, Jacob. "Prints of the Thirties: Reflections on the Federal Art Project." *Artist's Proof* 11 (1971): 34–41.

PONCE DE LEON, MICHAEL (1922–   )

1970   Library of Congress. *American Prints in the Library of Congress: A Catalog of the Collection.* Compiled by Karen F. Beall. p. 406. Baltimore: The Library of Congress, The Johns Hopkins Press, 1970.

1973   Jane Haslem Gallery. *The Innovators: Renaissance in American Printmaking.* Washington, D.C., 1973.

POND, ARTHUR (1705–1758)

1922   Hake, Henry M. "Pond's and Knapton's Imitations of Drawings." *Print Collector's Quarterly* 9 (1922): 325–349.

POND, CLAYTON (1941–   )

1972   De Cordova Museum. *Clayton Pond: Paintings, Prints.* Lincoln, Mass., 1972.

1972   Heckscher Museum. *Artists of Suffolk County: Part 6, Contemporary Prints*. Huntington, N. Y., 1972.

PORTER, FAIRFIELD (1907–   )

1972   Heckscher Museum. *Artists of Suffolk County: Part 6, Contemporary Prints*. Huntington, N.Y., 1972.

1972   Schjeldahl, Peter. *Fairfield Porter: Recent Work*. New York: Hirschl and Adler Galleries, 1972.

1973   Harbor Gallery. *Fairfield Porter: Exhibition Catalogue*. Cold Spring Harbor, New York, 1973.

POSADA, JOSÉ GUADALUPE (1851–1913)

1944   Gamboa, F. *Posada: Printmaker to the Mexican People*. Chicago: Art Institute of Chicago, 1944.

1963   Ponce de Léon, Michael. "Homage to Posada." *Artist's Proof* 6 (1963): 46–49.

1972   Sotriffer, Kristian. *Expressionism and Fauvism*. New York: McGraw-Hill Book Co., 1972.

POTT, CONSTANCE MARY, R.E. (1862–   )

1906   Hardie, M. "Constance M. Pott." *The Queen* 8 September 1906.

POZZATTI, RUDY (1926–   )

1970   Library of Congress. *American Prints in the Library of Congress: A Catalog of the Collection*. Compiled by Karen F. Beall. p. 407. Baltimore: the Library of Congress, The Johns Hopkins Press, 1970.

1971   Geske, Norman. *Rudy Pozzatti, American Printmaker*. Lawrence, Kansas: The University Press, 1971.

1973   Jane Haslem Gallery. *The Innovators: Renaissance in American Printmaking*. Washington, D.C., 1973.

PRAMPOLINI, ENRICO (1896–1956)

1957   Peters, H. ed. *Die Bauhaus Mappen: Neue Europäische Graphik, 1921–1923*. Cologne: C. Czwiklitzer, 1957.

182 1965   Wingler, H. M. *Graphic Work from the Bauhaus*. Greenwich, Conn.: New York Graphic Society, 1965.

PRASSINOS, MARIO (1916–   )

1962   Ferrier, J. L. *Prassinos*. Paris: Musée de poche, 1962.

PRENDERGAST, MAURICE (1859–1924)

1960   Rhys, Hedley Howell. *Maurice Prendergast, 1859–1924*. Cambridge, Mass.: Harvard University Press, 1960.

1967   Phillips, M. *Maurice Prendergast, The Monotypes: Exhibition Catalogue*. New York: Bard College, 1967.

1970   Library of Congress. *American Prints in the Library of Congress: A Catalog of the Collection*. Compiled by Karen F. Beall. p. 408. Baltimore: The Library of Congress, The Johns Hopkins Press, 1970.

PRIEST, ALFRED (1810–1850)

1905   Dickes, William Frederick. *The Norwich School of Painting*. p. 567. London and Norwich, 1905.

PROUVÉ, VICTOR EMILE (1858–1943)

1970   Stein, Donna and Karshan, Donald. *L'Estampe Originale: A Catalogue Raisonné*. New York: The Museum of Graphic Art, 1970.

PRUD'HON, PIERRE-PAUL (1758–1823)

1876   Goncourt, Edmond de. *Catalogue raisonné de l'oeuvre peint, dessiné et gravé de P. P. Prud'hon*. Paris: Rapilly, 1876.

1924   Guiffrey, Jean. *L'oeuvre de P. P. Prud'hon*. Paris: Colin, 1924.

1928   Régamey, Raymond. *Prud'hon*. Paris: Rieder, 1928.

PURRMAN, HANS (1880–1966)

1966–67 Man, Felix H., ed. *Europäische Graphik*. Vol. 4, 5. Munich: Galerie Wolfgang Ketterer, 1966–67.

1971   Victoria and Albert Museum. *Homage to Senefelder*. Introduction by Felix H. Man. London, 1971.

PUVIS DE CHAVANNES, PIERRE (1824–1898)

1944   Johnson, Una E. *Ambroise Vollard, Éditeur*. New York: Wittenborn and Co., 1944.

1970   Kovler Gallery. *The Graphic Art of Valloton and the Nabis*. pp. 58–61. Chicago, Ill., 1970.

1970   Stein, Donna and Karshan, Donald.*L'Estampe Originale: A Catalogue Raisonné*. New York: The Museum of Graphic Art, 1970.

PUY, JEAN (1876–   )

1944   Johnson, Una E. *Ambroise Vollard: Editeur*. New York: Wittenborn and Co., 1944.

PYTLAK, LEONARD (1910–   )

1949   Reese, Albert. *American Prize Prints of the 20th Century*. p. 165. New York: American Artists Group, 1949.

1970   Library of Congress. *American Prints in the Library of Congress: A Catalog of the Collection*. Compiled by Karen F. Beall. p. 409. Baltimore: The Library of Congress, The Johns Hopkins Press, 1970.

QUIEN, JEAN (18th C.)

1927   Hardie, Martin. "A Note on Jean Quien." *Print Collector's Quarterly* 14 (1927): 95–97.

QUINTANILLA, LUIS (1895–   )

1935   Burdett, Basil. "The Drypoints of Luis Quintanilla." *Print Collector's Quarterly* 22 (1935): 265–278.

RACHOU, HENRI (1856–   )

1970   Stein, Donna and Karshan, Donald. *L'Estampe Originale: A Catalogue Raisonné*. New York: The Museum of Graphic Art, 1970.

RAFFAËLLI, JEAN-FRANÇOIS (1850–1924)

1923   Delteil, Loys. *Le Peintre-Graveur Illustré: Raffaëlli*. Vol. 16. Paris: Chez l'auteur, 1923.

1967   Kovler Gallery. *Forgotten Printmakers of the 19th Century*. Chicago, 1967.

1969   Delteil, Loys. *Le Peintre-Graveur Illustré: Raffaëlli*. Vol. 16. 1923. Reprint. New York: Da Capo Press, 1969.

1970   Stein, Donna and Karshan, Donald. *L'Estampe Originale: A Catalogue Raisonné*. New York: The Museum of Graphic Art, 1970.

184   **RAFFET, AUGUSTE (1804–1860)**

1862   Giacomelli, H. *Raffet, Son Oeuvre Lithographie . . . Eaux-fortes.* Paris: Bureau de la Gazette des beaux-arts, 1862.

1903   Curtis, A. *Auguste Raffet.* New York: Frederick Keppel and Co., 1903.

1917   Wickenden, Robert J. "Auguste Raffet (1804–1860)" *Print Collector's Quarterly* 7 (1917): 25–54.

1971   Victoria and Albert Museum. *Homage to Senefelder.* Introduction by Felix H. Man. London, 1971.

RAINER, ARNULF (1929–   )

1971   Breicha, O. *Arnulf Rainer, Katalog des Druckgraphischen Werks.* Vienna, 1971.

1972   Sotriffer, Kristian. *Expressionism and Fauvism.* New York: McGraw-Hill Book Co., 1972.

RAJON, PAUL ADOLPHE (1842–1888)

1916   Wickenden, Robert J. "Paul Adolphe Rajon (1842–1888)," *Print Collector's Quarterly* 6 (1916): 411–434.

RAMONDOT, JACQUES (1928–   )

1968   Frapier, J. *Galerie des Peintres-Graveurs.* Catalogue 5. Paris: Galerie Jacques Frapier, 1968.

1969   Avati, M. *Album des Peintres-Graveurs français, 80ᵉ anniversaire.* Paris, 1969.

RAMSAY, ALLAN (1713–1784)

1931   Sanderson, Kenneth. "Engravings after Allan Ramsay." *Print Collector's Quarterly* 18 (1931): 105–128.

RAMSAY, DAGA (1924–   )

1972   Heckscher Museum. *Artists of Suffolk County: Part 6, Contemporary Prints.* Huntington, N. Y., 1972.

RANFT, RICHARD (1862–1931)

1970   Stein, Donna and Karshan, Donald. *L'Estampe Originale: A Catalogue Raisonné.* New York: The Museum of Graphic Art, 1970.

1954 Humbert, A. *Les Nabis et Leur Époque, 1888–1900. Geneva: P. Cailler, 1954.*

1970 Kovler Gallery. *The Graphic Art of Valloton and the Nabis.* pp. 62–64. Chicago, Ill., 1970.

1970 Stein, Donna and Karshan, Donald. *L'Estampe Originale: A Catalogue Raisonné.* New York: The Museum of Graphic Art, 1970.

RASKIN, SAUL (1878–1966)

1949 Reese, Albert. *American Prize Prints of the 20th Century.* p. 166. New York: American Artists Group, 1949.

1970 Library of Congress. *American Prints in the Library of Congress: A Catalog of the Collection.* Compiled by Karen F. Beall. p. 411. Baltimore: The Library of Congress, The Johns Hopkins Press, 1970.

RATTNER, ABRAHAM (1895–   )

1970 Library of Congress. *American Prints in the Library of Congress: A Catalog of the Collection.* Compiled by Karen F. Beall. p. 412. Baltimore: The Library of Congress, The Johns Hopkins Press, 1970.

1972 Heckscher Museum. *Artists of Suffolk County: Part 6, Contemporary Prints.* Huntington, N.Y., 1972

RAUSCHENBERG, ROBERT (1925–   )

1969 Fort Worth Art Center Museum. *Robert Rauschenberg: Selections.* Fort Worth, Texas, 1969.

1970 Institute of Contemporary Art. *Rauschenberg: Graphic Art.* Philadelphia: University of Pennsylvania, 1970.

1970 Library of Congress. *American Prints in the Library of Congress: A Catalog of the Collection.* Compiled by Karen F. Beall. p. 412. Baltimore: The Library of Congress, The Johns Hopkins Press, 1970.

1970 The Minneapolis Institute of Arts. *Robert Rauschenberg: Prints 1948/1970: Exhibition Catalogue.* Minneapolis, Minn., 1970.

1974 University of South Florida Library Gallery. *Rauschenberg at Graphicstudio.* Tampa, Fla., 1974.

RAVERAT, GWENDOLEN (1885–1957)

1931   Fletcher, John Gould. "The Woodcuts of Gwendolen Raverat."
        Print Collector's Quarterly 18 (1931): 331–350.

        RAYNES, SYDNEY (1907–   )

1949   Reese, Albert. *American Prize Prints of the 20th Century*. p. 167.
        New York: American Artists Group, 1949.

        RAYO, OMAR (1928–   )

1970   Library of Congress. *American Prints in the Library of Congress: A
        Catalog of the Collection*. Compiled by Karen F. Beall. p. 413.
        Baltimore: The Library of Congress, The Johns Hopkins Press,
        1970.

1971   Oniciu, A. P. *Omar Rayo Prints/Grabados 1960–1970*. Bogota,
        Colombia, 1971. [American distributor: New York: Wittenborn
        and Co.]

1972   Pizarro, Agueda. *Omar Rayo: Blind Knot/Nudo Ciego*. 1972.
        [American distributor: New York: Wittenborn and Co.]

        READ, DAVID CHARLES (1790–1851)

1832   *Catalogue of Etchings by D. C. Read*. Salisbury, 1832. Manuscript in
        the British Museum.

        REDON, ODILON (1840–1916)

1913   Mellerio, André. *Odilon Redon*. Paris: Société pour l'Étude de la
        Gravure Française, 1913.

1920   Pach, Walter. "The Etchings and Lithographs of Odilon Redon."
        Print Connoisseur 1 (1920): 45–63.

1923   Mellerio, André. *Odilon Redon: peintre, dessinateur et graveur*.
        Paris: Floury, 1923. Reprint. New York: Plenum, 1923. Reprint.
        New York: Da Capo Press, 1968.

1924   Mellerio, André *Odilon Redon: peintre, dessinateur et graveur*. 2nd
        ed. Paris, 1924. Reprint. New York: Da Capo Press, 1968.

1935   Roger-Marx, Claude. "The Engraved Work of Odilon Redon."
        Print Collector's Quarterly 22 (1935): 167–188.

1937   Sterner, Albert. "Odilon Redon." *Prints* 8 (1937): 63–70.

1944   Johnson, Una E. *Ambroise Vollard, Éditeur*. New York: Witten-
        born and Co., 1944.

1966   De Cordova Museum. *Odilon Redon: Graphics.* Lincoln, Mass.,   **187**
        1966.

1968   Mellerio, André. *Odilon Redon.* Paris, 1924. Reprint. New York:
        Da Capo Press, 1968.

1969   Werner, Alfred. *The Graphic Works of Odilon Redon.* New York:
        Dover, 1969.

1970   Kovler Gallery. *The Graphic Art of Valloton and the Nabis.* pp.
        65–67. Chicago, Ill., 1970.

1970   Stein, Donna and Karshan, Donald. *L'Estampe Originale: A
        Catalogue Raisonné.* New York: The Museum of Graphic Art,
        1970.

1973   Bairati, Eleonora. "Poetic Symbolism in the Graphic Work of
        Redon." *Print Collector* [Milan: Grafica Sipiel, s.r.] 4 (1973): 16–35.

1973   Brion, Marcel. *Quatre Siècles de Surréalisme: L'Art Fantastique
        dans la Gravuere.* Paris: Pierre Belfond, 1973. [American distrib-
        utor: New York: Wittenborn and Co.]

REED, DOEL (1894–   )

1949   Reese, Albert. *American Prize Prints of the 20th Century.* p. 168.
        New York: American Artists Group, 1949.

1970   Library of Congress. *American Prints in the Library of Congress: A
        Catalog of the Collection.* Compiled by Karen F. Beall. p. 413.
        Baltimore: The Library of Congress, The Johns Hopkins Press,
        1970.

REED, EARL HOWELL (1863–1931)

1970   Library of Congress. *American Prints in the Library of Congress: A
        Catalog of the Collection.* Compiled by Karen F. Beall. p. 413.
        Baltimore: The Library of Congress, The Johns Hopkins Press,
        1970.

REINHARDT, AD (1913–1967)

1970   Library of Congress. *American Prints in the Library of Congress: A
        Catalog of the Collection.* Compiled by Karen F. Beall. p. 414.
        Baltimore: The Library of Congress, The Johns Hopkins Press,
        1970.

REMINGTON, FREDERIC (1861–1909)

1947   McCracken, H. *Frederic Remington: Artist of the Old West.*
        Philadelphia and New York: J. B. Lippincott Co., 1947.

188 1970   Wister, O. *The Illustrations of Frederic Remington.* New York: Crown Publishers, 1970.

RENOIR, PIERRE-AUGUSTE (1841–1919)

1923   Delteil, Loys. *Le Peintre-Graveur Illustré: Pissarro, Sisley, Renoir.* Vol. 17. Paris: Chez l'auteur, 1923.

1944   Johnson, Una E. *Ambroise Vollard, Éditeur.* New York: Wittenborn and Co., 1944.

1951   Roger-Marx, Claude. *Les lithographies de Renoir.* Monte Carlo: A. Sauret, 1951.

1969   Delteil, Loys. *Le Peintre-Graveur Illustré: Pissarro, Sisley, Renoir.* Vol. 17. 1923. Reprint. New York: Da Capo Press, 1969.

1970   Stein, Donna and Karshan, Donald. *L'Estampe Originale: A Catalogue raisonné.* New York: The Museum of Graphic Art, 1970.

1972   Leymarie, Jean and Melot, Michel. *The Graphic Works of the Impressionists: The Complete Prints of Monet, Pissarro, Renoir, Cézanne and Sisley.* New York: Abrams, 1972.

RENOUARD, CHARLES PAUL (1845–1924)

1922   Clément-Janin. "Paul Rénouard." *Print Collector's Quarterly* 9 (1922): 129–188.

1970   Stein, Donna and Karshan, Donald. *L'Estampe Originale: A Catalogue Raisonné.* New York: The Museum of Graphic Art, 1970.

REVERE, PAUL (1735–1818)

1954   Brigham, Clarence Saunders. *Paul Revere's Engravings.* Worcester, Mass.: American Anitiquarian Society, 1954.

1969   Brigham, Clarence Saunders. *Paul Revere's Engravings.* 2nd ed. New York: Atheneum, 1969.

1970   Library of Congress. *American Prints in the Library of Congress: A Catalog of the Collection.* Compiled by Karen F. Beall. pp. 415–416. Baltimore: The Library of Congress, The Johns Hopkins Press, 1970.

REYNARD, GRANT TYSON (1887–1967)

1949   Reese, Albert. *American Prize Prints of the 20th Century.* p. 169. New York: American Artists Group, 1949.

1970   Library of Congress. *American Prints in the Library of Congress: A*   **189**
        Catalog of the Collection. Compiled by Karen F. Beall. p. 416.
        Baltimore: The Library of Congress, The Johns Hopkins Press,
        1970.

REYNOLDS, FREDERICK THOMAS (1882–   )

1920   "List of Plates Engraved by Frederick Reynolds." *The Print
        Connoisseur* 1 (1920): 18–23.

REYNOLDS, SIR JOSHUA (1755–1822)

1874   Hamilton, Edward. *A Catalogue Raissoné of the Engraved Works,
        1755–1820, of Sir Joshua Reynolds.* London: P. and D. Colnaghi,
        1874.

1884   Hamilton, Edward. *A Catalogue Raisonné of the Engraved Works,
        1755–1820, of Sir Joshua Reynolds.* 2nd ed. London: P. and D.
        Colnaghi, 1884.

1973   Hamilton, Edward. *A Catalogue Raisonné of the Engraved Works,
        1755–1820, of Sir Joshua Reynolds.* 1884. Reprint. Amsterdam: G.
        W. Hissink & Co., 1973.

RIBOT, THÉODULE (1823–1891)

1855   Fourcard, L. de. *Maîtres Modernes: Théodule Ribot, sa vie et ses
        oeuvres.* Paris, 1855.

1891   Béraldi, Henri. *Les Graveurs du XIXᵉ Siècle.* Vol. 11. Paris: L.
        Conquet, 1891.

1891   Lefort, Paul. "Les artistes contemporains: Théodule Ribot." *Ga-
        zette des Beaux-Arts,* October 1891, pp. 298–309.

RICH, FRANCIE (1947–   )

1973   Roswell Art Museum. *Francie Rich: Hand Colored Etchings.*
        Roswell, New Mexico, 1973.

RICHARDS, CERI (1903–   )

1963   Thompson, D. *Ceri Richards.* London: Methuen, 1963.

1973   Sanesi, R. *The Graphic Works of Ceri Richards.* Milan, 1973.

RICHARDS, F. DE BERG (1903–   )

1970   Library of Congress. *American Prints in the Library of Congress: A
        Catalog of the Collection.* Compiled by Karen F. Beall. pp. 416–417.
        Baltimore: The Library of Congress, The Johns Hopkins Press,
        1970.

190   **RICHARDS, FRED, R. E. (1878–1932)**

1918   Gibson, Frank. "Etchings of Fred Richards." *Studio* 72 (1918): 17.

RICHMOND, GEORGE, R.A. (1809–1896)

1930   Dodgson, Campbell. "The Engravings of George Richmond, R.A., and Welby Sherman." *Print Collector's Quarterly* 17 (1930): 353.

RICHTER, HANS THEO (1902–1969)

1962   Schmidt, W. H. T. *Richter*. Dresden, 1962.

1971   Victoria and Albert Museum. *Homage to Senefelder*. Introduction by Felix H. Man. London, 1971.

RICKETTS, CHARLES (1866–1931)

1927   French, Cecil. "The Wood-engravings of Charles Ricketts." *Print Collector's Quarterly* 14 (1927): 195–217.

1970   Stein, Donna and Karshan, Donald. *L'Estampe Originale: A Catalogue Raisonné*. New York: The Museum of Graphic Art, 1970.

RIGAUD, HYACINTHE (1659–1743)

1924   Thomas, Thomas H. "Rigau and his Engravers." *Print Connoisseur* 4 (1924): 195.

RIGGS, ROBERT (1896–1966)

1949   Reese, Albert. *American Prize Prints of the 20th Century*. p. 170. New York: American Artists Group, 1970.

1970   Library of Congress. *American Prints in the Library of Congress: A Catalog of the Collection*. Compiled by Karen F. Beall. pp. 418–419. Baltimore: The Library of Congress, The Johns Hopkins Press, 1970.

RIPPL-RONAI, JOZEF (1861–1927)

1944   Johnson, Una E. *Ambroise Vollard, Éditeur*. New York: Wittenborn and Co., 1944.

RIST, LUIGI (LOUIS G.) (1888–1959)

1949   Reese, Albert. *American Prize Prints of the 20th Century*. p. 171. New York: American Artists Group, 1949.

1970   Library of Congress. *American Prints in the Library of Congress: A Catalog of the Collection.* Compiled by Karen F. Beall. p. 420. Baltimore: The Library of Congress, The Johns Hopkins Press, 1970.

RIVE-KING MILLER, LOUISE *See* BOYER, LOUISE

RIVERA, DIEGO (1886–1957)

1939   Wolfe, B. D. *Diego Rivera: His Life and Times.* London: Hale, 1939.

RIVERS, LARRY (1923–   )

1970   Hunter, Sam. *Larry Rivers.* New York: Harry N. Abrams, 1970.

1970   Library of Congress. *American Prints in the Library of Congress: A Catalog of the Collection.* Compiled by Karen F. Beall. p. 420. Baltimore: The Library of Congress, The Johns Hopkins Press, 1970.

1972   Heckscher Museum. *Artists of Suffolk County: Part 6, Contemporary Prints.* Huntington, N.Y., 1972.

RIVIÈRE, BENJAMIN JEAN PIERRE HENRI (1864–1951)

1970   Stein, Donna and Karshan, Donald. *L'Estampe Originale: A Catalogue Raisonné.* New York: The Museum of Graphic Art, 1970.

ROBBINS, FREDERICK GOODRICH (1893–   )

1970   Library of Congress. *American Prints in the Library of Congress: A Catalog of the Collection.* Compiled by Karen F. Beall. pp. 420–421. Baltimore: The Library of Congress, The Johns Hopkins Press, 1970.

ROBERTSON, BRUCE

1917   "Bruce Robertson." *Art in Australia* (1917): 44.

ROBINS, WILLIAM P., R.E. (1882–1958)

1922   Salaman, M. C. "Etchings and Drypoints of W. P. Robins." *Bookman's Journal* 5 (1922): 113.

1925   Dodgson, Campbell. "The English Landscapes of W. P. Robins, R.E." *Bookman's Journal* 12 (1925): 93.

192   **ROBINSON, BOARDMAN (1876–1952)**

1946   Christ-Janer, Albert. *Boardman Robinson*. Chicago, Illinois: The University of Chicago Press, 1946.

1970   Library of Congress. *American Prints in the Library of Congress: A Catalog of the Collection*. Compiled by Karen F. Beall. p. 422. Baltimore: The Library of Congress, The Johns Hopkins Press, 1970.

ROBINSON, SIR JOHN CHARLES (1824–1913)

1906   Hind, A. M. "Etchings of Sir John Charles Robinson." *Studio* 26 (1906): 300.

1921   Allhusen, E. L. "Sir J. C. Robinson's Etchings." *Print Collector's Quarterly* 8 (1921): 299–322.

ROCHE, PIERRE (1855–1922)

1970   Stein, Donna and Karshan, Donald. *L'Estampe Originale: A Catalogue Raisonné*. New York: The Museum of Graphic Art, 1970.

ROCKER, FERMIN (20th C.)

1949   Reese, Albert. *American Prize Prints of the 20th Century*. p. 172. New York: American Artists Group, 1949.

1970   Library of Congress. *American Prints in the Library of Congress: A Catalog of the Collection*. Compiled by Karen F. Beall. pp. 422–423. Baltimore: The Library of Congress, The Johns Hopkins Press, 1970.

RODIN, FRANÇOIS-AUGUSTE-RENE (1840–1917)

1910   Delteil, Loys.*Le Peintre-Graveur Illustré: Rude, Barye, Carpeaux, Rodin*. Vol. 6. Paris: Chez l'auteur, 1910.

1944   Johnson, Una E. *Ambroise Vollard, Éditeur*. New York: Wittenborn and Co., 1944.

1969   Delteil, Loys. *Le Peintre-Graveur Illustré: Rude, Barye, Carpeaux, Rodin*. Vol. 6. 1910. Reprint. New York: Da Capo Press, 1969.

1970   Stein, Donna and Karshan, Donald. *L'Estampe Originale: A Catalogue Raisonné*. New York: The Museum of Graphic Art, 1970.

1967   Man, Felix H., ed. *Europäische Graphik*. Vol. 5. Munich: Galerie
        Wolfgang Ketterer, 1967.

ROGALSKI, WALTER R. (1925–   )

1954   Cleveland Museum of Art. *Prints and Drawings by Walter R.
        Rogalski*. Foreword by Louise S. Richards. Cleveland, 1954.

1970   Library of Congress. *American Prints in the Library of Congress: A
        Catalog of the Collection*. Compiled by Karen F. Beall. p. 423.
        Baltimore: The Library of Congress, The Johns Hopkins Press,
        1970.

ROHLFS, CHRISTIAN (1849–1938)

1950   Vogt, Paul. *Christian Rohlfs, Oeuvre Katalog der Druckgraphik*.
        Gottingen, 1950.

1957   Peters, H., ed. *Die Bauhaus Mappen: Neue Europäische Graphik
        1921–1923*. Cologne: C. Czwiklitzer, 1957.

1960   Vogt, Paul. *Chistian Rohlfs: das graphische werk*. Recklinghausen:
        A. Borgers, 1960.

1965   Wingler, H. M. *Graphic Work from the Bauhaus*. Greenwich,
        Conn.: New York Graphic Society, 1965.

1972   Sotriffer, Kristian. *Expressionism and Fauvism*. New York:
        McGraw-Hill Book Co., 1972.

ROHSE, OTTO (1925–   )

1972   Vogel, Carl et al. *Otto Rohse: Werkverzeichnis der Holzstiche,
        1951–1971*. 1972 [American distributor: New York: Wittenborn
        and Co.]

ROMANO, CLARE (MRS. ROSS) (1922–   )

1970   Library of Congress. *American Prints in the Library of Congress: A
        Catalog of the Collection*. Compiled by Karen F. Beall. p. 424.
        Baltimore: The Library of Congress, The Johns Hopkins Press,
        1970.

ROPS, FÉLICIEN (1833–1898)

1887   Ramiro, Evastène. *Catalogue déscriptif et analytique de l'oeuvre
        gravé de Félicien Rops*. Brussels: Daman and Paris: Conquet, 1887.

194   1921   Galerie Georges Giroux. *Félicien Rops: Vente publique et aux enchères de tableaux, aquarelles, dessins, eaux-fortes et lithographies.* [From the collection of Dr. Ottokar Mascha.] Brussels, 1921.

1928   Exsteens, Maurice. *L'Oeuvre Gravé et Lithographié de Félicien Rops.* Paris: Editions Pellet, 1928.

1968   Associated American Artists. *Félicien Rops: A Major Exhibition of Etchings and Lithographs.* New York, 1968.

1970   Stein, Donna and Karshan, Donald. *L'Estampe Originale: A Catalogue Raisonné.* New York: The Museum of Graphic Art, 1970.

ROSENBERG, LOUIS CONRAD (1890–   )

1925   Salaman, M. C. *Apollo* (1925): 256.

1928   Judge, Max. "The Constantinople Etchings of L. C. Rosenberg." *Print Collector's Quarterly* 15 (1928): 201–208.

1929   Salaman, Malcolm C. *Louis Conrad Rosenberg.* Modern Masters of Etching Series, no. 22. London: The Studio, Ltd., 1929.

1930   *Louis C. Rosenberg.* American Etchers Series. Vol. 10. New York: The Crafton Collection; London: P. and D. Colnaghi and Co., 1930.

1935   Arms, John Taylor. "The Drypoints of Louis Conrad Rosenberg, A.N.A." *Prints* 5 (1935): 1–9.

1949   Reese, Albert. *American Prize Prints of the 20th Century.* p. 173. New York: American Artists Group, 1949.

1970   Library of Congress. *American Prints in the Library of Congress: A Catalog of the Collection.* Compiled by Karen F. Beall. p. 425. Baltimore: The Library of Congress, The Johns Hopkins Press, 1970.

ROSENQUIST, JAMES (1933–   )

1970   Library of Congress. *American Prints in the Library of Congress: A Catalog of the Collection.* Compiled by Karen F. Beall. p. 426. Baltimore: The Library of Congress, The Johns Hopkins Press, 1970.

1972   Heckscher Museum. *Artists of Suffolk County: Part 6, Contemporary Prints.* Huntington, N. Y., 1972.

1973   Bernstein, Roberta. "Rosenquist Reflected: The Tampa Prints." *Print Collector's Newsletter* 4 (1973): 6–8.

1929   *Albert Rosenthal, Painter, Lithographer, Etcher*. Phil.: Privately printed, 1929.

1970   Library of Congress. *American Prints in the Library of Congress: A Catalog of the Collection*. Compiled by Karen F. Beall. p. 426. Baltimore: The Library of Congress, The Johns Hopkins Press, 1970.

ROSENTHAL, DORIS (–1970)

1949   Reese, Albert. *American Prize Prints of the 20th Century*. p. 174. New York: American Artists Group, 1949.

1970   Library of Congress. *American Prints in the Library of Congress: A Catalog of the Collection*. Compiled by Karen F. Beall. p. 426. Baltimore: The Library of Congress, The Johns Hopkins Press, 1970.

ROSENTHAL, MAX (1833–1918)

1921   "Catalogue Raisonné of the Mezzotints of Max Rosenthal." *Print Connoisseur* 2 (1921): 9.

1970   Library of Congress. *American Prints in the Library of Congress: A Catalog of the Collection*. Compiled by Karen F. Beall. p. 426. Baltimore: The Library of Congress, The Johns Hopkins Press, 1970.

ROSS, JOHN (1921–   )

1970   Library of Congress. *American Prints in the Library of Congress: A Catalog of the Collection*. Compiled by Karen F. Beall. p. 427. Baltimore: The Library of Congress, The Johns Hopkins Press, 1970.

ROSS, PIERRE SANFORD (1907–1954)

1949   Reese, Albert. *American Prize Prints of the 20th Century*. p. 175. New York: American Artists Group, 1970.

1970   Library of Congress. *American Prints in the Library of Congress: A Catalog of the Collection*. Compiled by Karen F. Beall. p. 427. Baltimore: The Library of Congress, The Johns Hopkins Press, 1970.

ROSSETTI, DANTE GABRIEL (1828–1882)

1915   Cary, Elisabeth Luther. "Dante Gabriel Rossetti, Illustrator." *Print Collector's Quarterly* 5 (1915): 317–339.

ROTH, ERNEST DAVID (1879–1964)

1911   "Catalogue of the Etched Work of Ernest D. Roth." *Print Collector's Quarterly* 1 (1911): 455–456.

1911   Mather, Frank Jewett, Jr. "The Etchings of Ernest D. Roth." *Print Collector's Quarterly* 1 (1911): 443–454.

1914   Madden, E. "A Rising Young Etcher." *Fine Arts Journal* [Chicago] (1914): 433.

1914   Madden, E. "Some Etchings by Ernest D. Roth." *Studio* 64 (1914): 13.

1929   *Ernest D. Roth.* American Etchers Series. Vol. 1. New York: The Crafton Collection; London: P. and D. Colnaghi, 1929.

1938   Arms, John Taylor. "Ernest D. Roth: Etcher." *Print Collector's Quarterly* 25 (1938): 33–57.

1949   Reese, Albert. *American Prize Prints of the 20th Century.* p. 176. New York: American Artists Group, 1949.

1970   Library of Congress. *American Prints in the Library of Congress: A Catalog of the Collection.* Compiled by Karen F. Beall. pp. 427–429. Baltimore: The Library of Congress, The Johns Hopkins Press, 1970.

ROTHENSTEIN, SIR WILLIAM (1872–1945)

1970   Stein, Donna and Karshan, Donald. *L'Estampe Originale: A Catalogue Raisonné.* New York: The Museum of Graphic Art, 1970.

ROUALT, GEORGES (1871–1958)

1926   Maritain, J. *Georges Rouault, Peintre et Graveur.* Paris, 1926.

1931   Roger-Marx, C. *L'Oeuvre gravé de Rouault.* Byblis, 1931.

1938   Wheeler, N. "The Prints of Roualt." *Art News* (1938).

1944   Johnson, Una E. *Ambroise Vollard, Éditeur.* New York: Wittenborn and Co., 1944.

1945   Soby, James Thrall. *Georges Roualt: Paintings and Prints.* New York: Museum of Modern Art, 1945.

1947   Soby, J. T. *Georges Roualt: Paintings and Prints.* 2nd. ed. New York: Museum of Modern Art, 1947.

1951   Morel, Abbé. *Le Miserère de Georges Roualt.* Paris, L'Etoile filante, **197**
        Le Seuil, 1951.

1956   *Roualt, Peintures, Gouaches, Miserère: Exposition.* Albi, 1956.

1962   Courthion, P. *Georges Roualt.* London and Paris: Flammarion,
        1962.

1963   Blunt, Anthony. *Georges Roualt: Miserère.* Boston Book and Art,
        1963.

1965   Marchiari, G. *Georges Roualt.* Paris: La Bibliothèque des Arts,
        1965.

1966   Kornfeld and Klipstein. *Georges Roualt: Graphik und Illustrierte
        Bücher.* Berne, 1966.

1972   Agustoni, F. "The Graphic Work of Georges Roualt." *Print
        Collector* [Milan: Grafica Sipiel, s. r.] 1 (1972): 14–35.

1972   Agustoni, F. and Bellini, Paolo. *Georges Roualt: Uomo e Artista.*
        With catalogue of graphics. Milan, 1972. [American distributor:
        New York: Wittenborn and Co.]

1972   Porter, D. *The Graphic Work of Georges Roualt: Exhibition
        catalogue.* South Bend, Ind.: University of Notre Dame, 1972.

1972   Sotriffer, Kristian. *Expressionism and Fauvism.* New York:
        McGraw-Hill Book Co., 1972.

ROUSSEAU, PIERRE-ÉTIENNE-THÉODORE (1812–1867)

1906   Delteil, Loys. *Le Peintre-Graveur Illustré: Millet, Rousseau, Dupré,
        Jongkind.* Vol. 1. Paris: Chez l'auteur, 1906.

1969   Delteil, Loys. *Le Peintre-Graveur Illustré: Millet, Rousseau, Dupré,
        Jongkind.* Vol. 1. 1906. Reprint. New York: Da Capo Press, 1969.

ROUSSEL, KER XAVIER (1867–1944)

1931   Werth, L. *Ker Xavier Roussel.* Paris, 1931.

1944   Johnson, Una E. *Ambroise Vollard, Éditeur.* New York: Witten-
        born and Co., 1944.

1965   Busch, D. Günter and Helms, H. *Gemälde, Handzeichnungen,
        Druckgraphik: Collection Salomon.* Bremen: Kunsthalle, 1965.

1967   Salomon, Jacques. *Ker Xavier Roussel.* Paris: La Bibliothèque des
        Arts, 1967.

198   1968   Chartier, Émile (Alain), and Salomon, Jacques. *L'Oeuvre Gravé de Ker Xavier Roussel*. Paris: Mercure de France, 1968.

1970   Kovler Gallery. *The Graphic Art of Valloton and the Nabis*. pp. 68–70. Chicago, Ill., 1970.

1970   Stein, Donna and Karshan, Donald. *L'Estampe Originale: A Catalogue Raisonné*. New York: The Museum of Graphic Art, 1970.

ROUSSEL, THEODORE (1847–1926)

1927   Dodgson, Campbell. "The Etchings of Theodore Roussel." *Print Collector's Quarterly* 14 (1927): 325–346.

ROWLANDSON, THOMAS (1756–1827)

1880   Grego, Joseph. *Rowlandson, the Caricaturist*. 2 vols. London: Chatto and Windus, 1880.

1886   Thornber, H. *Thomas Rowlandson and his Work*. Manchester, 1886.

1902   Grego, Joseph. "Our Graphic Humourists: Thomas Rowlandson." *Magazine of Arts* (1902): 210.

1903   Nevill, R. "Thomas Rowlandson." *The Printseller* 1 (1903): 63.

1909   Doin, J. "Thomas Rowlandson." *Gazette des Beaux-Arts* 1 (1909): 287.

1912   Mather, Frank Jewett, Jr. "Some Drawings by Thomas Rowlandson." *Print Collector's Quarterly* 2 (1912): 389–406.

1932   Rienaecker, Victor. "Rowlandson's Prints." *Print Collector's Quarterly* 19 (1932): 11–30.

1949   Falk, Bernard. *Thomas Rowlandson; his Life and Art*. London: Hutchinson, 1949.

RUDE, FRANÇOIS (1784–1855)

1910   Delteil, Loys. *Le Peintre-Graveur Illustré: Rude, Barye, Carpeaux, Rodin*. Vol. 6. Paris: Chez l'auteur, 1910.

1969   Delteil, Loys. *Le Peintre-Graveur Illustré: Rude, Barye, Carpeaux, Rodin*. Vol. 6. 1910. Reprint. New York: Da Capo Press, 1969.

RUELLAN, ANDREE (1905–   )

1949   Reese, Albert. *American Prize Prints of the 20th Century*. p. 177. New York: American Artists Group, 1949.

1970   Library of Congress. *American Prints in the Library of Congress: A* **199**
        Catalog of the Collection. Compiled by Karen F. Beall. p. 429.
        Baltimore: The Library of Congress, The Johns Hopkins Press,
        1970.

1972   Kraushaar Galleries. *Exhibitions.* New York, 1972.

1973   Mt. Holyoke College Art Museum and the Weyhe Gallery. *14*
        American Women Printmakers of the 30's and 40's. S. Hadley, Mass.
        and New York, 1973.

RUSCHA, EDWARD (1937–   )

1972   Larson, Philip. "Ruscha in Minneapolis." *Print Collector's News-*
        letter 3 (1972): 52–54.

1973   Pindell, Howardena. "Words with Ruscha." *Print Collector's News-*
        letter 3 (1973): 125–128.

RUSHBURY, HENRY, A.R.A., R.E. (1889–   )

1923   Schwabe, Randolph. "Etchings of Henry Rushbury." *Print Col-*
        lector's Quarterly 10 (1923): 403–443.

1928   Salaman, Malcolm C. *Henry Rushbury.* Modern Masters of Etching
        Series, no. 18. London: The Studio, Ltd., 1928.

RUTH, JAN DE *See* DE RUTH, JAN

RUZICKA, RUDOLPH (1883–   )

1948   Grolier Club. *The Engraved and Typographic Work of Rudolph*
        Ruzicka: an Exhibition. New York, 1948.

1970   Library of Congress. *American Prints in the Library of Congress: A*
        Catalog of the Collection. Compiled by Karen F. Beall. pp. 430–431.
        Baltimore: The Library of Congress, The Johns Hopkins Press,
        1970.

RYAN, ANNE (1889–1954)

1970   Library of Congress. *American Prints in the Library of Congress: A*
        Catalog of the Collection. Compiled by Karen F. Beall. p. 431.
        Baltimore: The Library of Congress, The Johns Hopkins Press,
        1970.

RYDER, CHAUNCEY FOSTER (1868–1949)

1949   Reese, Albert. *American Prize Prints of the 20th Century.* p. 178.
        New York: American Artists Group, 1949.

200   1970   Library of Congress. *American Prints in the Library of Congress: A Catalog of the Collection.* Compiled by Karen F. Beall. p. 432. Baltimore: The Library of Congress, The Johns Hopkins Press, 1970.

RYERSON, MARGERY AUSTEN (1886–   )

1922   "Etchings of Miss Margery Ryerson." *Art in America* 10 (1922): 257.

1933   "Prints of Children." *Art Digest* 7 (1933): 22.

1970   Library of Congress. *American Prints in the Library of Congress: A Catalog of the Collection.* Compiled by Karen F. Beall. p. 432. Baltimore: The Library of Congress, The Johns Hopkins Press, 1970.

1973   Mt. Holyoke College Art Museum and the Weyhe Gallery. *14 American Women Printmakers of the 30's and 40's.* S. Hadley, Mass. and New York, 1973.

RYSELBERGHE, THEO VAN (1862–1926)

1944   Johnson, Una E. *Ambroise Vollard, Éditeur.* New York: Wittenborn and Co., 1944.

1970   Stein, Donna and Karshan, Donald. *L'Estampe Originale: A Catalogue Raisonné.* New York: The Museum of Graphic Art, 1970.

RYSSEL, PAUL VAN *See* GACHET, PAUL

SAINT AUBIN, AUGUSTIN de (1736–1807)

1931   Francis, Eric C. "Augustin de Saint Aubin." *Print Collector's Quarterly* 18 (1931): 151–173.

SAINT-AUBIN, GABRIEL de (1724–1780)

1914   Dacier, E. *L'Oeuvre Gravé de Gabriel de Saint-Aubin: Notice Historique et Catalogue Raisonné.* Paris, 1914.

1964   Adhémar, Jean. *Graphic Art of the 18th Century.* New York: McGraw-Hill Book Co., 1964.

SALLBERG, HARALD (1895–   )

1935   Jungmarker, Gunnar. "Harald Sallberg." *Print Collector's Quarterly* 22 (1935): 348–360.

1892   Monkhouse, Cosmo. "The Sandby's." *Portfolio* 23 (1892): 194.

1892   Sandby, William. *Thomas and Paul Sandby, Royal Academicians.* London: Seeley and Co., 1892.

SANDYS, FREDERICK (1832–1904)

1917   Cary, Elisabeth Luther. "Frederick Sandys." *Print Collector's Quarterly* 7 (1917): 201–216.

SANDZEN, SVEN BIRGER (1871–1964)

1923   "Catalogue Raisonné of the Work of Birger Sandzen." *Print Connoisseur* 3 (1923): 227–236.

1923   Powell, Minna K. "Sandzen's Lithographs of the Smoky Valley." *Print Connoisseur* 3 (1923): 221.

1923   Smalley, Carl J. "The Prints of Birger Sandzen." *Print Connoisseur* 3 (1923): 215.

1970   Library of Congress. *American Prints in the Library of Congress: A Catalog of the Collection.* Compiled by Karen F. Beall. p. 433. Baltimore: The Library of Congress, The Johns Hopkins Press, 1970.

SANSÒ, JUVENAL

1964   Cleveland Museum of Art. *An Exhibition of Works by Juvenal Sansò: Including a Complete Checklist of his Prints.* Foreword by Louise S. Richards. Cleveland, Ohio, 1964.

SANTOMASO, GIUSEPPE (1907–   )

1959   Apollonio, U. *Giuseppe Santomaso.* Amriswil: Bodensee Vlg., 1959.

SARGENT, JOHN SINGER (1856–1925)

1926   Belleroche, Albert. "The Lithographs of Sargent." *Print Collector's Quarterly* 13 (1926): 31–44.

1926   Dodgson, Campbell. "Catalogue of the Lithographs of John Singer Sargent, R. A." *Print Collector's Quarterly* 13 (1926): 44–45.

1970   Library of Congress. *American Prints in the Library of Congress: A Catalog of the Collection.* Compiled by Karen F. Beall. p. 434. Baltimore: The Library of Congress, The Johns Hopkins Press, 1970.

SAUER, LEROY D. (1894–1959)

1949   Reese, Albert. *American Prize Prints of the 20th Century*. p. 179.
New York: American Artists Group, 1949.

1970   Library of Congress. *American Prints in the Library of Congress: A
Catalog of the Collection*. Compiled by Karen F. Beall. p. 434.
Baltimore: The Library of Congress, The Johns Hopkins Press,
1970.

1972   June 1 Gallery of Fine Art. *Leroy D. Sauer's America: A
Retrospective of Etchings and Linocuts by an Artist of the American
Scene*. Washington, D.C., 1972.

SAVELLI, ANGELO (1911–   )

1965   Farrar, Joan. "The Embossed Lithographs of Angelo Savelli."
Artist's Proof 8 (1965): 41–42.

SCHANKER, LOUIS (1903–   )

1943   The Brooklyn Museum. *Abstractions: The Woodblock Color Prints
of Louis Schanker*. Brooklyn, N.Y., 1943.

1970   Library of Congress. *American Prints in the Library of Congress: A
Catalog of the Collection*. Compiled by Karen F. Beall. p. 436.
Baltimore: The Library of Congress, The Johns Hopkins Press,
1970.

1973   Jane Haslem Gallery. *The Innovators: Renaissance in American
Printmaking*. Washington, D.C., 1973.

SCHARFF, EDWIN (1887–1955)

1956   Hamburg Kunstverein. *Catalogue of the Retrospective Exhibition
Staged in Memory of Scharff*. Hamburg, 1956.

1957   Peters, Heinz, ed. *Die Bauhaus Mappen: Neue Europäische Graphik
1921–1923*. Cologne, Czwiklitzer, 1957.

1965   Wingler, H. M. *Graphic Work from the Bauhaus*. Greenwich,
Conn.: New York Graphic Society, 1965.

1970   Library of Congress. *American Prints in the Library of Congress: A
Catalog of the Collection*. Compiled by Karen F. Beall. p. 436.
Baltimore: The Library of Congress, The Johns Hopkins Press,
1970.

SCHIELE, EGON (1890–1918)

1966   Kallir, Otto. *Egon Schiele: Oeuvre Catalogue*. New York: Crown,
1966.

1970   Kallir, Otto. *Egon Schiele: The Graphic Work*. New York: Crown,   **203**
1970.

1972   Sotriffer, Kristian. *Expressionism and Fauvism*. New York:
McGraw-Hill Book Co., 1972.

SCHILLING, ALEXANDER (1859–1937)

1937   Cortissoz, Royal; Walker, Horatio; Giles, Howard, and others. *The Book of Alexander Schilling*. New York: The Paisley Press, Inc., 1937.

1970   Library of Congress. *American Prints in the Library of Congress: A Catalog of the Collection*. Compiled by Karen F. Beall. pp. 436–438. Baltimore: The Library of Congress, The Johns Hopkins Press, 1970.

SCHLEMMER, OSKAR (1888–1943)

1957   Peters, Heinz, ed. *Die Bauhaus Mappen: Neue Europäische Graphik 1921–23*. Cologne: Czwiklitzer, 1957.

1965   Grohmann, Will. *Oskar Schlemmer: Zeichnungen und Graphik-Oeuvre Katalog*. Stuttgart: G. Hatje, 1965.

1965   Wingler, H. M. *Graphic Work from the Bauhaus*. Greenwich, Conn.: New York Graphic Society, 1965.

        Nachbauer, Wenzel. *Oskar Schlemmer: Das Graphische Werk*. A complete catalogue raisonné. Edited by Tut Schlemmer and Dieter Keller. Amsterdam: Erasmus.

SCHMIDT-ROTTLUFF, KARL (1884–   )

1924   Schapire, Rosa. *Karl Schmidt-Rottluffs graphisches Werk bis 1923*. Berlin: Euphorion-Verlag, 1924. Reprint. Hamburg: Hauswedell, 1965.

1957   Peters. Heinz *Die Bauhaus Mappen: Neue Europäische Graphik 1921–23*. Cologne: C. Czwiklitzer, 1957.

1964   Rathenau, Ernst. *Karl Schmidt-Rottluffs: das graphische werk nach 1923*. [A sequel to the above.] Hamburg, 1964.

1965   Schapire, Rosa. *Karl Schmidt-Rottluffs graphisches Werk bis 1923*. 1924. Reprint. Hamburg: Hauswedell, 1965.

1965   Wingler, H. M. *Graphic Work from the Bauhaus*. Greenwich, Conn.: New York Graphic Society, 1965.

1972   Sotriffer, Kristian. *Expressionism and Fauvism*. New York: McGraw-Hill Book Co., 1972.

SCHMUTZER, FERNINAND (1870–1928)

1922   Weixlgärtner, Arpad. *Das Radierte Werk von Ferdinand Schmutzer 1896–1921: ein Verzeichnis.* Vienna: F. Mandel, 1922.

1930   Weixlgärtner, Arpad. "Ferdinand Schmutzer." *Print Collector's Quarterly* 17 (1930): 375–394.

SCHNEIDER, GÉRARD (1896–   )

1959   Pobé, M. *Gérard Schneider.* Paris: Musée de poche, 1959.

SCHRAG, KARL (1912–   )

1949   Reese, Albert. *American Prize Prints of the 20th Century.* p. 180. New York: American Artists Group, 1949.

1960   Gordon, John. *Karl Schrag.* New York: American Federation of Arts, 1960.

1970   Library of Congress. *American Prints in the Library of Congress: A Catalog of the Collection.* Compiled by Karen F. Beall. p. 438. Baltimore: The Library of Congress, The Johns Hopkins Press, 1970.

1972   Syracuse University. *Karl Schrag: A Catalogue Raisonné of the Graphic Works 1939–1970.* Syracuse, N.Y., 1972.

1973   Jane Haslem Gallery. *The Innovators: Renaissance in American Printmaking.* Washington, D.C., 1973.

SCHREIBER, GEORGES (1904–   )

1949   Reese, Albert. *American Prize Prints of the 20th Century.* p. 181. New York: American Artists Group, 1949.

1970   Library of Congress. *American Prints in the Library of Congress: A Catalog of the Collection.* p. 439. Baltimore: The Library of Congress, The Johns Hopkins Press, 1970.

SCHREYER, LOTHAR (1886–1966)

1957   Peters, H. ed. *Die Bauhaus Mappen: Neue Europäische Graphik 1921–23. Cologne: C. Czwiklitzer, 1957.*

1965   Wingler, H. M. *Graphic Work from the Bauhaus.* Greenwich, Conn.: New York Graphic Society, 1965.

SCHULTHEISS, CARL M. (1885–1963)

1949   Reese, Albert. *American Prize Prints of the 20th Century.* p. 182. New York: American Artists Group, 1949.

1970   Library of Congress. *American Prints in the Library of Congress: A Catalog of the Collection.* p. 439. Baltimore: The Library of Congress, The Johns Hopkins Press, 1970.

SCHUMACHER, EMIL (1912–   )

1958   Schultze-Vellinghausen, A. *Emil Schumacher.* Cologne: Du Mont Schauberg, 1958.

SCHWABE, CARLOZ (1866–1926)

1970   Stein, Donna and Karshan, Donald. *L'Estampe Originale: A Catalogue Raisonné.* New York: The Museum of Graphic Art, 1970.

SCHWARTZ, AUBREY (1928–   )

1970   Library of Congress. *American Prints in the Library of Congress: A Catalog of the Collection.* Compiled by Karen F. Beall. p. 440. Baltimore: The Library of Congress, The Johns Hopkins Press, 1970.

1972   Heckscher Museum. *Artists of Suffolk County: Part 6, Contemporary Prints.* Huntington, N.Y., 1972.

SCHWIND, MORITZ von (1804–1861)

1906   Weigmann, Otto Albert, ed. *Schwind, des meisters Werke in 1265 abbildungen.* Stuttgart und Leipzig: Deutsche Verlags-anstalt, 1906.

1971   Victoria and Albert Museum. *Homage to Senefelder.* Introduction by Felix H. Man. London, 1971.

SCHWITTERS, KURT (1887–1948)

1963   Steinitz, Kate T. *Kurt Schwitters: Erinnerungen aus den jahren 1918–1930.* Zurich: Arche, 1963.

1965   Wingler, H. M. *Graphic Work from the Bauhaus.* Greenwich, Conn.: New York Graphic Society, 1965.

1967   Schmalenbach, Werner. *Kurt Schwitters: Leben und werk.* Cologne: Du Mont Schauberg, 1967.

SEEWALD, RICHARD (1889–   )

1972   Sotriffer, Kristian. *Expressionism and Fauvism.* New York: McGraw-Hill Book Co., 1972.

SEGONZAC, ANDRÉ DUNOYER DE *See* DUNOYER DE SEGONZAC, ANDRÉ

206   SÉGUIN, ARMAND (1869–1903)

1944   Johnson, Una E. *Ambroise Vollard, Éditeur*. New York: Witten-
         born and Co., 1944.

1970   Stein, Donna and Karshan, Donald. *L'Estampe Originale: A
         Catalogue Raisonné*. New York: The Museum of Graphic Art,
         1970.

SELIGMANN, KURT (1900–1964)

1970   Gimpel and Weitzenhoffer Ltd. *Original Prints of the Surrealists*.
         New York, 1970.

1970   Library of Congress. *American Prints in the Library of Congress: A
         Catalog of the Collection*. Compiled by Karen F. Beall. p. 441.
         Baltimore: The Library of Congress, The Johns Hopkins Press,
         1970.

1973   Frumkin Gallery. *Kurt Seligmann*. Chicago, Ill., 1973.

1973   La Boetie Gallery. *Kurt Seligmann: His Graphic Work*. New York,
         1973.

SENEFELDER, ALOYS (1771–1834)

1818   Senefelder, Aloys. *Vollständiges Lehrbuch der Steindruckerey*.
         Munich: Thienemann, 1818.

1819   Senefelder, Aloys. *L'art de la lithogrphie*. Paris: Treuttel and Würtz,
         1819.

1819   Senefelder, Aloys. *A Complete Course of Lithography*. London: R.
         Ackermann, 1819.

1925   Dussler Luitpold. *Die Incunabeln der Deutschen Lithographie*.
         Berlin: H. Tiedemann, 1925.

1971   Victoria and Albert Museum. *Homage to Senefelder*. Introduction
         by Felix H. Man. London, 1971.

SÉRUSIER, LOUIS PAUL HENRI (1863–1927)

1970   Kovler Gallery. *The Graphic Art of Valloton and the Nabis*. pp.
         71–72. Chicago, Ill., 1970.

1970   Stein, Donna and Karshan, Donald *L'Estampe Originale: A
         Catalogue Raisonné*. New York: The Museum of Graphic Art,
         1970.

1974   Weisberg, Gabriel P. *Social Concern and the Worker: French Prints*   **207**
from 1830–1910. Salt Lake City, Utah: Utah Museum of Fine Arts,
1974.

SEVERINI, GINO (1883–1966)

1957   Peters, Heinz, ed. *Die Bauhaus Mappen: Neue Europäische Graphik
1921–23*. Cologne: C. Czwiklitzer, 1957.

1965   Wingler, H. M. *Graphic Work from the Bauhaus*. Greenwich,
Conn.: New York Graphic Society, 1965.

SEWARDS, MICHELE BOURQUE (1944–   )

1974   Roswell Museum and Art Center. *Michele Bourque Sewards:
Lithographs and Drawings*. Roswell, N. Mex., 1974.

SHAHN, BEN (1898–1969)

1957   Peck, Edward S. "Ben Shahn: His 'Personal Statement' in Drawings and Prints." *Impression,* September 1957, pp. 6–13.

1957   Soby, James Thrall. *Ben Shahn: Graphic Work*. London: Cory,
Adams and MacKay, 1957.

1959   Farr, Dennis. "Graphic Work of Ben Shahn at the Leicester
Galleries." *Burlington Magazine* [London] December 1959, p. 470.

1965   Soby, James Thrall. *Ben Shahn: Graphic Work*. 1957. 2nd printing.
London: Cory, Adams and MacKay, 1965.

1967   McNulty, Kneeland. *The Collected Prints of Ben Shahn*. Philadelphia: The Philadelphia Museum of Art, 1967.

1970   Library of Congress. *American Prints in the Library of Congress: A
Catalog of the Collection*. Compiled by Karen F. Beall. pp. 442–443.
Baltimore: The Library of Congress, The Johns Hopkins Press,
1970.

1973   Prescott, C. W. *The Complete Graphic Works of Ben Shahn*. New
York: Quadrangle Books, 1973.

SHANNON, CHARLES HAZELWOOD (1863–1937)

1910   Ricketts, Charles. *L'Art et les Artistes*. [Paris] 10 (1910).

1914   Derby, Georges. "The Lithographs of Charles Hazelwood Shannon." *Print Collector's Quarterly* 4 (1914): 393–420.

1920   Walker, R. A. and Derry, George. *The Lithographs of Charles
Shannon; With a Catalogue of Lithographs Issued Between the Years
1904–1918*. London, 1920.

208

1938   P. and D. Colnaghi. *Exhibition of the Lithographs of the Late Charles Shannon.* London, 1938.

1944   Johnson, Una E. *Ambroise Vollard, Éditeur.* New York: Wittenborn and Co., 1944.

1970   Stein, Donna and Karshan, Donald *L'Estampe Originale: A Catalogue Raissonné* New York: The Museum of Graphic Art, 1970.

SHAPIRO, DAVID (1916–   )

1949   University of British Columbia Art Gallery. *David Shapiro: Recent Work.* Vancouver, B.C., 1949.

1963   Milch Galleries. *David Shapiro: Recent Work.* New York, 1963.

1970   Library of Congress. *American Prints in the Library of Congress: A Catalog of the Collection.* Compiled by Karen F. Beall. p. 443. Baltimore: The Library of Congress, The Johns Hopkins Press, 1970.

1971   Galleria Dell'Orso. *David Shapiro: Paintings, Prints, Drawings.* Milan, 1971.

1971   Micheli, Mario de. *David Shapiro: Dipinti, Disegni, Incisioni.* Milano: Galleria Dell'Orso, 1971.

1971   Micheli, Mario de. *David Shapiro: Dipinti, Disegni, Incisioni.* Giugno: Galleria Blue Chips, 1971.

SHARP, WILLIAM (1900–1961)

1949   Reese, Albert. *American Prize Prints of the 20th Century.* p. 183. New York: American Artists Group, 1949.

1970   Library of Congress. *American Prints in the Library of Congress: A Catalogue of the Collection.* Compiled by Karen F. Beall. pp. 443–444. Baltimore: The Library of Congress, The Johns Hopkins Press, 1970.

SHEELER, CHARLES (1883–1965)

1938   Rourke, Constance M. *Charles Sheeler: Artist in the American Tradition.* New York: Harcourt, 1938.

1939   Williams, William C. *Charles Sheeler: Paintings, Drawings, Photographs.* New York: Museum of Modern Art, 1939.

1963   Dochterman, L. N. "The Stylistic Development of the Work of Charles Sheeler." Ph. D. dissertation, State University of Iowa, 1963. Ann Arbor, Mich.: University Microfilms.

1970 Library of Congress. *American Prints in the Library of Congress: A Catalog of the Collection.* Compiled by Karen F. Beall. pp. 444–445. Baltimore: The Library of Congress, The Johns Hopkins Press, 1970.

SHEPPERSON, CLAUDE ALLIN, A. R. A., A. R. E. (1867–1921)

1923 Hardie, Martin. "Etchings and Lithographs of Claude Shepperson, A. R. A., R. E." *Print Collector's Quarterly* 10 (1923): 444–471.

SHERMAN, EFFIM H. (1889–)

1949 Reese, Albert. *American Prize Prints of the 20th Century.* p. 184. New York: American Artists Group, 1949.

1970 Library of Congress. *American Prints in the Library of Congress: A Catalog of the Collection.* Compiled by Karen F. Beall. p. 444. Baltimore: The Library of Congress, The Johns Hopkins Press, 1970.

SHERMAN, WELBY (19th C.)

1930 Dodgson, Campbell. "The Engravings of George Richmond, R. A., and Welby Sherman." *Print Collector's Quarterly* 17 (1930): 353.

SHIRLOW, JOHN

1916–17 Lindsay, Lionel. "John Shirlow." *Art in Australia* (1916–17): 14.

SHOKLER, HARRY (1896–)

1949 Reese, Albert. *American Prize Prints of the 20th Century.* p. 185. New York: American Artists Group, 1949.

1970 Library of Congress. *American Prints in the Library of Congress: A Catalogue of the Collection.* Compiled by Karen F. Beall. p. 449. Baltimore: The Library of Congress, The Johns Hopkins Press, 1970.

SHORT, SIR FRANK JOB, R. A., P. R. E. (1857–1945)

1906 Strange, Edward Fairbrother. "Mezzotint and Etched Work of Frank Short." *Studio* 38 (1906): 50.

1908 Strange, Edward Fairbrother. *Etched and Engraved Work of Frank Short, A. R. A., R. E.* London: G. Allen & Sons, 1908.

1923 Wilder. F. L. "Undescribed States of Etchings and Mezzotints by Sir Frank Short." *Bookman's Journal* 7 (1923): 174.

1924 Laver, James. "Sir Frank Short, R. A., P. R. E." *Bookman's Journal* 10 (1924): 168.

210   1925   Salaman, Malcolm. *Sir Frank Short, R.A., P.R.E.* Modern Masters of Etching Series, no. 5. London: The Studio, Ltd., 1925.

1938   Hardie, Martin. *The Liber Studiorum mezzotints of Sir Frank Short, R.A., P.R.E., after J. M. W. Turner, R.A.* Vol 1. London: Print Collector's Club, 1938.

1939   Hardie, Martin. *The Mezzotints and Aquatints of Sir Frank Short, R.A., P.R.E., Other Than Those for the Liber Studiorum.* Vol. 2. London: Print Collector's Club, 1939.

1940   Hardie, Martin. *The Etchings, Drypoints, Lithographs of Sir Frank Short, R.A., P.R.E.* Vol. 3. London: Print Collector's Club, 1940.

SHOULBERG, HARRY (1903–   )

1949   Reese, Albert. *American Prize Prints of the 20th Century.* p. 186. New York: American Artists Group, 1949.

1970   Library of Congress. *American Prints in the Library of Congress: A Catalog of the Collection.* Compiled by Karen F. Beall. p. 447. Baltimore: The Library of Congress, The Johns Hopkins Press, 1970.

SICKERT, WALTER RICHARD, A.R.A., A.R.E. (1860–1942)

1923   Murry, J. Middleton. "The Etchings of Walter Sickert." *Print Collector's Quarterly* 10 (1923): 31.

1929   Gaunt, W. "The Etched Work of W. Richard Sickert." *Studio* 97 (1929): 337.

1941   Emmons, Robert. *The Life and Opinions of Walter Richard Sickert.* London: Faber, 1941.

1947   Sickert, Walter R. *A Free House: or the Artist as Craftsman.* London: MacMillan, 1947.

SIGNAC, PAUL (1863–1935)

1921   Roger-Marx, Claude. *Signac.* Vienna, 1921.

1922   Couturier, L. *Signac.* Paris. Crès, 1922.

1944   Johnson, Una E. *Ambroise Vollard, Éditeur.* New York: Wittenborn and Co., 1944.

1962   Roger-Marx, Claude. *La Gravure originale au XIXᵉ siècle.* Paris: Somogy, 1962.

1962   Wick, Peter. "Some Drawings related to Signac Prints." *Prints*. edited by Carl Zigrosser. New York: Holt, Rinehart and Winston, 1962.

1970   Stein, Donna and Karshan, Donald. *L'Estampe Originale: A Catalogue Raisonné*. New York: The Museum of Graphic Art, 1970.

1974   Kornfeld, E. W. and Wick, Peter A. *Catalogue Raisonné de l'oeuvre gravé et lithographié de Paul Signac*. Berne: Editions Kornfeld et Klipstein, 1974.

SILVA, VIEIRA DA (1908–   )

1964   Calruccio, L. *Vieira da Silva: Catalogue of the Exhibition at the Galleria Civica d'Arte Moderna*. Turin, 1964.

SILVERMAN, MEL (1931–1966)

1964   Associated American Artists. *Mel Silverman: Woodcuts*. New York, 1964.

1967   Cole, Sylvan, Jr. *Mel Silverman: Memorial Exhibition*. New York: Associated American Artists, 1967.

SIMKHOVITCH, SIMKA (1893–1949)

1949   Reese, Albert. *American Prize Prints of the 20th Century*. p. 187. New York: American Artists Group, 1949.

SIMMONS, WILLIAM FRANCIS BERNARD (1884–1949)

1921   Rihani, Ameen. "Will Simmons and his Animals." *Print Connoisseur* 2 (1921): 95.

1921   "Catalogue Raisonné of the Etchings of Will Simmons." *Print Connoisseur* 2 (1921): 111.

1925   Simmons, Will. "Etching Wild Life." *American Magazine of Art* 16 (1925): 185.

SIMON, LUCIEN (1861–   )

1944   Johnson, Una E. *Ambroise Vollard, Éditeur*. New York: Wittenborn and Co., 1944.

SIMPSON, BRANTINGHAM

1924   Laver, James. "Mr. Brantingham Simpson's Estampes Galantes." *Bookman's Journal* 9 (1924): 174.

212   **SIMPSON, JOSEPH (1879–1939)**

1932   Fell, H. Granville. "The Etched Work of Joseph Simpson." *Print Collector's Quarterly* 19 (1932): 213–233.

SIMS, CHARLES, R.A. (1873–1928)

1931   Dodgson, Campbell. "The Engraved Work of Charles Sims, R.A." *Print Collector's Quarterly* 18 (1931): 375–387.

SINGIER, GUSTAVE (1909–   )

1958   Schmückinger, R. *Das graphische Werk.* Braunschweig: Schmücking, 1958.

SIQUEIROS, DAVID ALFARO (1898–1974)

1957   Haab, Armin. *Mexikanische Graphik.* Teufen: A. Niggli, 1957.

1957   Haab, Armin. *Mexican Graphic Art.* English edition. Switzerland: C. C. Palmer, 1957.

1961   Tibol, Raquel. *Siqueiros: introductor de realidades.* Mexico: University Press, 1961.

1972   Sotriffer, Kristian *Expressionism and Fauvism.* New York: McGraw-Hill Book Co., 1972.

SISLEY, ALFRED (1839–1899)

1923   Delteil, Loys. *Le Peintre-graveur Illustré: Pissarro, Sisley, Renoir.* Vol. 17. Paris: Chez l'auteur, 1923.

1944   Johnson, Una E. *Ambroise Vollard, Éditeur.* New York: Wittenborn and Co., 1944.

1969   Delteil, Loys. *Le Peintre–graveur Illustré: Pissarro, Sisley, Renoir.* Vol. 17. 1923. Reprint. New York: Da Capo Press, 1969.

1972   Leymarie, Jean and Melot, Michel. *The Graphic Works of the Impressionists: The Complete Prints of Manet, Pissarro, Renoir, Cézanne, and Sisley.* New York: Abrams, 1972.

SLEVOGT, MAX (1868–1932)

1921   Waldmann, Emil. *Max Slevogt's graphische kunst.* Dresden: Arnold, 1921.

1936   Rümann, Arthur. *Verzeichnis der Graphik von Max Slevogt in Büchern und Mappenwerken.* Hamburg: Gesellschaft der Bücherfreunde zu Hamburg, 1936.

1936   Waldmann, Emil. "The Graphic Art of Max Slevogt." *Print Collector's Quarterly* 23 (1936): 191–210.

1962   Sievers, J. and Waldmann, E. *Max Slevogt.* Heidelberg and Berlin, 1962.

1971   Victoria and Albert Museum: *Homage to Senefelder.* Introduction by Felix H. Man. London, 1971.

SLOAN, HELEN FARR (1911–   )

1973   Mount Holyoke College Art Museum and the Weyhe Gallery *14 American Women Printmakers of the 30's and 40's.* South Hadley, Mass, and New York, 1973.

SLOAN, JOHN (1871–1951)

1949   Reese, Albert. *American Prize Prints of the 20th Century.* p. 188. New York: American Artists Group, 1949.

1956   Zigrosser, Carl. "John Sloan Memorial: His complete Graphic Work." *The Philadelphia Museum Bulletin* 51 (1956).

1969   Morse, Peter. *John Sloan's Prints: A Catalogue Raisonné of the Etchings, Lithographs, and Posters.* New Haven, Conn.: Yale University Press, 1969.

1970   Library of Congress. *American Prints in the Library of Congress: A Catalog of the Collection.* Compiled by Karen F. Beall. pp. 449–457. Baltimore: The Library of Congress, The Johns Hopkins Press, 1970.

SMILLIE, JAMES D. (1833–1909)

1881   Koehler, S. R. *American Art Review* 2 (1881): 58.

1894   "James D. Smillie: Etcher." *Quarterly Illustrator* July, 1894.

1910   The Century Association. *Some Work by James D. Smillie.* New York, 1910.

SMITH, JOHN RAPHAEL (1752–1812)

1883   Smith, John Chaloner. *British Mezzotint Portraits.* London: H. Sotheran & Co., 1883.

1902   Frankau, Julia. *John Raphael Smith: His Life and Work.* 1902.

1922   Hall, Mark W. "George, Prince of Wales, by J. R. Smith, after Thomas Gainsborough." *Print Collector's Quarterly* 9 (1922): 315–320.

SMITH, JULES ANDRÉ (1880–   )

1914   Laurvik, J. N. "J. André Smith." *Print Collector's Quarterly* 4 (1914): 167–182.

1969   Andrew D. White Museum. *André Smith*. Ithaca, N.Y.: Cornell University, 1969.

1970   Library of Congress. *American Prints in The Library of Congress: A Catalog of the Collection*. Compiled by Karen F. Beall. pp. 458–459. Baltimore: The Library of Congress, The Johns Hopkins Press, 1970.

SMITH, MOISHE (1929–   )

1970   Library of Congress. *American Prints in the Library of Congress: A Catalog of the Collection*. Compiled by Karen F. Beall. pp. 459–460. Baltimore: The Library of Congress, The Johns Hopkins Press, 1970.

1974   Associated American Artists. *Moishe Smith*. Introduction by Alan Fern. New York, 1974.

SMITH, PERCY JOHN (1882–   )

1921   Dodgson, Campbell. "Mr. Percy Smith's 'Dance of Death'." *Print Collector's Quarterly* 8 (1921): 323.

1921   Leake, Stafford. "War and Peace in the Etchings and Drawings of Percy Smith." *Bookman's Journal* 8 (1926): 215.

SODERBERG, YNGVE EDWARD (1896–   )

1949   Reese, Albert. *American Prize Prints of the 20th Century*. p. 189. New York: American Artists Group, 1949.

1970   Library of Congress. *American Prints in the Library of Congress: A Catalog of the Collection*. Compiled by Karen F. Beall. pp. 460–461. Baltimore: The Library of Congress, The Johns Hopkins Press, 1970.

SOFFICI, ARDENGO (1879–   )

1961   Bartolini, Sigfrido. *Ardengo Soffici: Engravings*. Milan: Prandi, 1961.

SOLES, WILLIAM (1914–   )

1949   Reese, Albert. *American Prize Prints of the 20th Century*. p. 190. New York: American Artists Group, 1949.

1970   Library of Congress. *American Prints in the Library of Congress: A*   **215**
             Catalog of the Collection. Compiled by Karen F. Beall. p. 461.
             Baltimore: The Library of Congress, The Johns Hopkins Press,
             1970.

SOMM, HENRY (1844–1907)

1970   Stein, Donna and Karshan, Donald. *L'Estampe Originale: A*
             Catalogue Raisonné. New York: The Museum of Graphic Art,
             1970.

SONDERBORG, KURT (1923–   )

1964   Man, Felix H., ed. *Europäische Graphik.* Vol. 2. Munich: Galerie
             Wolfgang Ketterer, 1964.

SOPER, EILEEN (1905–   )

1923   Salaman, Malcolm C. "Miss Eileen Soper's Etchings." *Studio* 85
             (1923): 262.

SOPER, GEORGE THOMAS, R.E. (1870–   )

1920   Salaman, Malcolm C. "Etchings and Dry-Points of George Soper,
             R.E." *Studio* 80 (1920).

SOULAGES, PIERRE (1919–   )

1958   Juin, H. *Soulages.* Paris: Musée de poche, 1958.

SOYER, MOSES (1899–1974)

1970   Library of Congress. *American Prints in the Library of Congress: A*
             Catalog of the Collection. Compiled by Karen F. Beall. p. 461.
             Baltimore: The Library of Congress, The Johns Hopkins Press,
             1970.

1972   Heckscher Museum. *Artists of Suffolk County: Part 6, Contemporary*
             Prints. Huntington, N.Y., 1972.

SOYER, RAPHAEL (1899–   )

1942   Zigrosser, Carl. *The Artist in America: 24 Close-ups of Contemporary*
             Printmakers. New York: Alfred A. Knopf, 1942.

1949   Reese, Albert. *American Prize Prints of the 20th Century.* p. 191.
             New York: American Artists Group, Inc., 1949.

1967   Cole, Sylvan, Jr. *Raphael Soyer: Fifty Years of Printmaking,*
             1917–1967. New York: Da Capo Press, 1967.

216   1970   Library of Congress. *American Prints in the Library of Congress: A Catalog of the Collection*. Compiled by Karen F. Beall. p. 462. Baltimore: The Library of Congress, The Johns Hopkins Press, 1970.

SPACAL, LUIGI (1907–   )

1968   Palluchini, R. and Russoli, F. *Opera Grafica 1936–1967*. Milan: Scheiwiller, 1968.

SPARE, AUSTIN OSMON (1888–   )

1908   Sketchley, R. E. "Austin Spare." *Art Journal* (1908): 50.

SPELLMAN, COREEN (1905–   )

1949   Reese, Albert. *American Prize Prints of the 20th Century*. p. 192. New York: American Artists Group, 1949.

SPENCE, ROBERT, R.E. (1871–   )

1917   Gibson, F. "Etchings of Robert Spence, R.E." *Studio* 69 (1917): 29.

SPRUANCE, BENTON (1904–1967)

1942   Zigrosser, Carl. *The Artist in America: 24 Close-ups of Contemporary Printmakers*. New York: Alfred A. Knopf, 1942.

1949   Reese, Albert. *American Prize Prints of the 20th Century*. p. 193. New York: American Artists Group, 1949.

1970   Library of Congress. *American Prints in the Library of Congress: A Catalog of the Collection*. Compiled by Karen F. Beall. p. 463. Baltimore: The Library of Congress, The Johns Hopkins Press, 1970.

1972   June 1 Gallery of Fine Art. *Benton Spruance: A Retrospective: Four Decades of Lithography*. Washington, D.C., 1972.

STAEGER, FERDINAND (1880–   )

1939   Binder, Bruno. "The Graphic Art of Ferdinand Staeger." *Print Collector's Quarterly* 26 (1939): 193–207.

STAMOS, THEODOROS (1922–   )

1972   Heckscher Museum. *Artists of Suffolk County: Part 6, Contemporary Prints*. Huntington, N.Y., 1972.

1972   Corcoran Gallery of Art. *Julian Stanczak: Serigraphs and Drawings 1970–1972*. Washington, D.C., 1972.

STARK, JAMES (1794–1859)

1905   Dickes, W. F. *The Norwich School of Painting*. P. 453. London and Norwich, 1905.

STEINBERG, SAUL (1914–)

1972   Heckscher Museum. *Artists of Suffolk County: Part 6, Contemporary Prints*. Huntington, N.Y., 1972.

STEINHARDT, JAKOB (1887–1968)

1959   Kolb, Leon. *Jakob Steinhardt: Complete Catalogue of Woodcuts*. San Francisco, Cal.: Genuart Co., 1959.

1962   Kolb, Leon. *The Woodcuts of Jakob Steinhardt*. Philadelphia: Jewish Publication Society of America, 1962.

1963   Gamzu, H. *Jakob Steinhardt: A Critical Appreciation*. New York and London: Thomas Yoseloff, 1963.

1972   Sotriffer, Kristian. *Expressionism and Fauvism*. New York: McGraw-Hill Book Co., 1972.

STEINLEN, THÉOPHILE ALEXANDRE (1859–1923)

1913   Crauzat, Ernest de. *L'oeuvre gravé et lithographié de Steinlen*. Paris: Société de propagation des livres d'art, 1913.

1931   Clément-Janin. "Steinlen." *Print Collector's Quarterly* 18 (1931): 33–55.

1953–54 *An Exhibition of Drawings, Engravings, and Book Illustration*. Paris: Bibliothèque Nationale, 1953, and London: Great Britain Arts Council, 1954.

1967   Kovler Gallery. *Forgotten Printmakers of the 19th Century*. Chicago, 1967.

1974   Weisberg, Gabriel P. *Social Concern and the Worker: French Prints from 1830–1910*. Salt Lake City, Utah: Utah Museum of Fine Arts, 1974.

STELLA, FRANK (1936–)

1967   Rose, B. *American Art since 1900*. New York: F. A. Praeger, 1967.

STELLA, JOSEPH (1880–1946)

1970   Library of Congress. *American Prints in the Library of Congress: A Catalog of the Collection.* Compiled by Karen F. Beall. p. 466. Baltimore: The Library of Congress, The Johns Hopkins Press, 1970.

STERNBERG, HARRY (1904–   )

1942   Zigrosser, Carl. *The Artist in America: 24 Close-ups of Contemporary Printmakers.* New York: Alfred A. Knopf, 1942.

1949   Reese, Albert. *American Prize Prints of the 20th century.* p. 194. New York: American Artists Group, 1949.

1957   University Gallery. *The Prints of Harry Sternberg.* Minneapolis, Minn.: University of Minnesota, 1957.

1970   Library of Congress. *American Prints in the Library of Congress: A Catalog of the Collection.* Compiled by Karen F. Beall. p. 467. Baltimore: The Library of Congress, The Johns Hopkins Press, 1970.

STERNER, ALBERT EDWARD (1863–1946)

1916   Birnbaum, Max. "Albert Sterner's Lithographs." *Print Collector's Quarterly* 6 (1916): 213–224.

1927   Flint, Ralph. *Albert Sterner: His Life and his Art.* New York: Payson and Clark, 1927.

1932   Jewell, Edward Alden. "Albert Sterner's Prints." *Print Collector's Quarterly* 19 (1932): 253–266.

1970   Library of Congress. *American Prints in the Library of Congress: A Catalog of the Collection.* Compiled by Karen F. Beall. p. 467. Baltimore: The Library of Congress, The Johns Hopkins Press, 1970.

STEVENSON, BEULAH (–1965)

1973   Mount Holyoke College Art Museum and the Weyhe Gallery. *14 American Women Printmakers of the 30's and 40's.* South Hadley, Mass. and New York, 1973.

STEWARD, DONN H. (20th C.)

1972   Heckscher Museum. *Artists of Suffolk County: Part 6, Contemporary Prints.* Huntington, N.Y., 1972.

1935   Binder, Bruno. "Oskar Stoessel and his Graphic Art." *Print Collector's Quarterly* 22 (1935): 245.

STOWASSER, FRIEDRICH *see* HUNDERTWASSER, FRIEDRICH

STRANG, IAN, A.R.E. (1886–   )

1920   *Etchings and Dry-Points by Ian Strang.* London, 1920.

1931   Walker, R. A. "The Etchings of Ian Strang." *Print Collector's Quarterly* 18 (1931):129–149.

STRANG, WILLIAM (1859–1921)

1912   William Strang: C *Catalogue of Etched Work: 1882–1912.* Glasgow, 1912.

1921   Binyon, Laurence. "Etchings and Engravings of William Strang." *Print Collector's Quarterly* 8 (1921): 349–376.

1923   *William Strang: Supplement to Catalogue of Etched Work: 1912–1923.* Glasgow: Maclehose, Jackson & Co., 1923.

1937   Strang, David. "The Etchings of William Strang, R.A." *Print Collector's Quarterly* 24 (1937): 395–409.

1948   Dodgson, Campbell. "The Lithographs of William Strang." *Print Collector's Quarterly* 29 (1948): 43–54.

1948   "Catalogue of the Work of William Strang." *Print Collector's Quarterly* 29 (1948): 54–55.

STRUNCK, JUERGEN

1974   Tyler Museum of Art. *Juergen Strunck.* Tyler, Tex., 1974.

STUART, JAMES (1779–1849)

1942   Constable, W. G. "A Sketchbook by James Stuart in the Avery Library." *Print Collector's Quarterly* 29 (1942): 237.

STUBBS, GEORGE (1724–1806)

1898   Gilbey, Sir Walter. *Life of George Stubbs, R.A.* London, 1898.

STUCKENBERG, FRITZ (1881–1944)

1965   Wingler, H. M. *Graphic Work from the Bauhaus.* Greenwich, Conn.: New York Graphic Society, 1965.

STURGES, DWIGHT (1874–1940)

Work in progress for 100th anniversary by artist's daughter, Mrs. Butler.

SUGAI, KUMI (1919–   )

1960   Mandiargues, A. P. *Kumi Sugai*. Paris: Musée de poche, 1960.

SUMMERS, CAROL (1925–   )

1966   De Cordova Museum. *Carol Summers: Prints*. Lincoln, Mass., 1966.

1970   Library of Congress. *American Prints in the Library of Congress: A Catalog of the Collection*. Compiled by Karen F. Beall. p. 468. Baltimore: The Library of Congress, The Johns Hopkins Press, 1970.

1972   Associated American Artists. *Carol Summers: Checklist*. New York, 1972.

1973   Jane Haslem Gallery. *The Innovators: Renaissance in American Printmaking*. Washington, D.C., 1973.

SURENDORF, CHARLES FREDERICK (1906–   )

1949   Reese, Albert. *American Prize Prints of the 20th Century*. p. 195. New York: American Artists Group, 1949.

1970   Library of Congress. *American Prints in the Library of Congress: A Catalog of the Collection*. Compiled by Karen F. Beall. p. 469. Baltimore: The Library of Congress, The John Hopkins Press, 1970.

SURVAGE, LEOPOLD (1879–1968)

1965   Wingler, H. M. *Graphic Work from the Bauhaus*. Greenwich, Conn.: New York Graphic Society, 1965.

SUTHERLAND, GRAHAM (1903–   )

1929   Ogg, David. "The Etchings of Graham Sutherland and Paul Drury." *Print Collector's Quarterly* 16 (1929): 77–93.

1929   Walker, R. A. "A Chronological List of the Etchings and Drypoints of Graham Sutherland and Paul Drury." *Print Collector's Quarterly* 16 (1929): 94–96.

1962   Cooper, P. *The Work of Sutherland*. London: Lund Humphries, 1962.

1970   Man, Felix H., ed. *Graham Sutherland: Das Graphische Werk 1922–1970.* Munich: Galerie Wolfgang Ketterer, 1970.   **221**

1971   William Weston Gallery. *Graham Sutherland: Etchings and Lithographs 1925–1970.* London, 1971.

SUTTON, PHILIP (1928–   )

1967   London Arts Group. *Philip Sutton: Paintings, Sculpture, Prints: Exhibition Catalogue.* 1967.

SWANN, JAMES (1905–   )

1949   Reese, Albert. *American Prize Prints of the 20th Century.* p. 196. New York: American Artists Group, 1949.

1970   Library of Congress. *American Prints in the Library of Congress: A Catalog of the Collection.* Compiled by Karen F. Beall. p. 470. Baltimore: The Library of Congress, The Johns Hopkins Press, 1970.

SYKES, WILLIAM MALTBY (1911–   )

1949   Reese, Albert. *American Prize Prints of the 20th Century.* p. 197. New York: American Artists Group, 1949.

SYNGE, EDWARD MILLINGTON (1860–1913)

1913   Newbolt, F. "Etchings of E. M. Synge." *Studio* 60 (1913): 98.

TAIT, AGNES (MC NULTY) (1897–   )

1970   Library of Congress. *American Prints in the Library of Congress: A Catalog of the Collection.* Compiled by Karen F. Beall. p. 471. Baltimore: The Library of Congress, The Johns Hopkins Press, 1970.

1973   Mount Holyoke College Art Museum and the Weyhe Gallery. *14 American Women Printmakers of the 30's and 40's.* South Hadley, Mass. and New York, 1973.

TAKAL, PETER (1905–   )

1958   The Cleveland Museum of Art. *Recent Work of Peter Takal: Catalogue of an Exhibition.* Cleveland: The Print Club, 1958.

1970   Library of Congress. *American Prints in the Library of Congress: A Catalogue of the Collection.* Compiled by Karen F. Beall. pp. 471–472. Baltimore: The Library of Congress, The Johns Hopkins Press, 1970.

TAMAYO, RUFINO (1899–   )

1957   Haub, Armin. *Mexikanische Graphik*. Teufen, 1957.

1972   Sotriffer, Kristian. *Expressionism and Fauvism*. New York: McGraw-Hill Book Co., 1972.

TANGUY, YVES (1900–1955)

1970   Gimpel and Weitzenhoffer, Ltd. *Original Prints of the Surrealists*. New York, 1970.

1970   Library of Congress. *American Prints in the Library of Congress: A Catalog of the Collection*. Compiled by Karen F. Beall. p. 472. Baltimore: The Library of Congress, The Johns Hopkins Press, 1970.

TANNER, HENRY O. (1859–1937)

1970   National Collection of Fine Arts. *The Art of Henry O. Tanner*. Washington, D.C.: Smithsonian Institution, 1970.

TÀPIES, ANTONIO (1923–   )

1967   Gatt, C. *Antonio Tàpies*. Bologna: Cappelli, 1967.

1973   Galfetti, M. and Vogel, C. *Antonio Tàpies: Obra Grafica, 1947–1972*. New York: Wittenborn and Co., 1973.

TAYLOR, CHARLES W. (1875–   )

1936   Bliss, Douglas Percy. "The Engravings of Charles W. Taylor." *Print Collector's Quarterly* 23 (1936): 125–143.

TAYLOR, PRENTISS (1907–   )

1949   Reese, Albert. *American Prize Prints of the 20th Century*. p. 198. New York: American Artists Group, 1949.

1970   Library of Congress. *American Prints in the Library of Congress: A Catalog of the Collection*. Compiled by Karen F. Beall. pp. 473–474. Baltimore: The Library of Congress, The Johns Hopkins Press, 1970.

THAL, SAMUEL (1903–1964)

1949   Reese, Albert. *American Prize Prints of the 20th Century*. p. 199. New York: American Artists Group, 1949.

1970   Library of Congress. *American Prints in the Library of Congress: A Catalog of the Collection.* Compiled by Karen F. Beall. p. 474. Baltimore: The Library of Congress, The Johns Hopkins Press, 1970.

THIEBAUD, WAYNE (1920–   )

1968   Coplas, John. *Wayne Thiebaud: Graphics.* Pasadena, Cal.: Pasadena Art Museum, 1968.

1970   Library of Congress. *American Prints in the Library of Congress: A Catalog of the Collection.* Compiled by Karen F. Beall. p. 474. Baltimore: The Library of Congress, The Johns Hopkins Press, 1970.

1971   Corcoran Gallery of Art. *Wayne Thiebaud: Graphics. 1964–1971.* New York: Parasol Press, Ltd., 1971.

THOMA, HANS (1839–1924)

1920   Tannenbaum, H. *Hans Thoma: Graphische Kunst.* Dresden: E. Arnold, 1920.

1923   Beringer, J. A. *Hans Thoma: Radierungen.* Munchen: F. Bruckmann, 1923.

1971   Victoria and Albert Museum. *Homage to Senefelder.* Introduction by Felix H. Man. London, 1971.

THOMAS, BYRON (1902–   )

1949   Reese, Albert. *American Prize Prints of the 20th Century.* p. 200. New York: American Artists Group, 1949.

THOMSON, RODNEY (1878–1941)

1942   Whitmore, Elizabeth. "Rodney Thomson." *Print Collector's Quarterly* 29 (1942): 273.

1970   Library of Congress. *American Prints in the Library of Congress: A Catalog of the Collection.* Compiled by Karen F. Beall. p. 475. Baltimore: The Library of Congress, The Johns Hopkins Press, 1970.

THORNHILL, SIR JAMES (1676–1734)

1928   Oppé, A. P. "Sir James Thornhill's Invitation Card." *Print Collector's Quarterly* 15 (1928): 65.

TIEPOLO, GIOVANNI BATTISTA (1696–1770)

1906   Vesme, Alessandro Baudi de. *Le Peintre-graveur Italien*. Milan: U. Hoepli, 1906.

1921   Hind, A. M. "The Etchings of Giovanni Battista Tiepolo." *Print Collector's Quarterly* 8 (1921): 37–60.

TIEPOLO, GIOVANNI DOMENICO (1727–1804)

1939   Francis, Henry S. "Six Drawings from the Life of Pulcinella by the Younger Tiepolo." *Print Collector's Quarterly* 26 (1939): 361–363.

TISSOT, JAMES JACQUES JOSEPH (1836–1902)

1886   Tissot, J. J. *Eaux-fortes, Manière Noire, Pointes Sèches*. Paris, 1886.

1892   Béraldi, H. *Les Graveurs du XIXᵉ Siècle*. Vol. 12. pp. 125–134. Paris, 1892.

1967   Kovler Gallery. *Forgotten Printmakers of the 19th Century*. Chicago, 1967.

1968   Wentworth, M. *James Jacques Joseph Tissot: A Retrospective Exhibition*. Providence, R.I.: Museum of Art, Rhode Island School of Design and Toronto, Ontario: The Art Gallery of Ontario, 1968.

1972   Tunick, David. *Twenty-one Prints by Tissot*. New York, 1972.

        Wentworth, Michael J. Catalogue in preparation. Waltham, Mass.: Brandeis University, Rose Art Museum.

TITTLE, WALTER ERNEST (1883–   )

1949   Reese, Albert. *American Prize Prints of the 20th Century*. p. 201. New York: American Artists Group, 1949.

1970   Library of Congress. *American Prints in the Library of Congress: A Catalog of the Collection*. Compiled by Karen F. Beall. pp. 475–476. Baltimore: The Library of Congress, The Johns Hopkins Press, 1970.

TOBEY, MARK (1890–   )

1970   Library of Congress. *American Prints in the Library of Congress: A Catalog of the Collection*. Compiled by Karen F. Beall. p. 476. Baltimore: The Library of Congress, The Johns Hopkins Press, 1970.

TOOROP, JAN THEODOOR (1858–1928)

1944   Johnson, Una E. *Ambroise Vollard, Éditeur.* New York: Witten-
        horn and Co., 1944.

TOPP, ARNOLD (1887–1960)

1965   Wingler, H. M. *Graphic Work from the Bauhaus.* Greenwich,
        Conn.: New York Graphic Society, 1965.

TOULOUSE-LAUTREC, HENRI DE (1864–1901)

1920   Delteil, Loys. *Le Peintre-Graveur Illustré: Toulouse-Lautrec.* Vols.
        10 and 11. Paris: Chez l'auteur, 1920.

1922   Symons, Arthur. "Notes on Toulouse-Lautrec and his Litho-
        graphs." *Print Collector's Quarterly* 9 (1922): 351–372.

1939   Ingersoll, R. Sturgis. "The Posters of Toulouse-Lautrec." *Print
        Collector's Quarterly* 26 (1939): 471–490.

1944   Johnson, Una E. *Ambroise Vollard, Éditeur.* New York: Witten-
        born and Co., 1944.

1948   Roger-Marx, Claude. *Les Lithographies de Toulouse-Lautrec.* Paris:
        Hazan, 1948.

1951   Adhémar, Jean. *Oeuvre graphique de Toulouse-Lautrec.* Paris:
        Bibliothèque Nationale, 1951.

1959   Lecomte, M. *Lithographies de Toulouse-Lautrec: Collection of
        Maurice Loncle.* Paris: Galerie Charpentier, 1959.

1964   Munson-Williams-Proctor Institute. *Lithographs by Toulouse-
        Lautrec.* Utica, N.Y., 1964.

1965   Adhémar, Jean. *Toulouse-Lautrec: His Complete Lithographs and
        Drypoints.* New York: Harry N. Abrams, 1965.

1969   Delteil, Loys. *Le Peintre-Graveur Illustré: Toulouse-Lautrec.* Vols.
        10 and 11. 1920. Reprint. New York: Da Capo Press, 1969.

1970   Stein, Donna and Karshan, Donald. *L'Estampe Originale: A
        Catalogue Raisonné.* New York: The Museum of Graphic Art,
        1970.

TOWNLEY, HUGH (1923–   )

1969   De Cordova Museum. *Hugh Townley: Sculpture, Drawings, Prints.*
        Lincoln, Mass., 1969.

226   **TRÖKES, HEINZ (1905–   )**

1959   Groszmann, W. *Heinz Trökes.* Berlin: Safari Vlg., 1959.

TSCHUMI, OTTO (1904–   )

1957   Kornfeld, Marlies. *Otto Tschumi: Katalog der Graphik.* Berne: Klipstein and Co., 1957.

TUNNICLIFFE, C. F.

1927   Salaman, M. C. "Etchings of C. F. Tunnicliffe." *Studio* 93 (1927): 91.

TURNER, JOSEPH MALLORD WILLIAM (1775–1851)

1874   *List of Drawings, Engravings, and Etchings by J. M. W. Turner.* Cambridge, Mass., 1874.

1878   Rawlinson, W. G. *Turner's Liber Studiorum: A Description and a Catalogue.* London, 1878.

1908–13 Rawlinson, W. G. *Engraved Work of J. M. W. Turner.* 2 vols. London, 1908–1913.

1913   Richter, Emil. "Turner and the 'Liber Studiorum'." *Print Collector's Quarterly* 3 (1913): 395–413.

1914   Richter, Emil. "Turner and his Unpublished Series of Mezzotints." *Print Collector's Quarterly* 4 (1914): 303–324.

1916   *A Catalogue of the Collection of Prints from the Liber Studiorum of Joseph Mallord William Turner: A Catalogue Raisonné Showing the Various States of the Prints.* Boston, 1916.

1922   Finberg, A. J. "Turner's Etchings." *Studio* 84 (1922): 201.

1929   Finberg, A. J. "Turner's 'Southern Coast'." *Print Collector's Quarterly* 16 (1929): 165–181.

TUSHINGHAM, SIDNEY (1884–   )

1924   Konody, P. G. *Etchings and Dry-Points by Sidney Tushingham.* London, 1924.

1929   Etchings and Drypoints of Sidney Tushingham. Introduction by Malcolm C. Salaman. London, 1929.

1970   Library of Congress. *American Prints in the Library of Congress: A Catalog of the Collection.* Compiled by Karen F. Beall. pp. 477–479. Baltimore: The Library of Congress, The Johns Hopkins Press, 1970.

TWACHTMAN, JOHN HENRY (1853–1902)

1920   Ryerson, M. A. "John H. Twachtman's Etchings: Including Catalogue." *Art in America.* 8 (1920): 92–96.

1921   Wickenden, Robert J. *The Art and Etching of John Henry Twachtman.* New York: Frederick Keppel and Co., 1921.

1924   Clark, Eliot. *John Twachtman.* New York: Privately printed, 1924.

1931   Tucker, Allen. *John H. Twachtman.* New York: Whitney Museum of American Art, 1931.

1966   Baskett, Mary Welch. "John Henry Twachtman: Prints." *John Twachtman: A Retrospective Exhibition.* pp. 34–39. Cincinnati, Ohio: Cincinnati Art Museum, 1966.

1970   Library of Congress. *American Prints in the Library of Congress: A Catalog of the Collection.* Compiled by Karen F. Beall. p. 479. Baltimore: The Library of Congress, The Johns Hopkins Press, 1970.

UHLMANN, HANS (1900–   )

1964   Man, Felix H., ed. *Europäische Graphik.* Vol. 2. Munich: Galerie Wolfgang Ketterer, 1964.

ULREICH, NURA WOODSON *see* NURA

UNWIN, FRANCIS SYDNEY (1885–1925)

1927   Laver, James. "The Etched Work of Francis Unwin." *Studio* (1927): 250.

1928   Dodgson, Campbell. *Francis Unwin: Etcher and Draughtsman.* London: The Fleuron Ltd., 1928.

1934   Schwabe, Randolph. "Francis Sydney Unwin: Etcher and Lithographer." *Print Collector's Quarterly* 21 (1934): 59–91.

UNWIN, NORA SPICER (1907–   )

1970   Library of Congress. *American Prints in the Library of Congress: A Catalog of the Collection.* Compiled by Karen F. Beall. p. 481. Baltimore: The Library of Congress, The Johns Hopkins Press, 1970.

UTRILLO, MAURICE (1883–1955)

1925   Rey, R. *Utrillo: Peintre et Lithographe*. Paris, 1925.

1926   Tabarant, Adolphe. *Utrillo*. Paris: Bernheim, 1926.

1927   Gros, Gabriel J. *Maurice Utrillo*. Paris: Crès, 1927.

1944   Gauthier, M. *Utrillo*. Paris, 1944.

1952   Beachboard, R. *La Trinité Maudite: Valadon, Utter, Utrillo*. Paris: Amiot-Dumont, 1952.

1953   Roger-Marx, Claude. *Maurice Utrillo*. 1953.

1959   Pétrides, Paul. *L'Oeuvre complet de Maurice Utrillo*. Vol. 1. Paris: Pétrides, 1959.

1960   Frapier, Jacques. *Galerie des Peintres-Graveurs*. Catalogue no. 2. Paris, 1960.

1964   Frapier, Jacques *Galerie des Peintres-Graveurs*. Catalogue no. 4. Paris: Galerie Jacques Frapier, 1964.

VALADON, SUZANNE (1865–1938)

1929   Galerie Bernier. *Dessins et Gravures de Suzanne Valadon*. Paris, 1929.

1932   Roger-Marx, Claude. *Dix-huit planches originales de Suzanne Valadon (1895–1910) avec un essai de catalogue*. Paris: Daragnes, 1932.

1939   Roger-Marx, Claude. *La Gravure originale en France de Manet à nos Jours*. Paris: Hyperion, 1939.

1944   Johnson, Una E. *Ambroise Vollard, Éditeur*. New York: Wittenborn and Co., 1944.

1947   Jacometti, N. *Suzanne Valadon*. Geneva, 1947.

1952   Beachboard, R. *La Trinité maudite: Valadon, Utter, Utrillo*. Paris: Amiot-Dumont, 1952.

VALLOTON, FÉLIX (1865–1925)

1932   Godefroy, L. *L'Oeuvre gravé de Fe);a)lix Valloton*. Paris, 1932.

1944   Johnson, Una. *Ambroise Vollard, Éditeur*. New York: Wittenborn and Co., 1944.

1970 Stein, Donna and Karshan, Donald. *L'Estampe Originale: A Catalogue Raisonné.* New York: The Museum of Graphic Art, 1970.

1970 Valloton, Maxime. *The Graphic Art of Valloton and the Nabis.* Chicago: Kovler Gallery, 1970.

1972 Valloton, Maxime and Goerg, C. *Félix Valloton: Catalogue raisonné de l'oeuvre gravé et lithographie.* (English/French) *Catalogue Raisonné of the Printed Graphic Work.* Geneva: Les Éditions de Bonvent S. A., 1972.

VAN ABBÉ, S. *see* ABBÉ S. VAN

VAN GOGH, VINCENT *see* GOGH, VINCENT VAN

VAN LOAN, DOROTHY LEFFINGWELL (20th C.)

1949 Reese, Albert. *American Prize Prints of the 20th Century.* p. 202. New York: American Artists Group, 1949.

VAN VLIET, CLAIRE

1970 R. H. Fleming Museum. *Claire Van Vliet: Prints.* Burlington, Vt., 1970.

VASARELY, VICTOR (1908–   )

1965 Joray, Marcel, ed. *Vasarely.* Vol 1. Lucerne, Switzerland: Griffon, 1965.

1970 Joray, Marcel, ed. *Vasarely.* Vol. 2. Lucerne, Switzerland: Griffon, 1970.

Joray, Marcel, ed. *Vasarely.* Vol. 3. Lucerne, Switzerland: Griffon. Work in progress.

VAUX, RICHARD (1940–   )

1972 Heckscher Museum. *Artists of Suffolk County: Part 6, Contemporary Prints.* Huntington, N.Y., 1972.

VERNER, ELIZABETH O'NEILL (1883–   )

1970 Library of Congress. *American Prints in the Library of Congress: A Catalog of the Collection.* Compiled by Karen F. Beall. pp. 482–483. Baltimore: The Library of Congress, The Johns Hopkins Press, 1970.

VERNET, CARLE (1758–1836)

1898   Blanc, Charles. *Une famille d'artistes, les trois Vernet: Joseph, Carle, Horace*. Paris: Rénouard, 1898.

1925   Dayot, Armand P. M. *Carle Vernet: étude sur l'artiste, suivi d'un catalogue de l'oeuvre gravé et lithographie et du catalogue de l'exposition rétrospective de 1925*. Paris: Goupy, 1925.

VERNET, HORACE (1789–1863)

1898   Blanc, Charles. *Une famille d'artistes, les trois Vernet: Joseph, Carle, Horace*. Paris: Rénouard, 1898.

VERNET, JOSEPH (1712–1789)

1898   Blanc, Charles. *Une famille d'artistes, les trois Vernet: Joseph, Carle, Horace*. Paris: Rénouard, 1898.

1926   Ingersoll-Smouse, Florence. *Joseph Vernet: peintre de marine 1712–1789*. Paris: Bignou, 1926.

VERRECCHIA, ALFEO (1911–)

1949   Reese, Albert. *American Prize Prints of the 20th Century*. p. 203. New York: American Artists Group, 1949.

1970   Library of Congress. *American Prints in the Library of Congress: A Catalog of the Collection*. Compiled by Karen F. Beall. p. 483. Baltimore: The Library of Congress, The Johns Hopkins Press, 1970.

VERTÈS, MARCEL (1895–1961)

1961   Roger-Marx, Claude. *Variations*. Greenwich, Conn.: New York Graphic Society, 1961.

VETH, JAN PIETER (1864–1925)

1927   Huizinga, Johan. *Leven en werk van Jan Veth*. Haarlem: H. D. Tjeenk Willink and Zoon, 1927.

VICENTE, ESTABAN (1906–)

1970   Library of Congress. *American Prints in the Library of Congress: A Catalog of the Collection*. Compiled by Karen F. Beall. p. 483. Baltimore: The Library of Congress, The Johns Hopkins Press, 1970.

1972   Heckscher Museum. *Artists of Suffolk County: Part 6, Contemporary Prints*. Huntington, N.Y., 1972.

VIEILLARD, ROGER (1907–)

1958   Volboudt, Pierre. *Roger Vieillard 1958: burins*. Paris: Galerie Maeght, 1958.

1972   Bibliothèque Nationale. *Roger Vieillard: burins, reliefs*. Paris, 1972.

VIGNON, VICTOR ALFRED PAUL (1847–1909)

1970   Stein, Donna and Karshan, Donald. *L'Estampe Originale: A Catalogue Raisonné*. New York: The Museum of Graphic Art, 1970.

VILLON, JACQUES (GASTON DUCHAMP) (1875–1963)

1950 Auberty, J. and Perusseux, C. *Jacques Villon: Catalogue de son oeuvre gravé*. Paris: Prouté, 1950.

1953   Lieberman, William S. *Jacques Villon: his Graphic Art*. New York: Museum of Modern Art, 1953.

1957   Askeland, J. *Jacques Villon grafiske Arbeuder*. Copenhagen: Bibliothèque royale de Copenhagen, 1957.

1959   Adhémar, J. *Catalogue de l'oeuvre gravé de Jacques Villon*. Paris: Bibliothèque Nationale, 1959.

1964   Steegmuller, Francis. *Jacques Villon: Master Printmaker*. New York: R. M. Light and Co., Helene C. Seiferheld Gallery, 1964.

1964   Steegmuller, Francis. "Jacques Villon: Master Printmaker." 1964. Reprint. *Artist's Proof* 7 (1964): 11–22.

1964   Wick, Peter. *Jacques Villon: Master of Graphic Art*. Boston: Museum of Fine Arts, and New York: October House, Inc., 1964.

1970   Lucien Goldschmidt Gallery. *Jacques Villon: A Collection of Graphic Work 1896–1913 in Rare or Unique Impressions*. New York, 1970.

VINCENT, GEORGE (1796–1831)

1905   Dickes, W. F. *The Norwich School of Painting*. p. 508. London, 1905.

VLAMINCK, MAURICE DE (1876–1958)

1928   Werth, L. *Vlaminck: Peintre-Gravure*. Paris, 1928.

1956   Romand, J.-C. *Vlaminck: Oeuvre gravé: Catalogue de l'Exposition*. Paris: Galerie Sagot-Le Garrec, 1956.

232 1961 *Catalogue of the S. Pollag Collection.* Berne: Kunstmuseum, 1961.

1964 Frapier, Jacques. *Galerie des Peintres-Graveurs.* Catalogue no. 4. Paris, 1964.

1972 Sotriffer, Kristian. *Expressionism and Fauvism.* New York: McGraw-Hill Book Co., 1972.

Walterskirchen, K. von and Pollag, S. *Maurice de Vlaminck: das Graphische Werk.* In preparation. [American distributor: New York: Wittenborn and Co.]

VOGEL, DONALD S. (1917–   )

1949 Reese, Albert. *American Prize Prints of the 20th Century.* p. 204. New York: American Artists Group, 1949.

1970 Library of Congress. *American Prints in the Library of Congress: A Catalog of the Collection.* Compiled by Karen F. Beall. p. 484. Baltimore: The Library of Congress, The Johns Hopkins Press, 1970.

VUILLARD, EDOUARD (1868–1940)

1934 Marguery, Henri. "Essai d'un catalogue des Lithographies de Vuillard." *L'Amateur d'Estampes* [Paris] 1934.

1934 Roger-Marx, Claude. *Les Lithographies de Vuillard.* Paris: A. M. G., 1934.

1935 Marguery, Henri. *Les Lithographies de Vuillard.* Paris: Cabinet des Estampes, Bibliothèque Nationale, 1935.

1944 Johnson, Una E. *Ambroise Vollard, Éditeur.* New York: Wittenborn and Co., 1944.

1948 Roger-Marx, Claude. *L'Oeuvre Gravé de Vuillard.* Monte Carlo: André Sauret Editions du Livre, 1948.

1970 Kovler Gallery. *The Graphic Art of Valloton and the Nabis.* pp. 73–75. Chicago, Ill., 1970.

1970 Stein, Donna and Karshan, Donald. *L'Estampe Originale: A Catalogue Raisonné.* New York: The Museum of Graphic Art, 1970.

WADSWORTH, EDWARD (1889–1949)

1973 Christopher Drake Gallery, Ltd. *Edward Wadsworth: Early Woodcuts, 1913–1918.* London, 1973.

1944   Johnson, Una E. *Ambroise Vollard, Éditeur.* New York: Witten-
        born and Co., 1944.

1970   Stein, Donna and Karshan, Donald. *L'Estampe Originale: A
        Catalogue Raisonné.* New York: The Museum of Graphic Art,
        1970.

WALCOT, WILLIAM, R. E. (1874–1943)

1923   Salaman, M. C. "William Walcot's Etchings of the Old and New
        World." *Studio* 85 (1923): 311.

1927   Salaman, M. C. *William Walcot.* Modern Masters of Etching
        Series, no. 16. London: The Studio, Ltd., 1927.

WALES, GEORGE CANNING (1868–1940)

1922   Holman, Louis A. *George C. Wales, Etcher of the Sea.* Boston,
        Mass.: Charles E. Goodspeed and Co., 1922.

1923   "List of Etchings by George C. Wales." *The Print Connoisseur* 3
        (1923): 19–22.

1923   Walker, C. Howard. "Etchings of Ships by George C. Wales." *Print
        Connoisseur* 3 (1923): 3.

1927   Walker, C. H. and Pentecost, Capt. E. H. *Etchings and Lithographs
        of American Ships by George C. Wales.* Boston, 1927.

WALKER, FREDERICK (1840–1875)

1917   Cary, Elisabeth Luther. "Frederick Walker." *Print Collector's
        Quarterly* 7 (1917): 385–405.

WALKER, WILLIAM, A. R. E. (1791–1867)

1913   "Etchings and Drypoints by William Walker." *Studio* 59 (1913):
        271.

1932   Daniell, Frederick. "William Walker and his Family." *Print
        Collector's Quarterly* 19 (1932): 321–340.

WALKOWITZ, ABRAHAM (1878–1965)

1970   Library of Congress. *American Prints in the Library of Congress: A
        Catalog of the Collection.* Compiled by Karen F. Beall. p. 486.
        Baltimore: The Library of Congress, The Johns Hopkins Press,
        1970.

234 1971 Reich, Sheldon. "Abraham Walkowitz: Pioneer of American Modernism." *The American Art Journal* 3 (1971): 72–82.

1973 Zabriskie Gallery. *Abraham Walkowitz: The Early Years.* New York, 1973.

WARD, JAMES, R. A. (1769–1859)

1909 Grundy, Cecil Reginald. *James Ward, R. A.* London: Otto Limited, 1909.

1971 Victoria and Albert Museum. *Homage to Senefelder.* Introduction by Felix H. Man. London, 1971.

WARD, LESLIE M., A. R. E. (1851–1922)

1925 "Three Etchings ... by Leslie M. Ward." *Studio* 89 (1925): 203.

WARD, LYND (1905–   )

1936 Haas, Irvin. "A Bibliography of the Work of Lynd Ward." *Prints* 7 (1936): 84–92.

1949 Reese, Albert. *American Prize Prints of the 20th Century.* p. 206. New York: American Artists Group, 1949.

1970 Library of Congress. *American Prints in the Library of Congress: A Catalog of the Collection.* Compiled by Karen F. Beall. pp. 486–487. Baltimore: The Library of Congress, The Johns Hopkins Press, 1970.

1974 Associated American Artists. *Lynd Ward: Wood-engravings 1929–1974.* Foreword by Lincoln Rothschild. New York, 1974.

1974 *Storyteller without Words: The Wood Engravings of Lynd Ward.* New York: Harry N. Abrams, 1974.

WARHOL, ANDY (1930–   )

1970 Crone, Rainer. *Andy Warhol.* New York: Praeger, 1970.

1971 Brown, Andreas. *Andy Warhol: His early work 1947–1959.* New York: Gotham Book Mart Gallery, 1971.

1971 Malanga, Gerard. "A Conversation with Andy Warhol." *Print Collector's Newsletter* 1 (1971): 125–127.

WASHBURN, CADWALLADER (1866–1965)

1911 Washburn, C. "Notes of an Etcher in Mexico and Maine." *Print Collector's Quarterly* 1 (1911): 465–481.

1916   Laurvik, John Nilson. *The Graphic Work of Cadwallader Washburn.*
San Francisco: H. Tolerton, 1916.

1970   Library of Congress. *American Prints in the Library of Congress: A Catalog of the Collection.* Compiled by Karen F. Beall. pp. 488–490. Baltimore: The Library of Congress, The Johns Hopkins Press, 1970.

WATSON, CHARLES JOHN, R. E. (1846–1927)

1896   White, Gleeson. "The Work of Charles Watson." *Studio* 9 (1896): 3.

WATTEAU, JEAN-ANTOINE (1684–1721)

1875   Goncourt, Edmond de. *Catalogue raisonné de l'oeuvre peint, dessiné et gravé d'Antoine Watteau.* Paris: Rapilly, 1875.

1921–29 Dacier, Émile. *Jean de Jullienne et les graveurs de Watteau au 18ᵉ siècle.* 3 vols. Paris: Societé pour l'Etude de la Graveur Française, 1921–1929.

1943   Brinckmann, Albert E. *J. A. Watteau.* Vienna: Schroll, 1943.

1943   Gillet, Louis. *Watteau, un grand maître du 18ᵉ siècle.* Paris: Plon, 1943.

1950   Adhémar, Hélène. *Watteau, sa vie, son oeuvre.* Paris: Tisne, 1950.

WAUER, WILLIAM (1866–1962)

1957   Peters, Heinz, ed. *Die Bauhaus-Mappen: Neue Europäische Graphik 1921–1923.* Cologne: C. Czwiklitzer, 1957.

1965   Wingler, H. M. *Graphic Work from the Bauhaus.* Greenwich, Conn.: New York Graphic Society, 1965.

WAYNE, JUNE (1918–   )

1969   Baskett, Mary Welsh. *The Art of June Wayne.* New York: Harry N. Abrams, Inc., 1969.

1970   Library of Congress. *American Prints in the Library of Congress: A Catalog of the Collection.* Compiled by Karen F. Beall. pp. 492–493. Baltimore: The Library of Congress, The Johns Hopkins Press, 1970.

1973   Municipal Art Gallery. *June Wayne.* Los Angeles, Cal., 1973.

WEBER, ALBERT PAUL (1893–)

1965   Eichenberg, Fritz. "The Satirical Lithographs of A. Paul Weber." *Artist's Proof* 8 (1965): 38–39.

1965   Weber, A. Paul. *Albert Paul Weber: Lithographien.* Schretstaken: Clou Presse, 1965.

1970   Library of Congress. *American Prints in the Library of Congress: A Catalog of the Collection.* Compiled by Karen F. Beall. p. 493. Baltimore: The Library of Congress, The Johns Hopkins Press, 1970.

WEBER, MAX (1881–1961)

1930   Cahill, H. *Max Weber.* New York: Downtown Gallery, 1930.

1949   Goodrich, Lloyd. *Max Weber: Retrospective Exhibition.* New York: Whitney Museum of American Art, 1949.

1956   Weber, Max. *Woodcuts and Linoleum Blocks.* New York: E. Weyhe, 1956.

1970   Associated American Artists. *The Lithographs of Max Weber.* Foreword by Una Johnson; introduction by Sylvan Cole. New York, 1970.

1970   Library of Congress. *American Prints in the Library of Congress: A Catalog of the Collection.* Compiled by Karen F. Beall. p. 494. Baltimore: The Library of Congress, The Johns Hopkins Press, 1970.

WEBSTER, HERMAN ARMOUR, R. E. (1878–1970)

1912   "Etchings by American Artists in Paris, 1. Herman A. Webster." *Studio* 54 (1912): 208.

1912   Hardie, Martin. "Herman A. Webster." Print Collector's Quarterly 2 (1912): 56–73.

1970   Library of Congress. *American Prints in the Library of Congress: A Catalog of the Collection.* Compiled by Karen F. Beall. pp. 495–496. Baltimore: The Library of Congress, The Johns Hopkins Press, 1970.

1974   Flint, Janet. *Herman A. Webster: Drawings, Watercolors, and Prints.* Washington, D.C.: National Collection of Fine Arts, Smithsonian Institution, 1974.

WEDGWOOD, GEOFFREY HEATH, A. R. E.

1925   Laver, J. "The Etchings of Geoffrey Heath Wedgwood." *Book-man's Journal* 12 (1925): 231.

WEIDENAAR, REYNOLD HENRY (1915–   )

1949   Reese, Albert. *American Prize Prints of the 20th Century*. p. 207. New York: American Artists Group, 1949.

1970   Library of Congress. *American Prints in the Library of Congress: A Catalog of the Collection*. Compiled by Karen F. Beall. p. 496. Baltimore: The Library of Congress, The Johns Hopkins Press, 1970.

1973   June 1 Gallery of Fine Art. *Reynold Weidenaar*. Washington, D.C., 1973.

WEIR, JULIAN ALDEN (1852–1919)

1919–20 Ryerson, M. A. "J. Alden Weir's etchings." *Art in America* 8 (1919–1920): 243.

1923   Zimmerman, Agnes. "An Essay Towards a Catalogue Raisonné of the Etchings, Dry-points, and Lithographs of Julian Alden Weir." *The Metropolitan Museum of Art Papers*. Vol. 1, pt. 2. New York, 1923.

1923   Zimmerman, Agnes. "Julian Alden Weir—his Etchings." *Print Collector's Quarterly* 10 (1923): 289–308.

1927   Ely, Caroline Weir. *Catalogue of an Exhibition of Etchings by J. Alden Weir*. New York: Frederick Keppel and Co., 1927.

1968   Sheldon Art Gallery. *The Etchings of Julian Alden Weir*. Monographs on American Art, no. 1. Omaha, Nebraska: University of Nebraska, 1968.

1970   Library of Congress. *American Prints in the Library of Congress: A Catalog of the Collection*. Compiled by Karen F. Beall. pp. 497–501. Baltimore: The Library of Congress, The Johns Hopkins Press, 1970.

1972   Flint, Janet. *Alden Weir: An American Printmaker*. Washington, D.C.: National Collection of Fine Arts, and Provo, Utah: Brigham Young University Press, 1972.

WEISSBUCH, OSCAR (1904–1948)

1948   Munson-Williams-Proctor Inst. *Oscar Weissbuch: A Memorial Exhibition*. Utica, N.Y., 1948.

238 1970   Library of Congress. *American Prints in the Library of Congress: A Catalog of the Collection.* Compiled by Karen F. Beall. p. 501. Baltimore: The Library of Congress, Johns Hopkins Press, 1970.

WELTI, ALBERT (1862–1912)

1913   Wartmann, Wilhelm. *Albert Welti: volständiges verzeichnis des graphischen werkes mit den ver schiedenen Plattenzuständen und Drucken.* Zurich: Zürcher Kunst-Gesellschaft, 1913.

WENGENROTH, STOW (1906–   )

1942   Reece, Childe. "Stow Wengenroth." *Print Collector's Quarterly* 29 (1942): 91–103.

1949   Reese, Albert. *American Prize Prints of the 20th Century.* p. 208. New York: American Artists Group, 1949.

1969   McCord, David. *Stow Wengenroth's New England.* Introduction by Sinclair Hitchings. Barre, Mass.: Barre Publishers, 1969.

1970   Library of Congress. *American Prints in the Library of Congress: A Catalog of the Collection.* Compiled by Karen F. Beall. pp. 502–504. Baltimore: The Library of Congress, The Johns Hopkins Press, 1970.

1972   Heckscher Museum. *Artists of Suffolk County: Part 6, Contemporary Prints.* Huntington, N.Y., 1972.

1973   Stuckey, R. and J. *The Lithographs of Stow Wengenroth.* Barre, Mass.: Barre Publishers, 1973.

WEST, BENJAMIN (1738–1820)

1962   Man, Felix. H. "Lithography in England: 1801–1810." *Prints.* Edited by Carl Zigrosser. New York: Holt, Rinehart and Winston, 1962.

1970   Library of Congress. *American Prints in the Library of Congress: A Catalog of the Collection.* Compiled by Karen F. Beall. p. 505. Baltimore: The Library of Congress, The Johns Hopkins Press, 1970.

WEST, LEVON (1900–1968)

1930   Salaman, Malcolm C. *Levon West.* Modern Masters of Etching Series, no. 24. London: The Studio, Ltd., 1930.

1930   Torrington, Otto M. *A Catalogue of the Etchings of Levon West.* New York: Rudge, 1930.

1949   Reese, Albert. *American Prize Prints of the 20th Century*. p. 209.   **239**
        New York: American Artists Group, 1949.

1970   Library of Congress. *American Prints in the Library of Congress: A
        Catalog of the Collection*. Compiled by Karen F. Beall. p. 505.
        Baltimore: The Library of Congress, The Johns Hopkins Press,
        1970.

WETHERILL, ELISHA KENT KANE (1874–1929)

1970   Library of Congress. *American Prints in the Library of Congress: A
        Catalog of the Collection*. Compiled by Karen F. Beall. pp. 505–506.
        Baltimore: The Library of Congress, The Johns Hopkins Press,
        1970.

WHISTLER, JAMES ABBOTT McNEILL (1834–1903)

1896   Way, Thomas Robert. *Mr. Whistler's Lithographs: The Catalogue*.
        London: G. Bell and Sons, 1896.

1905   Way, Thomas Robert. *Mr. Whistler's Lithographs: The Catalogue*.
        2nd ed. London: G. Bell and Sons, 1905.

1910   Kennedy, Edward Guthrie. *The Etched Work of Whistler: Illus-
        trated by Reproductions in Collotype of the Different States of the
        Plates*. 6 vols. New York: The Grolier Club, 1910.

1911   "James A. McNeill Whistler." *Print Collector's Quarterly* 1 (1911):
        32.

1911   "List of Etchings and Dry-Points by Whistler (from the Tracy
        Dows Collection.)" *Print Collector's Quarterly* 1 (1911) 33–61.

1913   Mansfield, H. "Whistler as Critic of his Own Prints." *Print
        Collector's Quarterly* 3 (1913): 367–393.

1913   Way, Thomas Robert. "Whistler's Lithographs." *Print Collector's
        Quarterly* 3 (1913): 279–309.

1914   Mansfield, Howard. "Concerning a Whistler Portrait: 'Mr. Mann,'
        or 'Mr. Davis'?" *Print Collector's Quarterly* 4 (1914): 383–391.

1915   Gallatin, A. E. "Notes on Some Rare Portraits of Whistler." *Print
        Collector's Quarterly* 5 (1915): 433–445.

1916   Mansfield, Howard. "Whistler in Belgium and Holland." *Print
        Collector's Quarterly*. 6 (1916): 375–395.

1917   Dodgson, Campbell. "Two Unpublished Whistlers." *Print Collec-
        tor's Quarterly* 7 (1917): 217–220.

240   1922   Dodgson, Campbell. *The Etchings of James McNeill Whistler.* London: The Studio, Ltd., 1922.

1927   Salaman, Malcolm. *James McNeill Whistler.* Modern Masters of Etching Series, no. 13. 2 vols. London: The Studio, Ltd., 1927.

1937   Mayor, A. Hyatt. "An Early Whistler Lithograph." *Print Collector's Quarterly* 24 (1937): 305–307.

1941   Johnson, Una E. "The Wood Engravings of James McNeill Whistler." *Print Collector's Quarterly* 28 (1941): 275–287.

1941   Johnson, Una E. "Catalogue of the Wood Engravings of James McNeill Whistler." *Print Collector's Quarterly* 28 (1941): 289–291.

1944   Johnson, Una E. *Ambroise Vollard, Éditeur.* New York: Wittenborn and Co., 1944.

1948   Stubbs, B. A. *Painting, Pastels, Drawings, Prints and Copper Plates by and Attributed to American and European Artists, Together With a List of Original Whistleriana, in the Freer Gallery of Art.* Publication no. 3905. Washington, D.C.: Smithsonian Institution, 1948.

1950   Stubbs, B. A. *James McNeill Whistler: A Biographical Outline Illustrated from the Collections of the Freer Gallery of Art.* Publication no. 3994. Washington, D.C.: Smithsonian Institution, 1950.

1970   Library of Congress. *American Prints in the Library of Congress: A Catalog of the Collection.* Compiled by Karen F. Beall. pp. 506–523. Baltimore: The Library of Congress, The Johns Hopkins Press, 1970.

1970   Stein, Donna and Karshan, Donald. *L'Estampe Originale: A Catalogue Raisonné.* New York: The Museum of Graphic Art, 1970.

Kennedy, Edward Guthrie. *The Etched Work of Whistler.* Reprint in preparation. New York: Da Capo Press.

WHYDALE, HERBERT, A. R. E.

1914   "E. H. Whydale." *Studio* 57 (1914): 307.

WICKEY, HARRY NEWMAN (1892–   )

1941   Wickey, Harry. *Thus Far.* New York: American Artists Group, 1941.

1942   Zigrosser, Carl. *The Artist in America: 24 Close-Ups of Contemporary Printmakers.* New York: Alfred Knopf, 1942.

1949   Reese, Albert. *American Prize Prints of the 20th Century*. p. 210. New York: American Artists Group, 1949.

1970   Library of Congress. *American Prints in the Library of Congress: A Catalog of the Collection*. Compiled by Karen F. Beall. p. 524. Baltimore: The Library of Congress, The Johns Hopkins Press, 1970.

WILKIE, SIR DAVID (1785–1841)

1840   "Engraved Works of Sir David Wilkie, R. A." *Art Union Journal* 2 (1840): 10.

1875   Laing, D. *Etchings by Sir David Wilkie and Andrew Geddes*. Edinburgh: Edmonston & Douglas, 1875.

WILLE, JEAN-GEORGES (1715–1808)

1847   Le Blanc, Charles. *Catalogue de l'oeuvre de Jean-Georges Wille*. Leipzig: R. Weigel, 1847.

1857   Duplessis, Georges. *Memoires et Journal de Jean-Georges Wille*. Paris: Renouard, 1857.

1914   Metcalf, Louis R. "The Memoirs and Journal of Jean-Georges Wille." *Print Collector's Quarterly* 4 (1914): 131–165.

WILLETTE, ADOLPHE LÉON (1857–1926)

1970   Stein, Donna and Karshan, Donald. *L'Estampe Originale: A Catalogue Raisonné*. New York: The Museum of Graphic Art, 1970.

WILLIAMS, FRED (1927–   )

1968   Mollison, James. *Fred Williams: Etchings*. Woullahra, Australia: Rudy Komon Gallery, 1968.

1972   Victoria and Albert Museum. *Australian Prints*. London, 1972.

WILLIAMS, KEITH SHAW (1906–1951)

1949   Reese, Albert. *American Prize Prints of the 20th Century*. p. 211. New York: American Artists Group, 1949.

1970   Library of Congress. *American Prints in the Library of Congress: A Catalog of the Collection*. Compiled by Karen F. Beall. p. 524. Baltimore: The Library of Congress, The Johns Hopkins Press, 1970.

WILSON, BENJAMIN (1721–1788)

1903   "Wilson's Imitations of Rembrandt's Etching." *Connoisseur* 7 (1903): 124.

WILSON, JOHN (1922–   )

1949   Reese, Albert. *American Prize Prints of the 20th Century.* p. 212. New York: American Artists Group, 1949.

WILSON, SOL (1896–   )

1949   Reese, Albert. *American Prize Prints of the 20th Century.* p. 213. New York: American Artists Group, 1949.

1970   Library of Congress. *American Prints in the Library of Congress: A Catalog of the Collection.* Compiled by Karen F. Beall. p. 526. Baltimore: The Library of Congress, The Johns Hopkins Press, 1970.

WILSON, SYDNEY E. (1869–   )

1920   Bland, Harry MacNeill. "Sydney E. Wilson, An English Master of Mezzotint." *Print Connoisseur* 1 (1920): 185–194.

1920   Truesdell, Winfred Porter. "List of Mezzotints by Sydney E. Wilson." *Print Connoisseur* 1 (1920): 197–198.

WINKLER, JOHN W. (1890–   )

1924   Godefroy, Louis. "List of the Etchings of J. W. Winkler." *Print Connoisseur* 4 (1924): 186–191.

1924   Godefroy, Louis. "The Etchings of J. W. Winkler." *Print Connoisseur* 4 (1924): 169.

1934   Arms, John Taylor. "John W. Winkler: Master of Line." *Prints* 4 (1934): 1–13.

1949   Reese, Albert. *American Prize Prints of the 20th Century.* p. 214. New York: American Artists Group, 1949.

1970   Library of Congress. *American Prints in the Library of Congress: A Catalog of the Collection.* Compiled by Karen F. Beall. pp. 526–527. Baltimore: The Library of Congress, The Johns Hopkins Press, 1970.

WOICESKE, RONAU WILLIAM (1887–1953)

1949   Reese, Albert. *American Prize Prints of the 20th Century.* p. 215. New York: American Artists Group, 1949.

1970   Library of Congress. *American Prints in the Library of Congress: A* 　　　**243**
        Catalog of the Collection. Compiled by Karen F. Beall. pp. 528–529.
        Baltimore: The Library of Congress, The Johns Hopkins Press,
        1970.

WOOD, FRANKLIN T. (1887–1945)

1925   Thomas, T. H. "List of the Etchings of Franklin T. Wood." *The*
        Print Connoisseur 5 (1925): 240–245.

1970   Library of Congress. *American Prints in the Library of Congress: A*
        Catalog of the Collection. Compiled by Karen F. Beall. p. 529.
        Baltimore: The Library of Congress, The Johns Hopkins Press,
        1970.

WOOD, GRANT (1892–1942)

1944   Garwood, Darrell. *Artist in Iowa: A Life of Grant Wood.* New York:
        W. W. Norton & Company, 1944.

1949   Reese, Albert. *American Prize Prints of the 20th Century.* p. 233.
        New York: American Artists Group, 1949.

1959   University of Kansas. *Grant Wood: A Retrospective Exhibition.*
        Lawrence, Kansas, 1959.

1970   Library of Congress. *American Prints in the Library of Congress: A*
        Catalog of the Collection. Compiled by Karen F. Beall. p. 531.
        Baltimore: The Library of Congress, The Johns Hopkins Press,
        1970.

1973   Cedar Rapids Art Center. *The Grant Wood Collection.* Cedar
        Rapids, Iowa, 1973.

WOODBURY, CHARLES HERBERT (1864–1940)

1934   Arms, John Taylor. "Charles H. Woodbury: Etcher." *Prints* 5
        (1934): 20–33.

1970   Library of Congress. *American Prints in the Library of Congress: A*
        Catalog of the Collection. Compiled by Karen F. Beall. pp. 531–532.
        Baltimore: The Library of Congress, The Johns Hopkins Press,
        1970.

WOOLLARD, DOROTHY E. G., A.R.E.

1914   "Five Etchings by Dorothy E. G. Woollard." *Studio* 61 (1914): 123.

WOOLLETT, WILLIAM (1735–1785)

1885   Fagan, Louis. *William Woollett: A Catalogue Raisonné of the*
        Engraved Works. London, 1885.

WORLIDGE, THOMAS (1700–1766)

1907   Dack, Charles. *Sketch of the Life of Thomas Worlidge, Etcher and Painter, With a Catalogue of his Works.* Peterborough: Crown Printing Works for Peterborough Natural History, Scientific and Archeological Society, 1907.

WOTRUBA, FRITZ (1907–)

1967   Breicha, Otto, ed. *Um Wotruba. Schriften zum Werk.* Vienna, Frankfurt, Zurich: Europa-Verlag, 1967.

1969   Man, Felix H., ed. *Europäische Graphik.* Vol. 6. Munich: Galerie Wolfgang Ketterer, 1969.

WRIGHT, JOHN, A.R.E. (1857–1933)

1906   "John Wright." *Studio* 39 (1906): 69.

WRIGHT, JOSEPH, A.R.A. (1734–1797)

1932   Morris, Roy. "Engravings After Joseph Wright, A.R.A." *Print Collector's Quarterly* 19 (1932): 95–115.

WRIGHT, R. STEPHENS (1903–)

1935   Morrow, B. F. "Highlights of Copper: R. Stephens Wright." *Prints* 6 (1935): 86–89.

WUNDERLICH, PAUL (1927–)

1964   *Wegzeichen im Unbekannten: 19 Deutsche Maler zu Fragen der Zeitgenössischen Kunst.* Heidelberg: Edition Rothe, 1964.

1965   "The Rationale of Paul Wunderlich." Translated by Fritz Eichenberg from "Wegzeichen im Unbekannten: 19 Deutsche Maler zu Fragen der Zeitgenössischen Kunst," 1964. *Artist's Proof* 8 (1965): 14–17.

1966   Brusberg, Dieter. *Paul Wunderlich: Werk-verzeichnis der Lithographien von 1949–1965.* Hanover: Verlag der Galerie Dieter Brusberg, 1966.

WÜRALT, EDUARD (1898–)

1936   Burdett, Basil. "An Esthonian engraver." *Print Collector's Quarterly* 23 (1936): 145–160.

WYLLIE, WILLIAM LIONEL, R.A., R.E. (1851–)

1907   Bridge, Admiral Sir Cyprian. "William Lionel Wyllie, R.A." *Art Journal* (1907): 1.

1940   Addison Gallery of American Art, Phillips Academy. *Mahonri M. Young: Retrospective Exhibition.* Andover, Mass., 1940.

1942   Zigrosser, Carl. *The Artist in America: 24 Close-ups of Contemporary Printmakers.* New York: Alfred A. Knopf, 1942.

1949   Reese, Albert. *American Prize Prints of the 20th Century.* p. 216. New York: American Artists Group, 1949.

1970   Library of Congress. *American Prints in the Library of Congress: A Catalog of the Collection.* Compiled by Karen F. Beall. pp. 535–536. Baltimore: The Library of Congress, The Johns Hopkins Press, 1970.

YUNKERS, ADJA (1900–   )

1969   Johnson, Una and Miller, Jo. *Adja Yunkers: Prints 1927–1967.* American Graphic Artists of the 20th Century Series, Monograph no. 7. New York: Brooklyn Institute of Arts and Sciences, Shorewood Publishers, 1969.

1970   Library of Congress. *American Prints in the Library of Congress: A Catalog of the Collection.* Compiled by Karen F. Beall. p. 536. Baltimore: The Library of Congress, The Johns Hopkins Press, 1970.

ZADKINE, OSSIP (1890–1967)

1967   Czwiklitzer, Christophe. *Ossip Zadkine: le sculpteur-graveur de 1919–1967. Première partie: eaux-fortes. Deuxième partie: lithographes.* Paris: Fischbacher, 1967.

1968   Galerie Motte. *Ossip Zadkine: Oeuvre gravé.* Paris, 1968.

1969   Man, Felix H., ed. *Europäische Graphik.* Vol. 6. Munich: Galerie Wolfgang Ketterer, 1969.

ZAO, WOU-KI (1920–   )

1955   Jacometti, N. *Catalogue raisonné de l'oeuvre gravé et lithographié 1949–1954. Berne: Gütekunst u. Klipstein, 1955.*

ZIEMANN, RICHARD (1932–   )

1973   Jane Haslem Gallery. *The Innovators: Renaissance in American Printmaking.* Washington, D.C., 1973.

ZOELLNER, RICHARD CHARLES (1908–   )

1949   Reese, Albert. *American Prize Prints of the 20th Century*. p. 217. New York: American Artists Group, 1949.

1970   Library of Congress. *American Prints in the Library of Congress: A Catalog of the Collection*. Compiled by Karen F. Beall. p. 539. Baltimore: The Library of Congress, The Johns Hopkins Press, 1970.

ZORACH, MARGUERITE (1887–1968)

1973   Tarbell, Roberta, *Marguerite Zorach: The Early Years 1908–1920*. Washington, D.C.: National Collection of Fine Arts, 1973.

ZORACH, WILLIAM (1887–1966)

1964–65 *The Whitney Review: 1964–1965*. pp. 47–48. New York, 1964–65.

ZORN, ANDERS (1860–1920)

1909   Delteil, Loys. *Le Peintre-Graveur Illustré: Zorn*. Vol. 4. Paris: Chez l'auteur, 1909.

1911   Laurvik, J. Nilsen. "Anders Zorn: Painter, Etcher." *Print Collector's Quarterly* 1 (1911): 610–637.

1920   Asplund, Karl. *Anders Zorn: Complete Catalogue of Etchings*. New York: E. Weyhe, 1920.

1920   Rihani, Ameen. "Anders Zorn." *Print Connoisseur* 1 (1920): 159–182.

1920–21 Asplund, Karl. *Zorn's Engraved Work: A Descriptive Catalogue*. 2 vols. Stockholm, 1920–21.

1925   Salaman, Malcolm. *Anders Zorn*. Modern Masters of Etching Series, no. 3. London: The Studio, Ltd., 1925.

1949   Arms, John Taylor. "Seaward Skerries." *Print Collector's Quarterly* 29 (1949).

1952   Bibliothèque Nationale. *Zorn, 1830–1920: exposition de son oeuvre gravé*. Paris, 1952.

1969   Delteil, Loys. *Le Peintre-Graveur Illustré: Zorn*. Vol. 4. 1909. Reprint. New York: Da Capo Press, 1969.